Learning to Think Strategically

Strategic thinking has become a core competency for business leaders globally. Overused and under-defined, the term is often used interchangeably with other strategic management terms. This textbook delineates and defines strategic thinking as a conceptual cognitive capability, focusing on the nonlinear, divergent, and informal nature of strategic thinking.

In this third edition of a popular text, the author provides an unconventional definition and model for strategic thinking based on critical theory. This research-based book introduces the concept as the foundation of business strategy that is distinct from strategic planning and strategic implementation.

New features, including executive summaries and key critical reflective questions, along with new and updated figures, make the book vital reading for MBA, leadership development, and executive education students. The practical nature of this book also makes it valuable for business and policy executives, managers, and emerging leaders.

Julia Sloan is Principal of Sloan International Inc., a New York-based firm specializing in strategic thinking for leaders of businesses, government, and international agencies operating in markets of Asia, Europe, the Middle East, Africa, and North America. She received her doctorate in organizational leadership from Columbia University, where she teaches strategic thinking.

Sloan has written an exceptional, comprehensive book on the learning aspect of strategic thinking that makes a unique contribution to the strategy literature. Based on a masterful examination of how we learn to think strategically, this book offers an insightful, unconventional, and original proposition for developing strategic thinkers. Sloan is both erudite and practical in her approach. Highly recommended for policy and business leaders who aspire to strengthen strategic thinking.

Professor Kenneth Paul Tan, Vice Dean, Lee Kuan Yew School of Public Policy, National University of Singapore; author of forthcoming Routledge book *Governing Global-City Singapore*

At the heart of strategy is the strategist, so it follows both that the strategic thinking of individuals is worth developing. Julia's book clearly shows how people can learn to become better strategists, which is why it is so valuable for executive development.

Dr. Max McKeown, author of *The Strategy Book* and *#NOW*

The starting point for many writers who focus on strategy is on the process side of strategy-making. Sloan is a pioneer in helping us understand that process and planning are necessary, yet insufficient elements of what it takes to be a successful strategic thinker. In her third edition Sloan takes us further and deeper in our comprehension of what it means to think strategically within complex environments and how to build strategic capacity. A must-read for executives and leaders aspiring to build strategic organizations.

Professor Ross Harrison, School of Foreign Service, Georgetown University, USA; author of *Strategic Thinking in 3D: A Guide for National Security, Foreign Policy and Business Professionals*

Dr. Sloan uses her astute research acumen to judiciously detail the findings of how successful executives from different cultures learned to think strategically; then compiled them into this important book. This discerning and unconventional work will stimulate you to learn to think differently, and to eventually evolve your own strategy within an uncontrollable, unpredictable business environment. Most highly recommended book for business and policy leaders.

Ahmed Elsherbini A. Ibrahim, Brigadier General; former Egyptian Defense Attaché to Beijing, China

LEARNING TO THINK STRATEGICALLY

Third Edition

Julia Sloan

Routledge
Taylor & Francis Group

LONDON AND NEW YORK

Third edition published 2017
by Routledge
2 Park Square, Milton Park, Abingdon, Oxon OX14 4RN

and by Routledge
711 Third Avenue, New York, NY 10017

Routledge is an imprint of the Taylor & Francis Group, an informa business

First edition published by Butterworth-Heinemann 2006
Second edition published by Routledge 2014

British Library Cataloguing in Publication Data
A catalogue record for this book is available from the British Library

Library of Congress Cataloging in Publication Data
Names: Sloan, Julia, author.
Title: Learning to think strategically / by Julia Sloan.
Description: 3rd edition. | Abingdon, Oxon ; New York, NY : Routledge,
    2016. | Includes bibliographical references and index.
Identifiers: LCCN 2016016010| ISBN 9781138684768 (hardback) | ISBN
    9781138684751 (pbk.) | ISBN 9781315543642 (ebook)
Subjects: LCSH: Strategic planning.
Classification: LCC HD30.28.S53 2016 | DDC 658.4/012–dc23
LC record available at https://lccn.loc.gov/2016016010

ISBN: 978-1-138-68476-8 (hbk)
ISBN: 978-1-138-68475-1 (pbk)
ISBN: 978-1-315-54364-2 (ebk)

Typeset in Minion Pro
by Cenveo Publisher Services

Printed and bound by CPI Group (UK) Ltd, Croydon, CR0 4YY

Contents

Figures, Tables, and Boxes

Figures

Tables

Boxes

About the Author

Dr. Julia Sloan is a global executive development consultant, professor, and speaker working with leading corporations and international agencies. With more than two decades of expatriate corporate experience, Julia has lived and continues to work extensively in Asia, Europe, the Middle East, Africa, and North America. Her client base consists of the top most innovative companies and major businesses representing technology, manufacturing, consumer products, petroleum, and finance.

Julia's research interests include strategic thinking in relation to learning theory and social-culture theory. She teaches at Columbia University and has lectured at MIT, Tokyo University, the Brookings Institute, India Institute of Management, Beijing University, Central University of Finance and Economics in Beijing, King Saud University, and the Institute of Public Administration in Saudi Arabia, and was named as part of the Distinguished Lecture Series at Mohammed bin Rashid School of Government (UAE). In addition to working in the corporate sector, Julia also consults for the United Nations and UN Peacekeeping Operations.

Julia has received the Innovative Influence Award, Faculty Excellence Award, and Outstanding Teaching Award, and was awarded a Researcher in Residence fellowship for her work on learning to think strategically. She regularly presents at international business conferences and has addressed organizations including ASEAN (Association of South East Asian Nations), MITI (Japan's Ministry of International Trade and Industry), Fulbright Scholars, JETRO (Japan Export and Trade Organization), and the AFDB (African Development Bank). Additionally, she has been privileged to serve on the advisory boards for non-profit and technology start-up companies.

Residing in New York City, Julia holds a doctorate from Columbia University in organizational leadership development. Julia can be contacted at: Julia@sloaninternational consulting.com and jas127@columbia.edu.

Preface

Right before our wedding, my husband invited me to join him for an international hot air balloon competition in Umbria, Italy. A licensed international balloon pilot, he often travels to Europe, Asia, and other destinations to participate in various balloon races and fiestas. I stow away for the sheer pleasure, and I take special delight as an unofficial observer in the balloon basket. At that time I was toiling over research for my doctoral dissertation on learning strategy. Flying through blue skies over the sunflower fields of Umbria, watching the other balloons and observing the maneuvers of my husband, I couldn't help but notice how his piloting a balloon in a race mirrored the findings of the data that I was in the midst of analyzing. Ballooning became a metaphor for making global strategy and has continued to serve as an anchor metaphor for my studies more than a decade later.

Balloon flying is a very special kind of sport. Pilots have minimal control over their environments, and, to a high degree, the flight is unpredictable, uncontrollable, and risky. And a race is all about winning. A pilot can control only vertical movement of the balloon by using a propane burner to warm up the air inside the balloon envelope. The inertia of the huge balloon is a critical factor; it takes several minutes before it responds to any effort. And pilots are at the mercy of Providence and the weather—especially the winds. Balloons can shift horizontally only if taken by the wind; and, at different heights, the winds gust, veering direction without warning. Sure, there is some data from the weatherman, but trusting the weatherman with your life is like playing Russian roulette.

A good balloon pilot is a strategist "par excellence." I noticed that my husband ascended to a space far above the other balloons and, from this panoramic vantage point, calculatingly assessed the "Big picture": What balloon at what height is taken by the wind in which direction at what speed? Instruments and gauges are available, but they compete with time and are no substitute for "knowing." As other pilots were burning propane, bobbing up and down seeking the right wind to take them in the right direction, he suspended motion, carefully observed, and quickly decided his course. He "knew" when to ascend and descend ever so slightly. He had a "feel" for the subtleties and nuances required and trusted his judgment, learned from past experiences. Watching him pilot was like watching him perform an intimate dance with his balloon.

I am struck by how much this sport is reflected in making global strategy—watching the competition and learning from their successes and failures, rather than imitating the successes, or making or repeating their mistakes. Though I didn't think to mention the metaphor at the time, I was reminded of it several years later, in a conversation with my husband about how he proceeds with making strategy in his international business. He started by recounting how many of the strategic lessons he learned came from his ballooning experience. Recalling this metaphor, and the similar stories of so many clients, made me ever more curious to understand how successful strategists learn to think strategically. This was the initial research knot I needed to untie.

It wasn't strategy formulation or strategy implementation that compelled me to launch a systematic inquiry into strategic learning; it was my intense desire to understand what happens *before* strategy is made, about which I was truly curious. I wanted to find out how successful strategists learned to think strategically. I wanted to explore and to understand the first link in the strategy chain—learning how strategic thinking occurs.

Based on more than two decades of experience working as an international consultant with key corporate and public-sector executives and government leaders who are responsible for making global strategy, I came to the simple conclusion that there were those executives who were able to think strategically and those who were not. Given the impressive educational credentials and the equally impressive strategy budgets of the key strategy makers with whom I worked, it became clear that learning to think strategically was sufficiently more complex than being adept at problem solving, applying a model, or implementing a vision. These instrumental types of cognitive functions were skills the executives had mastered—with little effect on the success of their actual strategic thinking.

There was something curiously common about the thinking process of the successful key strategists with whom I worked in Asia, Africa, Eastern Europe, the Middle East, North America, and Western Europe, regardless of their respective cultural and business backgrounds. I couldn't help noticing a pattern among the successful strategists—something seemed to inform their thinking process. Having lived and worked abroad myself for much of my career, and being well versed in cross-cultural theory, I sensed that this learning process transcended culture.

It appeared that those who were able to make and remake successful strategy under very different circumstances had a particular way of thinking. I wanted to explore the nature of what that particular thinking process was. My quest was to understand how the successful strategists actually *learned* to think strategically, and I wanted to understand it from the perspective of the executives' own self reports.

This book is my journey on the road to understanding how the successful strategists learned to think strategically. In this book, I offer a synthesis of findings from several years of qualitative research in pursuit of three questions: How do successful executives learn to think strategically? What learning approaches do they use? What factors and conditions are essential for learning to think strategically? As part of an initial interpretive case study, I originally conducted in-depth interviews with nine successful executives in Japan, Poland, China, Germany, the United States, and Hong Kong to pursue this inquiry. Since the original research was conducted, the study has expanded into a body of data gathered from intensive interviews of 112 executives from 37 countries. I visited the executives in their work environments and outside of their offices to see what their worlds were like, to ask questions, to listen, and to observe.

Early on, I decided that to understand how these executives learn, I should ask them directly. So I did. The personal interviews paint an entirely different picture from the kind of information that is derived from a large-scale, check-box-style quantitative survey study. While there are many circumstances in which statistical quantitative surveys are an outstanding format for gathering data, for this particular research I believed personal interview offered a special depth and richness that no check-box questionnaire, however well designed, could deliver.

Personal interviews are loaded with details. It is one thing for an executive to check a box indicating that a particular experience or event had an impact on his thinking. It is another thing for me to understand why this experience had such power, how it occurred, and whether other executives can benefit in their work from the experience. The more illustrations and quotations an executive can offer to buttress a point, the better and more helpful that point is for others.

Each executive had a story to tell. Collectively, their narratives reveal certain common themes. Their stories emphasize the critical role of informal learning, the imperative of crucial reflective processes, and the importance of identification of five essential attributes required for learning to think strategically: imagination, broad perspective, "juggle," dealing with things which you have no control over, and a desire to win. It is striking that their learning was so similar in nature, given the diversity of backgrounds, industries, and histories.

I was impressed by the powerful, heartfelt, passionate stories about the subject: learning to think strategically. Interviewing these executives was a special pleasure for me. They had strong viewpoints and high expectations and were enthusiastic and productive. The best part was that all of them had suggestions for improving academic and business aspects to facilitate learning to think strategically. They constantly question what they do, and look for ways to do it better.

All the findings in this book came from structured, in-depth interviews. Every executive participated in several interviews, each preliminary interview lasting six to eight hours. Analyzing responses to each question of the in-depth interviews was a long, tedious, and fascinating process. Slowly but steadily I developed a process for categorizing schemas and experiences, coding the rich stories told by real executives. It was not the numbers and the statistical tests that told the truth of this research—it was the stories. The lessons of their experiences were vivid, emotional, and anything but objective.

Strong findings emerged that have influenced my professional practice of consulting, teaching, training, and advising, and I hope they will do the same for readers. Do these findings generalize? This is just a single series of interpretive qualitative research studies on a handful of successful global executives. Definitive conclusions cannot be drawn from the reporting of the results of the study—only insights and an understanding that will hopefully generate more studies. My work with other companies and organizations around the world has convinced me that the findings in this book do apply broadly. But this is up to the reader to decide. Is it their story as well?

I am struck by how much of what executives in other organizations say is similar to what the executives I interviewed for the study said. Maybe a select few findings will not generalize, but it is clear to me that most do so quite well. I know that enormous differences exist among organizations and individual executives. Yet nearly all of them have a wish to enhance their learning, to improve learning development initiatives, and to organize their businesses in such a way that they can make a positive contribution to the learning process of others. If the findings I present here help readers take a few steps toward achieving these outcomes, I will consider this book a great satisfaction.

Acknowledgments

I have been the beneficiary of the generous assistance, advice, encouragement, and support of so many people from around the world—most of whose names do not appear in this book, but whose contributions are embedded in the thoughts, insights, and examples within this text, and forever in my memory.

No book emerges as the sole manifestation of its author. Over the years many business clients, government leaders, academics, and graduate students have strongly influenced my thinking. Many people and circumstances have shaped the understanding and experience I have gained, and I owe an immense intellectual debt of gratitude to these special clients, colleagues, students, and friends. I could not have written this book without the dedicated assistance of so many people from across the globe.

I am greatly indebted to Michael Petty and Adrian Phillips for their technology assistance and graphics. Much of this book was written and revised in airports and en route to and from various countries—they made themselves available around the clock and across time zones. I owe much to their imagination, indefatigable organization skills, and uncanny ability to read my mind and convert my messy sketches into intelligible figures and tables.

My deep gratitude to Eileen Capone, who read the initial draft and was perceptive and ever tactful in her suggestions for revisions. Her wonderful energy and intellectual acumen prompted constructive changes that the reader will surely appreciate. I also want to thank Katharine Boies Smith for her eagle eye and thoughtful recommendations as she relentlessly waded through the chapters clearing the muddy waters.

My great appreciation to Christopher Croft for his expert advice and research on the military history of strategy, and for his generosity and quick wit in boomerang conversations. I also thank Michael Bulger for his willingness to share the creations of his vivid imagination and his willingness to engage in stretching thought boundaries.

My sincere gratitude to Westly LaFitte, David McLean, and David Weart for their unrelenting curiosity, their willingness to critique, their contribution to the summaries and questions, and their devotion to navigating new waters in the application of strategic thinking.

I also want to acknowledge the amazing research librarians at the New York Public Library for their enthusiasm and genuine interest in the subject and meaningful contributions to my thinking.

There were numerous people who volunteered to do anonymous "blind reads" of the manuscript at various stages. I would like to extend my deep appreciation to each of them for their candid, precise, and helpful suggestions.

Clients have been the greatest teachers in the conceptualization, content, and examples within this third edition of the book, bringing with them a sense of sincere interest and willingness to share what is important and relevant in their learning experiences regarding strategic thinking. They have taken a keen interest in my research and provided me with an understanding of their thinking and feeling, and the practices within their respective organizations. From them I have gleaned a tremendous collection of cases, examples, and stories. I am most grateful to them for sharing their time and experiences and hope I have represented them well. Many people from many countries have graciously agreed to be part of projects, experiments, studies, and interviews; this has added great value to my research and book. I owe them all a debt of thanks for their rich and generous contributions.

I also want to thank each of the wonderful, ambitious, and energetic graduate students from around the world for their boundless enthusiasm, serious contributions, and playful exploration of some very tedious and challenging topics.

The professional team at Routledge has been the best of the best to work with. My thanks to the experienced staff who steered the production process. The book would never have reached its present form without the dedication and integrity of the editorial team.

I am profoundly grateful to my many friends who have been loyal, patient, and most generous in their encouragement. And many thanks to my extended and very dear family for their sideline cheers and persistent telephone calls and emails requesting progress reports on the book revisions. Their encouragement and support nudged me to persevere.

Finally, there is my husband Oleg, who has been a pillar of support and understanding. Writing a book or revising an edition is an all-consuming endeavor—it takes on a life of its own that is both isolating and invigorating. I literally closed the door on him for countless days, most weekends, and far too many holidays. Without his encouragement, humor, sacrifice, candid insights, intellectual rigor, and love, the effort would have been nearly impossible to sustain. His affection and patience have endeared and inspired me.

Introduction

Learning to Think Strategically is structured around three key questions: (1) How do successful executives learn to think strategically? (Is it something they are taught? Where? By whom? How?) (2) What learning approaches are used by successful executive strategists? (3) What factors and conditions are essential for learning to think strategically?

One of the most frequent and impassioned requests I hear from executive leaders, regardless of industry or geographic location, is "How can I develop my people to think strategically?" As we discuss their observations and needs, these executives deftly identify their greatest need as being able to shift course, rapidly and effectively, and to have more strategic thinkers in the "pipeline." Their want, however, is to acquire a quick and easy, step-by-step model from which they can develop a foolproof strategic plan, once and for all.

Being strategically competitive in today's global, unpredictable, complex, and rapidly changing environment requires a different way of looking at how we develop strategic thinkers. The strategic landscape makes it difficult to distinguish and decide which of our interests are most vital at any given time. Paramount among the challenges facing leaders is how to help their organizations continually adapt and change in new directions, and to generate the momentum needed to propel strategic thinking. Understanding how we *learn* to think strategically is increasingly critical for sustaining competitiveness in a world that is becoming ever more turbulent.

The focus of this book is on the learning aspect of strategic thinking—moving beyond strategic planning and implementation models to a more expansive and complex notion that includes perpetual change. *Learning to Think Strategically* is intended for organizational leaders at all levels—experienced and emerging—around the world who are serious about increasing their capacity to think strategically in order to create, re-create, and sustain strategic effectiveness. It is also aimed at those who are tasked with and committed to leveraging learning to develop a steady "pipeline" of strategic thinkers in their organizations:

- Executives;
- Policy makers;

- Chief learning officers;
- Entrepreneurs;
- Government leaders;
- HRD and OD leaders;
- Senior line managers;
- Internal and external consultants;
- Professors;
- Graduate students.

This book attempts to provide an understanding of how we learn to think strategically in order to help leaders to better understand and develop strategic thinking. Although the strategic management literature clearly agrees on the importance of strategic thinking, there is a wide variation of thought and opinion on what it is and how to develop it. Learning is more often implied and inferred, than studied. Articles and books that contain a discussion of strategic thinking and provide a coherent framework are hard to find. An excessive focus is cast on what we *do*, rather than how we *learn* to do it.

While we seem to have no difficulty recognizing those who think strategically and those who do not, there is a gaping hole in the literature and in practice that we have not examined, about how strategic thinkers learn to think the way they do. Therefore, it is difficult to support the development of strategic thinking. An enormous collection of studies on the best practices of formal learning about strategy has emerged; but scant reference regarding the informal learning aspect of strategic thinking is available. I endeavor to address this vacuum by defining strategic thinking and detailing the underlying informal learning process that supports it.

Since the first and second editions of this book were published, my own interest, research, and practice have continued to grow and expand. This book represents a version of my current understanding about how we learn to think strategically, which has been influenced by my work with clients in corporations, governments, international agencies, entrepreneurial businesses, as well as my graduate students in many countries.

Based on my experience consulting and advising executives, and teaching strategic thinking to graduate MBA and doctoral students, I have noticed that executive development professionals, university faculty, and strategy consultants have become intent on the teaching aspect of strategic thinking, without first addressing the underlying learning supposition of thinking strategically.

Learning to think strategically is largely an informal, nonlinear, "messy" process that is reliant on a cognitive cluster that is distinctly different than the traditional cognitive cluster emphasized in conventional teaching approaches of strategic planning. Well-intentioned, overloaded executives understandably prefer to teach and be taught with the brevity of bullet points and sound bites, without the hassle of acquiring the necessary insight or understanding of how we learn what we need to know—wanting to "produce" a strategy, rather than generate a learning process of sustainable and re-creative capability.

Executives, consultants, and leadership development professionals often succumb to the business culture myth of simple and short with regard to strategic thinking, seeking a quick and tidy, how-to approach for even the most complex of problems.

Our unchallenged mantra is fast, faster, fastest equals good, better, best! The lure of the myth has enticed us to deny or ignore the complexity, ambiguity, paradoxes, and contradictions that are inherent in the learning process required to think strategically.

While leaders talk about wanting to develop organizational strategic capability that is sustainable and competitive, and they recognize internal strategic capability as the most valuable human capital asset, these same executives often cling to their habit of wanting to learn strategy as a "fast fix" planning model. Efficiency in the "production" of strategic thinking is rewarded and perpetuated in many business schools and organizational development programs, over a mucky, unpredictable learning process that can create a sustainable competitive advantage.

It is easy to be dismissive and avoidant of the extraordinarily complex factors of everyday business reality—voluminous data, contradictory and complex information, laser-speed decision making—which require a very different approach to factors of time, problem solving, discipline, and decision making. But the long-term return on investing in the learning process pays dividends by creating sustainable, innovative, agile, and adaptive organizational strategic capacity that creates and re-creates winning strategies.

As you will discover, this is not a how-to book. Learning to think strategically is hardly a quick, easy, or step-by-step formal learning process. Rather, the process rubs against the conventional grain and raises questions about much of what most of us have learned and been taught in traditional strategy courses.

Organization of the Book

This book is organized to reflect the informal and dynamic approach that I take toward the development of learning to think strategically, based on the findings of the research studies. Ten parts comprise the book in its entirety, with each part consisting of several chapters.

Part I sets the framework by presenting a very brief historical snapshot of Western strategy perspectives. Admittedly, Parts II, III, IV, and V are theoretical in nature, as they detail the informal learning process required of strategic thinking. The latter Parts VI, VII, VIII, IX, and X offer some thoughts on application of the foundational elements of learning to think strategically.

Part II posits a definition of strategic thinking and a model that I have created and work with. It also describes informal learning as the primary learning approach, while Part III illustrates a three-stage informal learning process. Part IV explores the concept of surf and dive learning domains; Part V expands on the deeper learning domain by introducing the role of critical dialogue and critical inquiry. Part VI positions intuition as a vital complement to analysis in learning to think strategically. The critically reflective processes along with framing, shattering, and reframing are described as methods that help to develop strategic thinking. Part VII links the roles of intuition and analysis with regard to strategic decision making.

Part VIII discusses socio-national culture as a factor of influence in learning to think strategically. Part IX identifies five essential attributes for learning to think strategically that emerged from the research findings. And finally, Part X puts forth some of the recommendations that I find useful to support the development of strategic thinking on the individual and organizational levels.

Although the list of possibilities is infinite, engagement in the arts is a learning process that I suggest as a starter, as it synthesizes the five attributes and critical reflective processes required of strategic thinking. The recommendations in Part X are not prescriptive, formal, or structured in nature, but rather broad and flexible in scope and depth, reflecting my professional belief that strategic thinking is a long-term informal development process, best learned from experiences outside the work environment and applied and supported within the work environment.

Two features distinguish this book from others. First, its focus on the *learning* aspect of thinking strategically, in contrast to an emphasis on planning and implementing strategy. The second point of differentiation is that this book invites the reader to select a strategic thinking development approach that is based on a cognitive cluster of an informal, nonlinear learning process rather than on a conventional approach that is structured according to a linear planning model.

There is a profound and urgent need to understand the underlying learning process of strategic thinking so that we can facilitate our own and others' strategic development. It is my intent that this third edition of *Learning to Think Strategically* provides just that. I hope that reading this book will generate questions and ideas that readers can use to create alternative ways of facilitating their own strategic development and contribute to the learning experience of others, and to the strategic success of their organization. My intention is for this book to be a starting point for further exploration of learning to think strategically.

1

HOW DID WE GET HERE?

Strategy:
A Snapshot

All men can see these tactics whereby I conquer,
but what none can see is the strategy out of which victory is evolved.

Sun-tzu (fourth century B.C.), Chinese military strategist

1

Chronology of Strategy

Developing organizational capability for strategic thinking can be one of the most significant contributions leaders can make to organizational performance. By developing a "pipeline" of strategic thinkers within their organization, companies can truly begin to harness human capital as their greatest asset and build sustainable organizational strategic capability.

Prior to discussing the learning aspect of strategic thinking, we will briefly review notions of strategy from the past. Although this book focuses on the learning aspect of thinking strategically, this preliminary overview of strategy will provide readers with a historical context from which Western strategy emerged. While there are many excellent texts and resources that provide detailed histories of strategy, my intent is simply to provide a useful sketch or snapshot—with some deliberate and obvious omissions.

Part I frames organizational strategy within a historical context, focusing on a learning perspective. Curiously, we will see that everything old is new again—or at least, understand that current trends in organizational strategic thinking are not incompatible with concepts of strategy in ancient Western civilization. In fact, current views of strategy are strikingly similar to veins of the past. Knowing a bit about strategy in ancient history can make the present debate on strategy less perplexing and inform current decisions.

Most often, discussions about the history of business strategy start with the twentieth century. Chapter 1, however, harks back much further and begins by tracing strategy from ancient Western civilization to the present. Chapter 2 discusses contemporary competing views of strategy, and Chapter 3 acknowledges some of the implications of the history of strategy for strategic thinking.

Although the term *strategy* is commonly and conveniently used, its meaning is far from shared. Despite volumes of academic research on the topic, there is remarkably little agreement on what strategy is. Essentially, its meaning depends on whether we are looking toward the future or back to the past. For those who look into the past, strategy is a repeated pattern on the path to a success; for those who look toward the future, strategy is a broad framework for actions that will culminate in a win. While strategy's complexity defies simple description, there is consensus on its basic characteristics. Regardless of any particular definition, all definitions imply a will to win, an element of competition, a process or framework for success, an extended time horizon, the determination of a broad and major aim, a unifying intent, and decisions about resource allocation.

Within Western civilization, the term *strategos* can be traced back to the ancient Greeks, for whom it meant "a chief magistrate and military commander-in-chief responsible for employing the science and art of the political, economic, psychological and military forces … to afford the maximum support to adopted policies in peace or war."[1]

The purpose here, however, is not to elaborate on the history of strategy but, rather, to provide a glimpse of history before highlighting the imperative of *learning to think strategically*.

Ancient Greek Concept of Strategy

The ancient Greeks, whose view of strategy influenced Western civilization, likened a military or political strategist to the helmsman on a seafaring vessel. These early strategists had to interpret their maps and their understanding of the prevailing currents in relation to their journey's purpose and their own skill at the rudder. The Greeks regarded strategic wisdom as oscillating between different positions and perspectives relative to a particular purpose.[2]

The concept of pre-modern strategy emphasized the personal and relational rather than the objective and rational qualities of spatial order. Consequently, pre-modern maps were evolving and "organic," in the sense that they could be added to, reinterpreted, and modified according to the traveler's experience. A depiction of mountains, valleys, or other important milestones could easily be added to the maps.[3] This subjective relativism had a significant influence on the ancient Greeks' concept of strategy.

While such relativism may be attributed to what is now deemed a lack of knowledge perspective, it was a reasonable byproduct of a pre-modern worldview and a different way of conceiving one's relationship with the world. Rather than the prevailing modern Western worldview of ascertaining objective knowledge from a detached perspective over and above particular events, the ancient Greeks saw the world subjectively. In other words, their relation with things *was* knowledge. And because they saw the individual human being as a microcosm of the universal macrocosm, the ancient Greeks sought knowledge by finding certain characteristics in themselves before going on to create relationships with other things.

There are cultures and societies today that hold a similar worldview, to varying degrees—cultures that are highly relational, contextual, subjective, and fatalistic in their perspective. If an executive holds this worldview, it could be difficult for him or her to conform to a contemporary Western view of strategy as detached, rational, and objective. While the frameworks and worldviews that influence the conception of strategy can be very different, these differing ways of thinking are not inferior in any way. Different worldviews are, however, manifested (and can be exacerbated) during conversations about strategy when conceptual expectations become explicit and possibly discordant. Over the years, I have found that understanding the learning process that supports strategic thinking can mitigate some of the fundamental conceptual differences.

Given the subjective, interpretative, and unfolding nature of knowing, wisdom was also perceived differently by the ancient Greeks. Furthermore, the ancient Greeks assumed an irresolvable tension between, and mutuality of, chaos and *cosmos* (order). While we have learned to see paradox and contradiction as something of an obstruction to strategy making today, the ancient Greeks saw paradox, ambivalence, and contradiction as natural and necessary.

Consequently, the Greeks did not see wisdom as the ability to represent the order of things with objective certainty in the interests of predictability and control but, rather, they saw it as *metos*. *Metos* referred to the ability to oscillate between the *cosmos* (a world of forms and laws) and chaos (a world that included the multiple, unstable, and unlimited nature of affairs) in order to map and steer a prudent course.[4]

In keeping with this concept of *metos*, strategy was about moving between order and uncertainty, and about detached long-term forethought, planning, and ordering in advance of action. At the same time, the front lines were the best place to get a feel for the "becoming" of events, to implement plans, or to adapt plans as circumstances changed. Strategists understood that strategy making also happened here, and were expected to be at or connected to the points where action took place in order to reinterpret things.[5]

Pre-modern strategy was focused on the interplay of seeming paradoxes and contradictions, playing off and balancing one another. *Metos* expresses nimble oscillation between *cosmos* and chaos, structure and circumstance, design and emergence.

Military Influence on Strategy

Throughout history, the concept of strategy has been closely associated with the military. The ancient Greek concept of *metos* survived through most of the Middle Ages; however, a slow, methodical process of change began to take place between the fifteenth and late nineteenth centuries. The expansion of the monetary-based economy had a dramatic impact on the agricultural aspects and mindset of medieval society. This forced a transformation from a feudal state into a more bureaucratic state, which "reached its climax in the eighteenth century."[6]

While there are many examples of successful strategists during this era, only a select few will be highlighted here, to accentuate their thinking and impact on the concept of strategy. Sixteenth-century Niccolò Machiavelli was "a theorist for the age of unregulated warfare," and made warfare and statecraft an art as well as a science. He made the study of war a "social science ... relating it to constitutional, economic, and political speculations."[7] While many of his specific ideas about conscription and his disdain for professional armies later proved to be mistaken, some of his ideas became the foundation of future thinking on strategy.

A legendary Renaissance military strategist of the seventeenth century was Sebastian LePrestre de Vauban, considered the greatest strategist of French king Louis XIV's reign.

During a military career of more than 50 years he designed several hundred fortifications and conducted many sieges. He had an intense dislike for what he perceived as unnecessary loss of life. An engineer by trade, Vauban devised a highly formalized and systematic method for defeating enemy fortifications. His theories remained active until well into the twentieth century and through World War I.[8]

The seventeenth century saw an unprecedented enlargement of armies, creating a need for orderly administration and control. Accordingly, emphasis was placed on discipline and the establishment of complex hierarchies of tactical units. It was during this period that military leaders became political figures. Prior to this, essentially, wars were fought between rulers; afterwards, war became "total"—a battle between nations of peoples.[9] It was in the "seventeenth century that we discovered the machine, its intricate precision, its revelation ... of mathematical reason in action."[10]

The eighteenth century placed a "Newtonian twist" on the machine notion and the nineteenth century simply "worshiped not the machine but power."[11] So began the transformation of military and civilian bureaucracies during this period—adapting qualities of the efficient machine to institutions and strategy. The march toward a machinist view accelerated as armies grew larger and more complex.

The eighteenth-century king Frederick the Great believed in a "single mind and will," and established that the king was the central figure in planning and strategy. He believed that military soldiers and staff must be trained repeatedly in drill and ceremony to ensure a mechanistic response in battle. Frederick never varied his military formation, but always left himself the "liberty in adapting to specific purposes."[12] He is widely considered to have been one of the greatest strategists of this period.[13]

Chief of the Prussian General Staff Helmuth von Moltke was the pre-eminent nineteenth-century military strategist who brought strategic thinking closest to the twentieth-century corporate view. Moltke stated that the "basic elements of strategy thought, hardly went beyond the propositions of common sense, but their correct execution required strength of character and the ability to make rapid decisions under stress."[14] Moltke is characterized by "his openness of mind and by the elastic changes from one device to the other."[15] He seemed to embrace the spirit of weaving through treacherous waters, while supporting structured organization and processes. With few exceptions, corporations in this era limited themselves to strategies used by the military to destroy, stabilize, build up, ratify, and sanction countries.

A hierarchical structure, strict discipline, and thinking teams, called General Staffs, were deemed necessary to achieve the desired results in battle. As the twentieth century began, military leaders were placed at the center of action, and many times their own fate affected the outcome of the campaign. However, gradually, separation of the leader from the action came about. With the vast increase in the size and complexity of armies, military organization became less relational and more process oriented. Numerous volumes analyzing every action of these military strategists and the increasing complexity of the battlefield underscore the significance of and change in thinking on strategy during the twentieth century.

The military analogy became popular within a business context during the 1950s as operational plans called for companies to "attack" the competitor, "conquer markets," "win product wars," and so on. Today, we can peruse a myriad of excellent books on strategy and entire libraries describing its history in detail, from such varied perspectives as those of Napoleon, Jomini, Clausewitz, Bismarck, and Mahan—to Winnie the Pooh and Dilbert, on the lighter side. For those who believe that business strategy is about creating competitive, sustainable development, the military analogy and its related imagery is no longer the only source on which to draw.

As we have seen, there was a conceptual disconnect between the pre-modern and contemporary definitions of strategy. Let us move forward and briefly examine strategy as it was conceived in the twentieth-century corporate context.

Twentieth-Century Corporate Strategy

If we fast-forward to the twentieth-century corporate environment, we find a rather different interpretation of strategy. Although today's business commentary is littered with references to "strategy," use of this word in a business context is a relatively recent phenomenon. Its occurrence in business discourse dates back to only the late nineteenth century, and its use in a competitive context can be traced back to the second half of the twentieth century.

Corporate strategy, as we tend to understand it today, came about in the late nineteenth century, at the height of the scientific, technical, and rational era, amidst modernist optimism and the second industrial revolution. The concept of strategy during this period was a clear reflection of its historical context, and was closely aligned with the scientific, technical rational mindset. Remarkably, this sense of strategy remains highly influential in strategy development circles today.

According to the model of *technical rationality*—the late nineteenth-century view of professional knowledge that shaped our thinking about professions and institutions relating to research, education, and business strategy—professional activity consists of instrumental problem solving, made rigorous by the application of scientific theory and technique.

Where does this dominant view of professional knowledge as the application of scientific theory and instrumental knowledge originate? It comes from the last 300 years of Western ideas and institutions. The term *technical rationality* emerged from the legacy of positivism, the powerful philosophical doctrine that dawned in the nineteenth century as a complement to the rise of science and technology. Technical rationality was also a social movement, aimed at employing the achievements of science and technology for humanity's prosperity. Technical rationality was institutionalized in modern universities during the late nineteenth century, when positivism was at its height, and in the professional schools that established themselves in those universities in the early twentieth century. There are many excellent sources detailing this era, so we will look at only a few key points here as they relate to shaping our notion of strategy.

According to the technical rational school of thought, the systematic knowledge base of a profession is understood to have four essential properties. The knowledge base is specialized, scientific, firmly bounded, and standardized. The notion of standardization is particularly important with regard to our conception of strategy because it explains the current analytic preoccupation with which many leaders struggle today when developing strategy.

Contemporary strategy making is grounded in systematic, fundamental knowledge, of which scientific methodology is the prototype. But what happens when the industry and business environments are unstable, constantly changing, and ambiguous? Rigidly or unknowingly adhering to an outmoded framework can further complicate an already complex problem. The ability to make successful strategy hinges upon one's willingness to embrace a whole new framework.

The first industrial revolution (mid-1700s to mid-1800s), driven largely by the development of international trade around commodities such as cotton, witnessed intense competition among industrial firms.[16] However, most private companies were unable to directly influence or impact upon the competitive marketplace. Political and economic turbulence during this period inspired economists such as Adam Smith to describe market forces as an "invisible hand" largely beyond the control of individual companies.

The second industrial revolution (late 1800s) saw the emergence of large-scale investment to exploit economies of scale in production and economies of scope and distribution.[17] In the United States after 1850, the construction of the railroads made the building of mass markets possible for the first time. A new type of vertically integrated firm began to emerge, first in the United States and then in Europe. These multidivisional corporations made large investments in manufacturing and marketing and created management hierarchies to coordinate those functions. Together with improved access to capital and credit, the emergence of mass markets encouraged companies to consider strategy as a way to control market forces and transform the competitive landscape.

Additionally, the second industrial revolution triggered the establishment of several elite business schools in the United States in response to the demand for trained managers, beginning with the founding of the Wharton School in 1881. The Harvard Business School, founded in 1908, was one of the first to promote the notion that managers should be trained to think strategically and not just act as functional administrators.[18]

Two decades later in the business arena, top executives of these multidivisional corporations first articulated the need for a formal approach to corporate strategy. In the 1930s, Chester Barnard, a senior executive at AT&T, argued that managers should pay especially close attention to "strategic factors" that depended on "personal or organizational action."[19]

The organizational challenges associated with fighting two world wars in the first half of the twentieth century provided a vital stimulus to the field of strategic development. The need to allocate scarce resources across an entire economy in wartime led to the use of quantitative analysis in formal strategic planning. The concept of the *learning curve* was first put forth in the military aircraft industry in the 1920s and 1930s, when the military noted that direct labor costs tended to decrease by a constant percentage as the cumulative quantity of aircraft produced doubled. Learning figured prominently as a factor of operational impact in subsequent wartime production and planning efforts.

The wartime disruption of non-U.S. multinational businesses, especially those in the European and Asian markets, enabled U.S. companies to profit from the post-World War

II boom without effective competition in many industries. Insights into the nature of strategy gleaned during World War II—that premeditated and formal planning enable an organization to exert some positive control over market forces—remained undeveloped until the early 1960s, when many large multinational corporations were forced to consider global competition as a factor in their planning.

Strategy and the Academy

On the academic front, in the late 1950s Harvard professor Kenneth Andrews argued that "every business organization, every subunit of an organization, and even every individual [ought to] have a clearly defined set of purposes or goals which keeps it moving in a deliberately chosen direction and prevents it drifting in undesired directions."[20] This argument became the banner under which the proponents of the design school of thought operated, and the goal to which businesses and consulting firms have rallied since the 1950s.

Design School

The design school, the most influential strategy concept since the 1960s, provided the basis for the business school curricula, consulting firm propositions, and corporate strategy approaches that we know today. Remnants of the school can still be identified in each school of strategy that has developed since that time.

Two sources credited with the thinking underlying the design school were Philip Selznick's 1957 book, *Leadership in Administration*, and Alfred Chandler's 1962 volume, *Strategy and Structure*. The idea of *distinctive competence* was introduced by Selznick, who highlighted the importance of synchronizing an organization's "internal state" with its "external expectations."[21] By the 1960s, academic discussions focused on identifying the strengths, weaknesses, opportunities, and threats that a company faced in the market. The exercise, commonly referred to as SWOT analysis, is still used to this day, with an explicit strategic goal of creating a "fit" by manipulating both external and internal factors.

A few years later, Alfred Chandler added to the design school, contributing the notion of business strategy and its structure. Chandler's classic 1962 definition of strategy focused on the determination of basic long-term goals and the objectives of an enterprise. He saw strategy as having "two specific characteristics: many distinct operating units, managed by a hierarchy of salaried executives."[22] In fact, a distinctive facet of the design school was its singular foundation in economics. The case study was institutionalized as its primary strategy-development technique. A highly structured, descriptive, and prescriptive tool, the case study provided second-hand data and business anecdotes as fodder for comparative analyses and implied following a "best" example.

The design school of the 1960s provided the basis for subsequent strategy tangents such as the planning and positioning schools. The premise of the design school continues to dominate strategy even into the twenty-first century.

The real momentum behind design school thinking came from the Harvard Business School. As Kenneth Andrews, eminent proponent of the design school, declared, the ensuing "establishment of business schools provided the basis for the education of strategic managers and the divisionalized structure of organizations provided the form for them to work within."[23]

Of note, in 1959 both the Carnegie and Ford foundations conducted studies on the curricula of business schools and concluded that "in order to counter the disparate 'organic' growth of programs with differing contributing 'specialisms,' it had to be realized that economics has traditionally provided the only theoretical framework for the study of business."[24] The foundations' research proposed that economics serves as the central stem from which all other courses in a management degree would branch. The Carnegie and Ford studies advocated for the standardization of the curricula's top level, or *sharp end*. They recommended *capstone courses* that would allow students to round off what they learned in various business fields, and courses in corporate strategy became the tip of the educational triangle.

The Carnegie and Ford foundations' reports on the curricula of business schools not only consolidated, but also perpetuated, an image of companies as triangular hierarchies. Ansoff's and Chandler's image of organizations was also that of a triangle. This "tip-of-the-triangle" vision was consistent with the design school notion that those at the top of an organization tend to know best, an idea that many organizations and business schools perpetuate even today.

The contextual background of the 1960s–1970s was conducive to such strategy schools as the design and planning schools. Strategy was perceived to be the responsibility of a select cadre of highly educated planners at the tip of the corporate triangle.

Planning School

Simultaneous to the dawn of the design school was the rise of the planning school, spearheaded by Igor Ansoff. Ansoff defined strategy as "a rule for making decisions pertaining to a firm's match to its environment" and set out to "enrich the theoretical conception of the firm."[25] Ansoff's seminal work of 1965, *Corporate Strategy*, identified a gap between increasingly complex business environments and the activities of multi-business firms. He suggested that this combination of factors positioned companies to use foresight in order to exploit environmental change and offered a theory based on the prevailing microeconomic conception of a business.

Proponents of the planning school detailed the differentiation between definitions for goals, objectives, values, and so on, and developed extensive procedures for construing elaborate quantitative metrics and methodical explanations. Exhaustive checklists and techniques for each procedural step, and tightly crafted diagrams, ensured an ability to control internal and external factors. Hundreds of forecasting and audit-analysis techniques and control measures have been developed to assess the hundreds of strategic planning models churned out.

While the planning school overlaps with most areas of the design school, it advocates a considerably more formal and systematic process—a nearly mechanical methodology that is deeply rooted in industrial-era beliefs. Strategy theorist Henry Mintzberg noted that the strategic planning process is based on the machine assumption, to "produce each of the component parts as specified, assemble them according to the blueprint, and the end product (strategy) will result."[26]

A recent outgrowth of the planning school has been scenario planning and strategic control as part of a risk-management portfolio. Scenario planning is based on the idea that if the future cannot be totally planned, then by planning several futures we may increase the likelihood that the right one will be selected. In addition to formal quantitative analysis, scenario planning expands analysis to incorporate insights gained from analyzing various factors in different scenarios. An extension of planning, called strategic control, aims to review, test, and manage the strategy that was planned. In short, if the strategy was not planned and cannot be measured, then it does not count.

The planning view saw organizations as manufacturers of strategy—turning resources into outputs through a production function—with the assumption that managers manipulated variables within their control to maximize profits. This strategy assumed that the "people at the top" were to carry out strategy, and that they were best positioned to have an objective global view, to forecast and represent changes in the environment, and to position and control corporate development accordingly.

Strategy and Consultancies

The 1960s and 1970s saw the rise of strategy consulting practices. The Boston Consulting Group (BCG), in particular, had a major impact on the field by applying quantitative research to problems of business and corporate strategy. BCG founder Bruce Henderson's underlying premise was that "good strategy must be based primarily on logic, not … on experience derived from intuition."[27] Henderson was convinced that a quantitative approach would someday lead to a set of universal rules for strategy development.

In the mid-1960s, BCG had devised a version of the learning curve that it called the *experience curve*. It implied that for a given product segment, "the producer … who has made the most units should have the lowest costs and the highest profits."[28] A second BCG tool, Portfolio Analysis, compared the relative potential for investment of a diversified company's business units by plotting their experience curves on a grid.

McKinsey & Company introduced a strategy planning system during the same period that divided a company into *natural business units*, later termed *strategic business units* (SBUs). The McKinsey system also presented an approach to portfolio planning called the Profit Impact of Market Strategies, or PIM program.

By the 1970s virtually every major American consulting firm applied some type of quantitative analysis to strategy making, pushing strategic thinking "down the line" to managers closer to the particular industry and its competitive conditions.[29] The design and planning strategy schools had been highly influential, and in complement to one another they provided an ideal platform for consulting firms. Their emphasis on quantitative measures produced an enormous inventory of analytical tools, models, and metrics for predicting, monitoring, and measuring strategic planning.

Shift in Corporate Strategy Role

Strategy can be viewed from several perspectives, including organizational strategy, hierarchical levels, structural strategy, and infrastructural strategy. The focus here is on the profound influence that corporate strategy had on organizational strategy.

Three themes that emerge from the strategy literature assembled over the centuries have specific implications for the functional role of corporate planning. First, no approach or school of thought, however sound, applies to all organizations at all times under all circumstances. Successful strategy reflects both a specific and a broad context. Second, each school of strategy has limitations when carried to extremes or used in exclusivity. Specific strategy schools appear to run a natural course, coming into and falling out of favor, and tend to be self-corrective either by blending into other schools or by transforming to accommodate the context. Third, across the centuries, successful strategy has proven to be dynamic and generative, not static and finite. These three observations indicate that organizational strategies need to be open and adaptable in order to be successful.

Throughout the mid-twentieth century, formal models of strategic planning gave rise to the creation of corporate planning staff functions in large companies. Corporate planners were tasked with exercising the design and planning concepts of corporate strategy. Beginning in the 1980s, however, many organizations reconsidered the value of these functions and moved to replace them with strategy planning at the business-unit level. So, while strategy, as a concept, continued to emphasize planning, the responsibility was dispersed.

Around that same time the role of corporate planning underwent change—from formulating strategy to supporting strategy by providing technical expertise and analysis. This trend has recently accelerated and has been further modified as companies move toward "intrapreneurial" and "entrepreneurial" business models—less vertically integrated structures that function more as internal market economies rather than planned economies.

In recent years, the notion of strategy-as-planning has begun to recede, while strategy-as-thinking has surfaced. With the surge of technological innovation, fluctuations in the globalized marketplace, and socio-political and environmental turmoil, organizations are starting to rethink their approaches to strategy development. They are beginning to acknowledge how the strategic thinking process encourages new challenges and tests their business. This process includes critical reflective processes as well as theories and models of creative and divergent thinking, rather than traditional frameworks and theories that lead to strategic imitation or planning.

Today, corporate leaders understand that being a bit better than the competition is no longer advantageous. While this notion is gaining traction in many places, the idea remains a daunting concept for executives who were brought up in an environment where incremental gains *were* strategic successes. In order to be strategically competitive today, leaders must be able to critically reexamine data and perceive information in novel ways, to dramatically shift perspectives, and to re-create and adapt continually. As I work with business and government leaders across the globe, I notice that leaders are taking particular interest in strategic thinking and are intensely curious about how people learn to think strategically.

Notes

1. *Webster's Third New International Dictionary of the English Language Unabridged*, 2256.
2. Cummings and Wilson, *Images of Strategy*, 6.
3. Cummings and Wilson, *Images of Strategy*, 6.
4. Cummings and Wilson, *Images of Strategy*, 6.
5. Cummings and Wilson, *Images of Strategy*, 9.
6. Palmer, "Frederick the Great, Guibert, Bülow: From Dynastic to National War," 91.
7. Gilbert, "Machiavelli: The Renaissance of the Art of War," 13.
8. Guerlac, "Vauban: The Impact of Science on War," 73–5.
9. Palmer, "Frederick the Great, Guibert, Bülow: From Dynastic to National War," 91–2.
10. Guerlac, "Vauban: The Impact of Science on War," 68.
11. Guerlac, "Vauban: The Impact of Science on War," 68.
12. Palmer, "Frederick the Great, Guibert, Bülow: From Dynastic to National War," 99–116.
13. Holborn, "The Prusso-German School: Moltke and the Rise of the General Staff," 299.
14. Holborn, "The Prusso-German School: Moltke and the Rise of the General Staff," 299.
15. Holborn, "The Prusso-German School: Moltke and the Rise of the General Staff," 295.
16. Chandler, *Scale and Scope: The Dynamics of Industrial Capitalism*.
17. Chandler, *Scale and Scope: The Dynamics of Industrial Capitalism*.
18. Botticelli, "Competition and Business Strategy in Historical Perspective."
19. Sloan, A., Jr., *My Years with General Motors*.
20. Andrews, *The Concept of Corporate Strategy*, 23.
21. Selznick, *Leadership in Administration: A Sociological Interpretation*, 67–74.
22. Chandler, *Strategy and Structure: Chapters in the History of the Industrial Enterprise*, 42.
23. Botticelli, "Competition and Business Strategy in Historical Perspective," 3.
24. Cummings and Wilson, *Images of Strategy*, 17.
25. Cummings and Wilson, *Images of Strategy*, 16.
26. Mintzberg, Ahlstrand, and Lampel, *Strategy Safari: A Guided Tour through the Wilds of Strategic Management*, 57.
27. Henderson, *The Logic of Business Strategy*, 10.
28. Conley, *Experience Curves as a Planning Tool*, 15.
29. Gluck and Kaufman, "Using the Strategic Planning Framework," 3–4.

2

Contemporary Competing Views of Strategy

As we consider the traditional approaches to strategy from 1960 forward, it may be useful to characterize them according to the Sloan School of Management's ten major schools of thought[1] (Table 2.1). These major strategy schools are commonly referred to in the strategy literature because of their influence on practice. While these ten schools depict fundamentally different aspects across similar strategy-making processes, they can be distilled into the two basic perspectives: the design school of strategy viewpoint, which we have already outlined in Chapter 1, and the emergent viewpoint, which is mentioned later in this chapter.

The ten schools of strategy represent a line of chronology through history, but not descent by replacement. The planning school, for example, may be a predecessor of the positioning school, but it has not disappeared. There is a tendency for previous schools of strategy to contribute to newer schools in complicated and often subtle ways. All of the schools continue to coexist today, infiltrating new frameworks under various guises and in different circumstances.

The biggest uproar from the 1980s through the present within the academic, business, and consulting fields has been over whether companies should select and design good strategies based on rational thought or whether better strategies emerge from experimentation and honed intuition.

Technical Rational Influence

On one side of the argument is the perspective of the design school of strategy, which was discussed in Chapter 1 and which was heavily influenced by the technical rational period of thought prevalent in the early nineteenth century, which continues through to today. This perspective is anchored in principles of industrialism and reflects one of modernity's key tenets—*objective representationalism*, the idea that the purpose of knowledge is to

TABLE 2.1 Ten Schools of Strategy Making*

	Sources	Base Discipline	Advocates	Intended Message	Realized Message
Design	Selznick; Andrews	None (architecture as metaphor)	Case study teachers (especially Harvard), leadership advocates (especially the U.S.)	Fit	Think (strategy making as case study)
Planning	Ansoff	Links to urban planning, systems theory, and cybernetics	"Professional" managers, MBAs, consultants, and government controllers (especially France and the U.S.)	Formalize	Program (rather than formulate)
Positioning	Porter; Purdue University (Schendel, Hatten)	Economics (industrial organization) and military history	Planning schools, consulting "boutiques," military writers (especially the U.S.)	Analyze	Calculate (rather than create or commit)
Entrepreneurial	Schumpeter; Cole	None (early writings from economists)	Popular business press, small businesses (especially Latin America and overseas Chinese)	Envision	Centralize (rather than hope)
Cognitive	Simon and March	Cognitive psychology	People with a psychological bent (pessimists and optimists—in opposite camps)	Cope or create	Worry (being unable to cope in either case)
Learning	Lindblom; Cyert and March; Weick; Quinn; Hamel and Prahalad	Some links to learning theory. Chaos theory in mathematics	People inclined to experimentation, ambiguity, adaptability (especially Japan and Scandinavia)	Learn	Play (rather than pursue)
Power	Alison; Pfeffer and Salancik; Astley	Political science	People who like power, politics, and conspiracy (especially France)	Promote	Hoard (rather than share)
Cultural	Rhenman; Normann	Anthropology	People who like the social, the spiritual, the collective (especially Scandinavia and Japan)	Coalesce	Perpetuate (rather than change)
Environmental	Hannan and Freeman; Pugh et al.	Biology	Population ecologists, some organization theorists, splitters, and positivists (especially Anglo-Saxon countries)	React	Capitulate (rather than confront)
Configuration	Chandler; Mintzberg; Miller and Friesen; Miles and Snow	History	Lumpers and integrators, change agents. (Configuration popular in the Netherlands, transformation popular in the U.S.)	Integrate, transform	Lump (rather than split, adapt)

represent, without logical contradiction, the "way things really are," or the linear, functional causes of actions.

As highlighted earlier, the design school has had a profound influence on the concept of strategy for governments and corporations. In this context, strategy is commonly perceived as oversight, separate from and levels above organizational action in a linear and hierarchical environment. The design school perspective lauds the development of the most accurate and most objective model possible, and then positions a company and formulates a rational plan for the future movement of the company.[2] Traditional ideas of rationality—diagnosis, prescription, and action—underlie the technical rational school of thought. Logic, control, and linear thinking support strategic assumptions, and thinking is separate from action.

Emergent Theory Influence

On the other side of the strategy argument is the emergent theory, a more intuitive strategy perspective, which was the technical rational triangular-hierarchical view of strategy as a top-down affair that strategy theorist Henry Mintzberg challenged in the early 1990s. Mintzberg's research found that managers were far less rational and foresightful strategy makers than the management literature supposed. This thinking led the way for proposals of a more "organic" view of organizations.[3]

Mintzberg's challenge to the classical design view of strategy argues that the perspective of Ansoff and others was dependent on "the fallacy of detachment," the belief that thinking and doing are separate. Managers, according to Mintzberg, are not rational, logical directors—their agendas and actions are influenced by politics, history, and human patterns of behavior over time.

Consequently, Mintzberg found that the interaction crucial to strategy does not occur between top executives and the environment; it happens where employees at the operational level of the organization interact with one another (at the coffee bar) and react to or anticipate customer needs and wants. Over time, the informal strategy making that occurs organically within various parts of the organization may create patterns of behavior that filter up to the apex to be formalized in plans. But, as Mintzberg discovered, strategy does not drop from the top.

Ansoff was equally adamant that the evidence he was gathering supported the planning school view, as mentioned in Chapter 1, of how strategy develops. This school of thought was adopted by Michael Porter, whose models are constructed on the premises of microeconomics and the design school, and are among the most popular strategy tools used today.

The debate between the emergent and design schools of strategy became increasingly polarized in the first half of the 1990s. By the late 1990s the debate had become colossal, and was a fundamental factor in the conceptual development of strategy. In his 1998 book, *Strategy Safari*, Mintzberg (along with Ahlstrand and Lampel) outlined many different approaches to strategy and concluded that no one is better than the others.[4]

Feuding Factions

By the late 1990s, the design-versus-emergent debate between Ansoff and Mintzberg had crescendoed. Eventually, Mintzberg framed the difference between the emergent approach that he advocated and Ansoff's analytical and formal approach by coining the phrase *strategy as learning*. Immediately, Ansoff countered by reframing his position and declaring that the debate was in fact about two contrasting views of strategy as learning. This position took the planning school's process of learning from being implicit to being explicit and opened the debate to new possibilities.

Today, the debate continues between strategy as a process of learning through hypothesis, generation, and revision, in accordance with the view of the design school, and strategy as a process of learning through exploration and discovery, from the perspective of the emergent school.

Mintzberg does not underrate the value of formal planning. Instead, he now argues that strategic planning is analysis, as opposed to strategic thinking—something that is considerably more.[5] Mintzberg proposes that the role of planners is not to discover the correct choice but, rather, to support strategy formulation by supplying the data and analyses for strategic thinking in order to inform and expand the issues considered during strategic discussions. He further develops his argument by pointing out that strategy making does not happen in isolation from the workings of the organization but, rather, involves the totality of everything that shapes the business.

Comparative Discussion

If we take the strategy debate back to the pre-modern perspective as a point of reference and trace strategy back to its ancient base, we can interpret the design-versus-emergent debate rather differently. Instead of viewing the two diametrically opposed schools of thought, in competition with each other, the design and emergent schools, taken together, can represent a well-developed version that mirrors the elemental strategy concept of the ancient Greeks. If the two schools continue to be perceived in opposition to each other, businesses themselves stand ultimately to lose strategically. If they are viewed as two parts of a whole, strategy takes on an expanded and constructive role. Further, businesses may be better served by viewing this inclusive approach to strategy as one that establishes a natural, synchronous movement between these two realms, which is essential to thinking strategically.

This is not to suggest that the ancient Greek concept of strategy is identical to the strategic thinking that is required today. While our current knowledge and perspective base has dramatically expanded, due to cumulative advances in information technology over the centuries, the basic nature of our complex reality suggests a need for inclusion, dealing with paradox and contradictory or incomplete information, and being able to juggle many different things at once. This complex reality represents the same basic nature as the reality that was confronted by the ancient Greeks.

Complexity Theory

Another indication that contemporary strategy is gradually moving toward a more inclusive and integrated approach is the growth of interest in a concept of natural science: complexity theory. The current interest in complexity theory is not new, but it is a new application in strategic thinking. In a nutshell, complexity theory focuses on the apparent random, disparate, and discontinuous nature of change. Complexity theory compares the nature of organizations to that of other living organisms, through a behaviorist and a Darwinian lens, referring to such naturally occurring organizations as "complex adaptive systems."

Complexity theory presumes that such systems inherently tend toward order rather than randomness and that this kind of nonlinear world is characterized more by discontinuity than by incremental change. Complexity theorists hold that when it comes to continuous adaptation, nature is the best teacher, and that forecasting the future is virtually impossible. Therefore, with regard to strategy, the expectation that companies can plan ahead is, fundamentally, an illusion, a waste of time and resources, and an exercise in futility.

Given that adaptation is inherent in sound strategy, complexity theory looks to the world of nature for cues to creating successful strategy. As in nature, the rules of survival in competitive global business are Darwinian—businesses must keep moving, and must continually develop advantageous variations in business to avoid irrelevance and extinction.

Among the most prominent places for the study of complexity theory as theoretical and mathematical modeling are the Institute of Advanced Study at Princeton University, the Santa Fe Institute, and Caltech. The theorists in these institutions believe that human organizations are also complex, adaptive systems that instinctively "know" how to act "strategically," if left to their own devices. These thinkers' studies suggest that the role of a corporate leader is to create conditions that will allow strategy to emerge—naturally. This process is what complexity theorists refer to as *self-organization*. Work conditions that encourage this kind of self-organization include decentralization, individual expression, and even chaos. It is believed that an abundance of top-down controls will ultimately doom the organization to failure. Complexity theorists insist that chaos is essential for ideas to flourish and suggest that virtually all controls should be eradicated, allowing a multitude of minds to contribute new ideas. The studies of the complexity theory perspective have very wide application in fields such as policy design and national defense strategy.[6]

A responsive and flexible process needs be established within organizations for chaos to emerge—one that encourages regular input, learning, and creativity throughout the organization in order to facilitate strategic thinking. Creativity, we know from current research, requires a subtle balance between chaos and order. To foster this equilibrium, support is necessary for an atmosphere that encourages novel insights, unusual perspectives, contrarian opinions, and an abundance of data to surface and be recognized.

Chaos Theory

Another contemporary, high-anxiety view of strategy is to perceive the future as totally unpredictable, uncontrollable, and chaotic. The chaos theory concept appeared first in the field of meteorology in the 1960s, when founder Edward Lorenz (of MIT) was working on a project to simulate weather patterns on a computer. Contrary to the technical rational school of thought, which has deluded executives into believing that strategy is a means of controlling the future, chaos theory refers to whether or not it is possible to make long-term predictions of any system if the initial conditions are substantially unknown.

Essentially, chaos theory contends that because the universe is a chaotic and unpredictable place, predicting what is going to happen at any given time or location is nearly impossible, because everything within a given system is ultimately connected. Therefore, an action in one place can have an effect in another place. Although chaotic systems appear to be random, beneath random behavior, patterns still emerge to suggest a kind of order. Oddly enough, chaotic systems can develop in modes that appear to be smooth and ordered.[7]

Acknowledging that the stock market is a nonlinear, dynamic, and chaotic system, chaos theory can be applied in order to determine the patterns behind market pricing. Aspects of chaos appear everywhere around the world. Mathematical equations for predicting how a system will act have been applied to other highly complex systems, such as ecological systems, biological systems, population growth, and epidemics, and experiments have been performed in human organizational systems. Chaos theory is really about making order from apparently random data.

From a scientific perspective, chaos theory is understandable and sensible. From a human organizational perspective, chaos theory can foster alienation and a feeling of powerlessness. From a strategic perspective, there is a certain perverted fatalism that can appeal: Why bother if things are going to unravel and unfold with or without my help?

Why is chaos theory relevant to our discussion of strategic thinking? One reason for its popularity in business strategy can be linked to the post-modern worldview of social change. The ancient Greeks believed life proceeded in cycles. In the nineteenth and twentieth centuries, social theorists believed life moved forward in stages. Current thinking has tended to swing in the direction of believing that functioning in the world is inherently something of a gamble, with direction left largely to luck. In terms of strategy, an extreme reaction to chaos theory could be phobia about the future, which might manifest itself in executive avoidance tactics such as over-analyzing ("Let's conduct just one more study"), through incrementalizing ("Let's just 'tweak' our existing strategy"), and through over-planning every minute detail ("Let's place each sub-phase of the timeline under the microscope lens").

Another reason for chaos theory's relevance to strategy is its shift in the approach to how businesses view the future. When the future was seen as a variation or a projection of the past, it was predictable; determination of the future was in the organization's hands, and an organization could control any significant diversion from the past. In recent years, political, social, and economic events have shifted dramatically and rapidly—beyond imagination and comprehension. This experience has given rise to feelings of unpreparedness, vulnerability, and powerlessness among business leaders. Curiously, the whims of chaos offer some comfort: If the future is the convergence of chaotic forces, then it is impossible to predict and control. So, why try? In some sense, there may be a natural reassurance that comes from being absolved of responsibility for the unknowable and uncontrollable future of an organization.

Interestingly and understandably, among the corporate clients with whom I work I have noticed a diminishing emphasis on long-term sustainable strategy whenever there is imminent chaos or a major economic hurdle on the horizon. Executives tend to shift their focus from a strategic horizon to a short-term, immediate, operational success. In some companies, those responsible for strategy have actually stepped back from their strategic responsibility in an effort to perform operational triage. Such a panicked emphasis on emergency, short-term results, coupled with obsessiveness about short-term financial strength, can eventually sever the companies' lifeline to a competitive future.

If the past is considered to be a less reliable predictor of the future than was previously believed, then chance or chaos becomes an appealing and relevant alternative to strategic planning—but not to strategic thinking. Strategic thinking becomes all the more compelling. Strategic thinking is a proposition that says we can affect the future through a strategic learning process that positions strategists as adaptive influencers in this ominously unpredictable environment, rather than as victims or as controllers.

Dealing with natural contradictions, paradoxes, and polarities is a central part of strategic thinking, especially within our globalized environment. Through the frameworks of natural order, ancient Greek history, and other cultures, contradictions, paradoxes, and polarities are not regarded as opposites with an objective to conquer, crush, or cancel. Rather, they are perceived as delicate yet durable parts of a whole that are necessary for natural strategic balance and sustainability.

The tension that is inherent in uncertainty and ambivalence is a constructive component for avoiding stagnation and maintaining a dynamic process. This same tension supports strategic thinking through its emphasis on learning, creativity, critical reflective processes, adaptability, and sustainability.

The learning theorists and the complexity theorists agree that our current competitive, unpredictable, and inconsistent business environment places unprecedented demands on our capacity to re-create resilient and sustainable strategy.

An interesting notion is to overlay complexity and chaos theories onto corporations, which are artificially constructed organizations comprised of humans—organisms of the highest level—and strategic thinking. While there are of course parallels, there are also points of diversion, namely that humans have the capacity to reflect, to think, and to feel. Although nature is extraordinarily creative and adaptive, it has, nonetheless, a vital flaw. Nature is unable to understand why it succeeds or fails.[8] The renewed interest in natural order, in ancient history, and in other cultures with regard to learning to think strategically points to an implicit need to explore beyond the means that we currently use to define strategy making, and hints at a willingness to extend our search for making meaning within a broader strategic context.

Strategic Planning and Strategic Thinking: Two Sides of the Coin

The changes in the corporate strategy function and role have implications not only for those responsible for facilitating the learning of strategic thinking, but also for all who are increasingly involved in strategic thinking. The highly analytical, data-based strategy decisions need to be strengthened with a process of challenge and testing that shifts from a linear planning model to a thinking model.

There is nothing wrong with any of the current linear planning models; they are simply insufficient for strategic thinking, unless they ride in tandem with divergent thinking, critical inquiry, critical dialogue, critical reflection, and critical thinking.

Table 2.2 provides a more detailed comparison of strategic planning and strategic thinking, including how the two approaches differ conceptually, who is typically tasked with leading them, and the kinds of analysis they draw on. Hopefully, the table will paint a compelling picture not only of how strategic planning and strategic thinking differ, but also of how they can complement one another in the competitive business environment.

TABLE 2.2   Contrast of Strategic Planning and Strategic Thinking

Factor	Strategic Planning	Strategic Thinking
Concept	A "product" Analysis, metrics, numbers Successful strategy is present tense and future tense Convergent	A "process" that is renewable, re-creative, generative, adaptable Insight, innovation, ideas Successful strategy is past tense Divergent
Key dimensions	Financial	Financial, social contribution, individual development, risk assessment, business, integrity
Anchor	Singular, exclusive Economics	Multiple, inclusive Economics, sociology, history, politics, science, arts, humanities
Formulation	Executive committee Corporate management team VPs Business unit heads	Corporate management team Business unit heads Functional heads "Pipeline" of strategists
Performance measures	Financial Money as key asset Static Quantitative	Comprehensive relationships are key asset Dynamic Qualitative and quantitative
Analysis	Convergent Quantitative Neutral Objective	Quantitative and qualitative Relationships Contextual Subjective and objective
People and organization development	Cost/expense Profitability	Investment/asset Sustainable growth

Notes

1. Mintzberg and Lampel, "Reflecting on the Strategy Process," 23–4.
2. Cummings and Wilson, *Images of Strategy*, 16–17.
3. Mintzberg, Ahlstrand, and Lampel, *Strategy Safari: A Guided Tour through the Wilds of Strategic Management*.
4. Mintzberg, Ahlstrand, and Lampel, *Strategy Safari: A Guided Tour through the Wilds of Strategic Management*.
5. Mintzberg, Ahlstrand, and Lampel, *Strategy Safari: A Guided Tour through the Wilds of Strategic Management*.
6. Foremost among the leaders of purely theoretical and mathematical modeling is the Santa Fe Institute. An extensive publication list on complexity theory from this perspective is available at www.santafe.edu. Caltech offers an interesting list of publications on the topic at www.cds.caltech.edu. And the Institute of Advanced Study (www.ias.edu) at Princeton is also among the most prominent places to host scholars in disciplines related to complexity theory, as it relates to management and strategy, not mathematics.
7. Research on complexity and chaos theory is prominent at ESSEC in France, the Center for Social Dynamics & Complexity (CSDC) at Arizona State University, the Center for Complexity in Business at the University of Maryland, the Harvard-MIT Observatory of Economic Complexity, and the Center for Social Complexity at George Mason University. Also, specific research on cognition/strategy has been carried out at the Center for the Study of Complex Systems and Cognition at the École Normale Supérieure, France.
8. Pietersen, *Reinventing Strategy: Using Strategic Learning to Create and Sustain Breakthrough Performance*, 51.

3

Implications of the History of Strategy for Strategic Learning

So what does our understanding of the history of strategy have to say about learning to think strategically? Interdisciplinary thinking (i.e., management, science, mathematics, education, anthropology, philosophy, and humanities) offers a degree of convergence on the current direction of learning and strategy. Although learning has intermittently been implied in strategy literature, the management development literature increasingly echoes this convergence as well.[1] At present, the pendulum appears to be moving toward a more integrated and inclusive approach to strategy, as an effective counterpoint to the highly analytic, rational, linear approach that has dominated the field since the modern industrial era of the early 1900s.

As we have seen from modern strategy history, learning figured prominently in U.S. wartime production planning efforts. The U.S. military financed studies, and subsequently developed instructional approaches to strategy development based on the current strategy concept—economic efficiency—which translated into operational efficiency for the military. Therefore, many of the strategy approaches to learning born of the U.S. military were based in the technical rational concept of strategy and were eventually modified for the corporate sector.

The history of organizational strategy has shown that learning became explicit when BCG articulated the experience curve in the 1970s. Learning models such as BCG's Growth Share Matrix implied continuous learning based on market-share analysis. Porter's popular "five forces" model of strategic positioning emphasized the need for learning as a means to discover strategic opportunities. Both models were outgrowths of the highly structured school of strategic planning that identified strategic issues as complex problems to be solved, and assumed that a "best" answer exists for a given problem. This learning assumption was supported by instructional development that promoted a multitude of skills-based problem-solving approaches and analysis techniques for various levels and types of problems, which we use extensively today.

Although acceptance of strategic thinking as an emergent process is gradually gaining momentum among academics and consulting firms and within the organizational development field, most textbooks, business school courses, and corporate development approaches do not yet fully differentiate between strategic planning and strategic thinking. The terms continue to be used almost interchangeably and with little differentiation.

Emergent strategy is aligned with a learning belief that strategy-making problems have no single correct answer—only action that is somewhat better or worse.[2] All too often, I see strategists move to solve a problem before they have broadly and critically scrutinized and diverged the issue at hand. Strategic thinking is about far more than problem solving; strategic thinking suspends strategic problem solving to engage in a critical examination of the underlying assumptions that support the premise and operations, rather than focus only on the problem-solving outcome. Strategic thinking relies on the concepts of critical theory to diverge thinking, and to challenge, test, and explore a strategic issue. Strategic thinking is an iterative and fluid process between divergent and convergent thinking and contains both critical and creative elements. The inherent tension of these cognitive processes requires complex cognitive functions.

The schism between strategic planning and strategic thinking is an important conceptual distinction for executives and those seeking to advocate a learning approach to strategy making for their organizations. Those responsible for facilitating strategic learning can draw from the history of strategy and the cautionary tales of leaders and organizations swept away by the next new approach or trend. Perhaps the strategy jargon has changed and the formula is updated, but is the premise dramatically new?

Furthermore, history suggests that we need not be afraid to integrate and realign bits and pieces from the various strategy approaches to imagine new configurations and experiment with possibilities. As previously mentioned, schools of strategy cycle in and out of favor, and strategy making is a dynamic and messy process. Intricate models, complicated jargon, and scientific formulas have a way of creating false security and an illusion of precision within the realm of strategy. New strategies are often a recasting of the old. In a sense, old strategic ideas never disappear entirely—they simply go underground and infiltrate new practices covertly.

While risk analysis is integral to the strategy-making process, our preoccupation with hyper-rationalization and control of what we do not understand or are unable to choose between runs counter to our human nature. On the contrary, as recalled from the ancient Greek concept of strategy, balancing "among" opposing and contradictory things is inherent to the complexity of our humanity.

Today we are at a critical juncture: we recognize that the approach to strategy that we have been using no longer generates what we need, yet we fear the unknown. We are stuck in a logical, rational planning framework, which has us spinning in our place.

If successful strategic thinking is regarded as a process of continuously asking challenging questions and critically and creatively thinking through the strategic issues, then learning to construct effective critical reflective processes is just as important as finding "the solution." Thus, we must invest as much (if not more) in learning to think strategically as we do in pursuing strategic plans.

Notes

1. Several researchers and authors, including Ross Harrison, Lara Jelenc, Jeanne Liedtka, Henry Mintzberg, Willie Pietersen, Julia Sloan, George Tovsiga, and Douglas Waters have all offered or implied a range of definitions of strategic thinking.
2. Revans, *The Origin and Growth of Action Learning*.

Summary and Questions

Contemporary Western strategy is rooted in technical rationality, the late nineteenth-century view of knowledge that was based on the philosophical legacy of positivism that sought to solve problems through rigorous application of scientific theory and methodology. This basis for contemporary strategy originated at the height of the industrial revolution and was profoundly influential in shaping the notion of strategy to the principles underlying technical rationality. Strategy, consistent with other notions of the day, needed to adhere to the tenants of proof and predictability, and resolve to be systematic, specialized, and standardized. Corporations, governments, and other organizations remain yoked to this worldview today despite the substantially more complex reality of today's world. Executives and leaders today must deal with vastly complex strategic problems that are rife with paradox, ambiguity, and contradiction.

The ancient Greeks saw these polar, paradoxical, complex, and competing elements of strategic problems as not only natural, but also entirely necessary for understanding their world and developing strategic thought. Successful armies and leaders of the time adopted the concept of *metos* and the subjective relational notion, but it was slowly lost to process-based approaches as both armies and nations grew. The same shift occurred in late twentieth-century corporations; strategy shifted to the concept of deliberate strategic planning that was formulated by a select few at the top of an organization.

Successful strategic thinkers seek to expose and rigorously challenge the underlying premise of a strategy by suspending solutions in an effort to identify the essence of the strategic problem. This suspension process naturally creates tension that is constructive and critical to enabling strategic thinking. It supports agility and innovative thought. Engaging in the critical reflective processes of critical inquiry, critical dialogue, critical reflection, and critical thinking is key to understanding the complexity of strategic problems. Yet, the process is often overlooked as leaders race to find an expeditious solution to a complex problem. Like the ancient Greeks, successful strategists must embrace paradox and find ways to move fluidly amongst the cognitive functions that support strategic thinking, strategic planning, and strategic implementation.

1. Are there elements of technical rationality that you notice within your organizational culture? How is the technical rational approach reinforced in your organization's approach to strategy?
2. How has the approach to strategy within your organization been influenced by trends within your industry? Discuss any aspects of those trends that may have been influenced by technical rationality.
3. Compare and contrast key factors of strategic planning and strategic thinking. How are they complementary and compatible?
4. Discuss some examples of how society at large reinforces a technical rational perspective?
5. What are the implications of the history of strategy on your strategic approach in today's complex and global environment?

HOW DO WE LEARN TO THINK STRATEGICALLY?

Formal Learning Takes a Backseat to Informal Learning

We receive three educations,
One from our parents,
One from our school-masters,
and
One from the world.
The third contradicts
All that the first two teach us.

Charles Louis de Secondat, Baron de Montesquieu (1689–1755),
French political philosopher

4

Definition of Strategic Thinking

Moving on to *how* we learn to think strategically, let's start with *what* strategic thinking is. As we look closely at what strategic thinking is, it can be quite perplexing to discover that the term *strategic thinking* has become a synonym or substitute for lots of vague notions. In other words, it is an over-used, mis-used, and under-defined term. While there are many definitions of strategic thinking—some competing and some complementary—I have created and work with the definition of strategic thinking as an intent-driven approach to strategy based on critical theory that is supported by a complex cluster of cognitive capabilities that are distinct and different from strategic planning. This cognitive cluster includes the critical reflective processes (critical inquiry, critical reflection, critical dialogue, and critical thinking) and a complex set of cognitive functions.

Furthermore, the purpose of strategic thinking is to suspend problem solving and engage in a rigorous process of diverging, testing, and challenging the underlying premise of the strategy, and to generate new options as a means to creating a winning, innovative, and sustainable strategy.

> *Strategic thinking is an intent-driven approach to strategy based on critical theory and supported by a complex cluster of cognitive capabilities that are distinct and different from strategic planning.*

Drawing on the critical theory of Jürgen Habermas, the pre-eminent twentieth-century German philosopher and scholar, I consider both a creative and a critical element to strategic thinking—a divergent and a deep, dive-thinking aspect. Habermas established the theory of *communicative reason*, which distinguishes itself from the rationalist tradition of a reliance on scientific experts and bureaucrats providing rational, instrumental, and efficient problem solving. His theory of communicative reason rests on the argument of universal pragmatism and democratic participation through the use of critical reflective processes in complex problem solving. In other words, Habermas perceived that organizations suppressed the communicative and critical reflective processes by permitting associations, the government, and markets to control complex decisions through the use of strategic and instrumental rationality, so that the logic of the system supplants the workings of the real-life world.[1]

In search of the Holy Grail, business and government sectors are inundated with strategy models, methodologies, and approaches. The focus, however, should not be to find the perfect model, as our strategy environment is far too unpredictable, unstable, and uncertain; rather, the focus needs to be on strengthening people's strategic thinking capability. We need to understand how to *learn* to think strategically. As strategic thinking researcher Lara Jelenc notes, "The strategy focus must change from the models to the subject of strategy—people."[2] Once we have an understanding of what strategic thinking is, we can proceed with endless options for development. In this way, people can become strategic assets in the most fundamental and sustainable way.

Cognitive Clusters of Strategic Thinking and Strategic Planning™

As mentioned in the definition I offer in the previous section, strategic thinking includes a specific set of complex cognitive capabilities and critical reflective processes that are distinctly different from those required of strategic planning. Figure 4.1 shows a cluster of cognitive functions that are required for strategic thinking. These cognitive functions include: conceptual, divergent, a-rational, generative, nonlinear, metaphoric, conceptual, abstract, panoramic, polarity, symbolic, intuitive, and creative cognitive processes, as well as critical reflective processes. The intent of these strategic thinking functions is to suspend problem solving in order to diverge and deep-dive with critical reflective processes. How often do we rush to solve a so-called strategic problem, without taking the time to explore and critically examine the fundamental premise and explore alternative perspectives and propositions?

The complexity of the cognitive functions required of strategic thinkers is interesting to note, as we recall how little of formal strategy course content and time are devoted to strengthening and enhancing this cluster. Creating a winning and sustainable strategy is dependent on this cluster, yet a scant amount of emphasis is given to this cluster in our traditional educational curriculum. Among the most challenging and necessary cognitive functions is polarity thinking, which thrives on the tension of competing and contradictory elements to fuel imagination and innovative thought. Another curious distinction of this cluster is the emphasis on "seeing" strategy. Strategic thinking requires the ability to draw from this entire cluster of cognitive functions.

By contrast, as indicated in Figure 4.1, strategic planning requires the cognitive functions of convergent, concrete, linear, analytical, rational, reductionist, literal, objective, and logical thinking. The intent of strategic planning is to solve a strategic problem.

While one cluster is not superior to the other, each cluster is distinctly different. Interestingly, the cognitive cluster that supports strategic planning can impede and even undermine the cognitive cluster required of strategic thinking, and vice versa.

Within our conventional formal education, the strategic planning cluster receives fair attention and support. Can the same be said about the strategic thinking cluster? What are the implications of this for the future of global business strategy? Government policy? Military strategy? National defense? Good strategists learn, develop, and are adept at both clusters, as the two clusters are complementary.

Strategy is considered to be among the most important leadership responsibilities.[3] Yet, the educational lens tends to zoom in on the cognitive cluster that rewards and supports strategic planning—with sparse attention given to the highly complex cluster that is essential for strategic thinking. Given our complex, unpredictable, constant, and rapidly changing environment, we need strategic leaders who are adept at both cognitive clusters and able to pendulate between the two with agility. My hope is that by understanding these cognitive clusters (Figure 4.1) and the accompanying informal learning process, leaders can build their strategic thinking capability and expand their cognitive repertoire as a means to enriching their contribution to strategy.

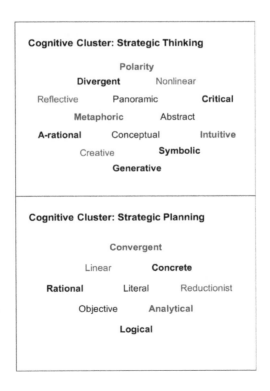

FIGURE 4.1   Cognitive Clusters for Strategic Thinking and Strategic Planning™

The Sloan Triad Model of Strategy™

As a practical way to clarify the considerable confusion around the term strategic thinking, I have created the following Sloan Triad Model of Strategy™ as a visual representation of strategic thinking, strategic planning, and strategic implementation. I have found the model to be helpful to position strategic thinking within a broader strategy framework, and as a means to support the learning of strategic thinkers. The following model can also be useful to identify individual, team, and organizational habits, strengths, and development needs.

This model is a rather simple illustration of how these three domains of strategic thinking, strategic planning, and strategic implementation are connected as part of a whole strategy process. Yet, as previously discussed, each domain is distinctly different in terms of the underlying cognitive cluster that supports it.

You will notice that this illustration is a "triangle." It is not a "circle" or a "line." Sometimes I find that executives confuse the triangle for a circle because there is a common, over-simplified, idealized misconception that strategy is a cycle—starting with strategic thinking during "strategy season," then moving to strategic planning, and predictably concluding with implementation. Another misconception is that strategy is a linear process consisting of three equal segments. It would be convenient if this were the case; but in our rapidly changing and constantly changing real business life, the process is actually a highly iterative, uneven, back-and-forth, boomerang process. It is dynamic, not static or invariable. Although there may appear to be a clean linear flow among the domains, it is not quite so simple or orderly. These domains are not separate or sequenced entities. In conversation with a Swedish technology CEO, he noted quite adamantly his experience with the strategy domains.

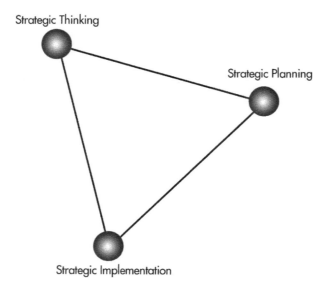

FIGURE 4.2 The Sloan Triad Model of Strategy™

I tell you honestly that two things happen when I work on my strategy. Yes, I make a tight plan to appease the investors and to put in[to] the report. (laughter) It looks like A-B-C-D! This is the easy part (more laughter). It is quite routine—anyone can do this. Then there is another part that is very different. I would say it is totally confusing; it is exciting—and it is when my adrenaline runs! Like a heavy working out to prepare for a new destination. I do not know how to describe it. I am in a different place in my head. I can only focus on one of these ways or the other at a time because the way I think when I am in this place is very different from the other. This idea that strategy is linear or that it follows a flow is false. It is not. It is risky and messy. For me, it is helpful to know which is my focus at the time. The actual process? It bounces between messy and messier! (laughter)

The characteristics of each strategy domain follow.

Strategic Thinking

Let us start with strategic thinking, since that is the emphasis of this book. As we discussed earlier in this chapter, the intent of strategic thinking is not to find solutions. Rather, the intent of strategic thinking is to *suspend* solutions, in order to diverge the problem and to dive deeply into the underlying premise of the issue in an attempt to challenge assumptions and to identify the correct strategic problem. While this may run counter to conventional approaches to strategy, it is not uncommon for businesses to be in the midst of a strategy implementation, only to discover that the real problem has not been addressed. Exasperating and frustrating, it is often an indication of the absence of strategic thinking.

Strategic thinking is often well outside the comfort zone of those tasked with developing a strategy. Strategic thinking is divergent in nature, non-linear, highly intuitive, and emotional, uses critical reflective processes (critical inquiry, critical dialogue, critical thinking, critical reflection), and is iterative, a-rational, and inefficient. Tension is an important part of strategic thinking.

Strategic Planning

In stark contrast to strategic thinking, the intent of strategic planning is to solve problems. It is convergent in nature, linear, rational, logical, devoid of emotion, analytical, reductionist, and efficient. In strategic planning, our aim is to eliminate tension in the form of a solution.

Strategic Implementation

And lastly, let us consider the characteristics of strategic implementation, as it tends to be everybody's favorite. Implementation is just "doing it!" Strategic implementation is also highly convergent, rational, logical, and linear in nature. Implementation is ultimately, the aim of any successful strategy. A quick reminder—while executives sometimes assume that there is nothing strategic about implementation, the intent of implementation is to be strategically aligned with a delineated strategic plan that has already been rigorously tested and challenged through strategic thinking.

The three domains on the Sloan Triad Model of Strategy™ are connected by imaginary "elastic bands" as a reminder that a successful strategy requires all three domains, though not in particular succession. The domains are inseparable and are inter-dependent upon each other. Each is significant to the business success, but each plays a different role and proceeds in and out of focus depending on the business need. And those who participate in strategy conversations need to inquire about the strategic focus.

Depending on the business need, one domain advances to the forefront at any given time, in a highly fragmented, oscillating manner, while the other two domains recede, as indicated in Figure 4.3. As previously mentioned, since strategy is a key leadership responsibility, it is a leader's role to determine and to state which strategy domain needs to be brought into focus and to zoom in and out accordingly—as the business circumstance requires. Leaders need to develop the habit of pressing the "pause button" at any point in the strategy process to advance the appropriate domain to the forefront; sometimes for a brief meeting and other times for a period of several months. Using the Sloan Triad Model of Strategy™ requires agility of thought, constant cognitive shifting, and getting comfortable with the fluidity that is inherent within the strategy framework.

The length of time given to any one domain of strategy is variable. It tends not to be the same duration or sequence twice. The rhythm of the movement among the domains is different with each strategy case because the particular factors and circumstances

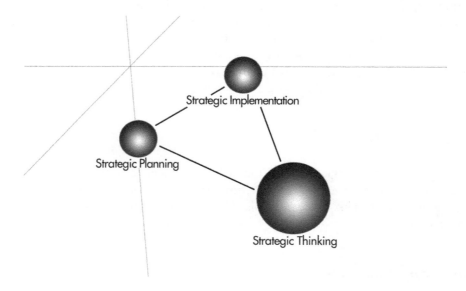

FIGURE 4.3 The Sloan Triad Model of Strategy™ in Operation, with Strategic Thinking in Focus at the Forefront

are different. As a favorite Indian proverb states, "When the pear is ripe, it falls from the tree." Executives often ask how long they should stay focused on one domain or the other. My answer usually is that it depends on the business need. This is part of the risk involved in leading strategy.

> *Despite strategic thinking being a highly informal,*
> *iterative, and social process, there is a rigor and*
> *discipline to learning it that is distinct and different*
> *from that which is required of strategic planning.*

The Sloan Triad Model of Strategy™ is highly dynamic. While thinking obviously occurs within all three domains, as we discussed earlier, the specific cognitive cluster that underlies each domain is distinctly different. Those who lead strategy conversations would do well to become adept and agile at all three; being capable of moving fluidly and seamlessly from one strategy domain to another based on the business need. Or, alternatively, to develop a cadre of capable and competent people within the company who are skillful at all three domains. One caveat that strategists want to avoid is an over-reliance on any one of the three domains.

Historically, most of the strategy literature has emphasized the importance of the domains of strategic planning and implementation, or the existing gap between these two domains. Yet, without an understanding of how successful strategists learn to think strategically, the gap between strategic planning and implementation will become only wider.

Despite strategic thinking being a highly informal, iterative, and social process, there is a rigor and discipline to learning it that is distinct and different from that which is required of strategic planning. My practice seeks to support learning to think strategically and to embed it within an organization. This is based on the belief and the findings from my studies that suggest strategic thinkers reside within all levels and across all functions and geographic locations of an organization. Strategic thinking is not the byproduct of position, precedence, or status. It is not an elitist function; rather it is learnable.

Notes

1. Habermas, *Between Facts and Norms: Contributions to a Discourse Theory of Law and Democracy.*
2. Jelenc, "The Impact of Strategic Management Schools and Strategic Thinking on the Performance of Croatian Entrepreneurial Practice," 6.
3. Brookings Institute, Center for Leadership Capacity Services. Office of Personnel Management. "Strategic Thinking," internal document 2011.1.

5

Informal and Formal
Learning Defined

So how do we actually learn to think strategically? The CEO of a leading privately owned Polish manufacturing company offered one explanation:

It's not so simple as step by step. [Strategy] is not a formula or a simple pattern. It is a complex, constantly developing process; it is not an ordered process. Making strategy is not a straight line—I don't sit at my desk and just build it like a model.

A Japanese financial executive declared:

I don't even like the word strategy. It seems to mean that it is a model or … fixed steps to follow. To be frank, I think all the models and theories, they are only complicated planning ideas. Strategy is not so orderly.

Throughout this book, informal learning is contrasted with formal learning because, as previously noted, it is the informal learning approach—rather than the formal one—that successful strategists credit with influencing their own learning. These preferences were echoed by the CEO of an American technology company who matter-of-factly stated:

It's a hard thing to describe—I wouldn't say it's at all step by step. It's more like a ball or something that's spinning. It's not even a single thing. And nothing truly strategic has ever occurred to me in the office. Never.

Another president of a manufacturing company endorsed strategic thinking as an informal process, noting:

It's not this kind of problem solving, formula, straight-line thinking—it's more about just opening up—seeing what kinds of opinions you can draw on. How many different perspectives can you find? What precedent has been set? Is there a new twist you can give? It's not very linear.

As explained in previous chapters, strategic thinking is nonlinear and a-rational and does not occur within a prescribed time and place. Drawing from the interviews I conducted with successful corporate strategists, clearly, we learn strategic thinking informally. In discussions about strategic thinking, learning is generally not the first word to pop up, and yet learning must be the foundation of strategic thinking if we are to have any hope of developing innovative, competitive, adaptive, and sustainable capacities within organizations. In order to encourage learning, we need to understand what informal learning is and how it applies to strategic thinking. To Henry Mintzberg, the essence of strategy making is the process of learning as we act. As he reminds us: "Strategies can develop inadvertently, without the conscious intention of senior management, often through a process of learning ... Learning inevitably plays *a*, if not *the*, crucial role in the development of novel strategies."[1]

Informal Learning

Informal learning warrants particular attention in order to understand how successful executives learn to think strategically, for the strategy and learning literature concur that it is informal learning, rather than formal learning, that most influences strategic thinking. However, current strategic development practices have not necessarily caught up with this notion.

During recent years, as informal learning has come into vogue, the term has sometimes been used to refer loosely to any "accidental" behavior outside predicted or anticipated norms—learning related or not. Day-to-day workplace banter makes little differentiation between informal and formal learning, and the word *informal* is becoming a convenient catch-all term among executive development practitioners.

This chapter establishes informal learning as the predominant learning approach used to think strategically. The next chapter presents the reflections of successful strategists on the impact of formal learning. The final chapter of this part discusses the factors of context and transfer on the strategic thinking process.

Several definitions are offered as a simple way of differentiating formal and informal learning. Informal learning is regarded as learning that is predominantly unstructured, unplanned, experiential, non-institutional, and non-routine. Informal learning takes place as people go about their daily activities at work, at play, or elsewhere. By contrast, formal learning is considered to be structured, planned, pre-programed, and institutionally sponsored classroom-based learning where a trainer, teacher, manager, professor, or some other "education agent" is responsible for planning, implementing, and evaluating the learning that occurs.

Let us not forget that we human beings are, by our very nature, learning beings. We learn all the time by identifying and solving problems, observing other people, asking questions of friends and colleagues, requesting advice and help, and accessing records of human experience, such as stories, books, and online information. Although many people associate learning with their educational experiences, most learning actually occurs outside any formal educational environment and is often simultaneous to our struggle with the challenges of daily life and work. Learning to think strategically also follows this informal pattern.

A Hong Kong technology executive explained that strategy

is not really a step-by-step process. It's not that black and white. It's more ongoing and not really a structured sort of thing. There isn't anything methodical or scientific about it. I don't think strategically in a meeting. It's just where I state my thinking—if I'm lucky!

According to adult learning theorists Victoria Marsick and Karen Watkins, informal learning is "predominantly experiential and non-institutional, non-routine, and often tacit."[2] By its nature, informal learning cannot be fully pre-programed. Informal learning arises spontaneously within the context of people following interests as they arise. Informal learning can be planned or unplanned and involves some degree of awareness that learning is taking place. Informal learning is driven by our everyday preferences, choices, and intentions. Self-directed learning, social learning, mentoring, coaching, networking, learning from mistakes, and trial and error are some common kinds of informal learning.

Incidental and Intentional Learning

Two subcategories of informal learning are particularly relevant to strategic thinking: *intentional* and *incidental* learning. Intentional learning is what we expect or anticipate we will learn. For example, if I have a phone conversation with the company's finance director to discuss a currency-valuation formula and I learn a new currency-valuation formula, then intentional learning has occurred.

> *Much of the learning involved in thinking strategically is informal—either incidental or intentional in nature.*

On the other hand, incidental informal learning is "a byproduct of some other activity, such as task accomplishment, interpersonal interaction, sensing the organization, trial-and-error experimentation, or even formal learning," as adult learning researchers Marsick and Watkins explain.[3]

Using our preceding example, I may incidentally learn not to trust the finance director's department because, during the conversation, I also hear that they have a very high staff turnover rate. I may become suspicious of the department because, in my belief system, longevity signifies stability and stability is an indicator of trust.

Incidental learning is unintentional and unexpected. We are virtually never conscious that it is occurring, as its modes include learning by doing, learning from mistakes, and learning through a series of covert interpersonal experiments. This type of learning is tacit, taken for granted, and implicit in its assumptions and actions.

As we will see in this chapter and the next, much of the learning involved in thinking strategically is informal—either incidental or intentional in nature. Table 5.1 outlines types of informal learning and describes some of the characteristics and examples of each type.[4]

In my practice, I notice that strategic thinking can be greatly enhanced by an awareness of intentional and incidental learning. Both influence our perceptions of situations, and we bring those perceptions to strategic discussions. A heightened awareness of intentional and incidental learning can help to eradicate our blind spots and lead to seeing new strategic possibilities for development.

Education theorist Peter Jarvis distinguishes formal, nonformal, and informal education by stating:

> *Formal [education] situations are bureaucratic, organized, nonformal situations but not necessarily in a bureaucratic environment, and informal situations are ones where there are no prespecified environments, although there are always covert, procedures of interaction.*[5]

Many of the executives I interviewed describe instances of incidental learning as they engaged in strategy making. The Hong Kong technology executive implied incidental learning in his process of information gathering when he explained:

TABLE 5.1 Description of Informal—Intentional and Incidental—Learning*

	Types of Informal Learning	
	Intentional	Incidental
Characteristics	Experiential Non-institutional Controlled by learner Somewhat planned, but may not be a primary aim Expect learning outcomes, but they may differ from those expected Non-classroom site Fair predictability of outcomes	Experiential Not planned Not intentional By-product of other activities Unclear, unpredictable outcomes
Examples	Self-directed learning Coaching Networking Personal study Mentoring Distance learning Feedback Performance planning Experimentation Research Trial and error	Involvement Mistakes Assumptions Beliefs, values Attributions Hidden curricula in formal learning

* Modified from Marsick and Watkins, *Informal and Incidental Learning in the Workplace.*

TABLE 5.2 Incidental and Intentional Learning Acquired from Information Gathering

Learning Source	Approach	Intentional Learning	Incidental/Actual Learning
Self-study	Journals Publications Newsletters Newspapers Professional papers Reports	Technical information Legal demographics Regulations Trends Projections Statistical data	Technical and professional information Not to trust all data or sources Inaccurate/misleading information Contradictions Hidden motive to publications Need to verify data
Professional meetings	Conferences Conventions Trade shows Lectures Government meetings Financial Currency meetings	Competitor reports Financial reports Industry standards Industry projections Regulatory policies Legal information	New ideas Different products and inventions Inside information/gossip "Political" savvy Need to withhold information Realistic data Intellectual stimulation Credibility "testing" of competitors Not to trust all official data One's position can create dangerous distance from reality—and skew projections
Colleagues	CEO President CFO COO Associates Partners	Specific information New ideas Different perspectives	Intellectual stimulation Reactions New ideas Different perspectives Gossip/agendas/hidden motives
Professional associates	Journalists Experts Other business leaders Government officials Politicians	New ideas Different information	Intellectual stimulation Challenge Testing New ideas Different perspectives
Strangers	Students Airline and train passengers Friends of friends People in stores People in coffee shops	Opinions Ideas Reactions Feedback	Reality check Different perspective New names of inventors/innovators/products New ideas Different, informal data Good questions Opinions Intellectual stimulation

What's happened to me a lot is, when I go for regulatory data or legal data, it's easy to get—straightforward. You know exactly what you need. Then I talk about it and play out different impact scenarios with people here, and also with counsel, and expert advisors ... and honestly, I've been burned a lot (laughter). And what I've really learned in looking back is that I can't trust anybody when it comes to data—not the analysts, not the publishers, not even my advisors or mates here. You just can't trust people with data. You have to look behind the curtain.

His *intentional* learning was retrieval of accurate data; what he learned *incidentally* through his experiences of gathering information was that he could not trust people involved in the data-collection process.

Interestingly, while we often intend to glean factual information from the data we gather, we also learn "other stuff" incidentally. In the case of the executives whom I interviewed, they all learned incidentally not to trust the media that publish the data, and sometimes even the data itself. Also, they learned incidentally to gauge boundaries among competitors and to weigh trust levels with colleagues and rivals—primarily through personal interactions and industry-culture mores when they attended trade shows, conferences, and meetings.

> *Thinking strategically does not tend to happen in meetings or at work—it occurs informally outside work in a very nonlinear manner.*

Coaching, feedback, networking, and personal study are some common forms of intentional learning. The incidental learning of the executives in my study is apparent in their differing responses presented in Table 5.2.[6]

Notes

1. Mintzberg, "The Fall and Rise of Strategic Planning."
2. Marsick and Watkins, *Informal and Incidental Learning in the Workplace*, 7.
3. Marsick and Watkins, *Informal and Incidental Learning in the Workplace*, 12.
4. Marsick and Watkins, *Informal and Incidental Learning in the Workplace*.
5. Jarvis, *Adult Learning in the Social Context*, 70.
6. Sloan, "A Case Study of How Nine Executives Learn Informally to Develop Strategy in a Global Context."

6

Formal Learning Refuted

What role do all the strategy courses and consulting seminars play in learning to think strategically? There is a seemingly weak and unconvincing role, according to the interview data. Again, differentiating between learning to *think strategically* and learning to *plan systematically* is important. As noted earlier, thinking strategically does not typically happen in meetings or at work—thinking strategically tends to occur informally, outside work, and in a nonlinear manner. This point is interesting for those responsible for strategic development. Thinking strategically is a considerably more conceptual and complex exercise than rational, sequential, and linear planning.

When senior executives were asked a series of questions about how they learned to make strategy, none referenced any formal learning approaches (e.g., courses, models, schools of thought, and theory), except through negative connotation. The executives were asked to identify background factors, particular people, or circumstances that influenced them, and to name the things to which they pay particular attention when thinking strategically. Not only were the executives negative in their recollections of formal strategy-making approaches, but also they discredited these formal approaches or assessed them as factors of non-influence.

Formal approaches to learning tended to be rejected in favor of an informal approach, which referred primarily to experience. The formal education and training that the executives received were dismissed outright as being irrelevant to their actual learning for how to make good strategy. Therefore, formal education for strategy making appears to have been neither an asset nor an impediment to their learning. Such irrelevance is sobering, especially if we consider the budgets that are allocated for strategy courses.

A Japanese financial executive concluded: "Most of what I learned in courses was only technique—like a nice craft." And a German manufacturing executive said: "I tell [junior executives] they must talk to many people and read everything. And I tell them not to worry about learning about the models of strategy. (*laughter*)" When asked to explain more about this, she continued:

> *You know, I have taken strategy courses in Germany from American consulting firms and I have read many books on how to make strategy. So I understand you have so many models to choose from. But they are not accurate to what really happens if you must be responsible for good strategy—because [strategic thinking] is not systematic.*

This specter of doubt regarding the contribution of formal learning was further reflected by a young president of a U.S. technology company who said:

> *I learned about strategy when I was getting my MBA, but it was mostly about, umm, you know, umm, well see, I can't even remember! (laughter) I think it was mostly just theories and models for analysis and whatever. This is not about thinking strategically. Maybe they're okay for planning.*
>
> *I will be honest with you, I haven't used any of [the models]. I don't think what I learned—all of these different models and theories—is practical. It's maybe okay for planning, but strategy is so much bigger, and I don't think this way. You know, I think it's much better—much better, to just teach people to talk to each other and to think in a hard way.*

When asked to name the most important points to include if he were teaching a course on making strategy, this same executive responded by saying: "I don't think I'd teach strategy as a separate course, I think that's a mistake. I'd want to use a more integrative approach—teach thinking and world affairs—that's how you get people to start thinking strategically."

Traditional approaches to developing strategic thinking have largely been formal and instrumental, ritualistic and mechanistic, with a lopsided emphasis on analytics. While such an emphasis is indeed valuable to strategic planning, this emphasis is only one side of the coin. A reaction to its failure is the growing interest in informal learning and its role in learning to think strategically. However, just because the influence of formal learning has been refuted and disregarded, we need not discard it from strategy development. In other words, there is no need to throw the baby out with the bath water. However, this questioning of the role of formal learning in strategy making presents an invitation to reconsider what is working and what is not in the disconnection of learning and development.

If one of the fundamental assumptions about "teaching" is that it supports learning, then we must better understand *how* we learn to think strategically, in order to "teach" or facilitate such learning. Those responsible for facilitating strategic thinking must leverage individual learning, organizational learning, and informal and formal learning in order to build capacity for sustainable, innovative, long-term strategic performance.

Learning alone does not produce such an outcome. Learning itself is not the end result of thinking strategically. Only when learning is specifically targeted toward the creation of an innovative, adaptable, and winning strategy does learning to think strategically contribute real value to an organization.

The traditional approach to developing strategic thinking is most often anchored in a *planning* model rather than in a *process-based* model for learning and creation. The planning model of strategic thinking offers very little emphasis on creative thinking, long-term thinking, critical reflection, critical dialogue, challenge, or testing. We must regard strategic thinking as a continuous learning process rather than as a sequence of steps resulting in a strategy "product."

As previously mentioned, formal learning was consistently refuted among the successful strategists as a primary source of influence on learning to think strategically. Reflecting on the factors that were most influential in his learning to think strategically, an executive of a Hong Kong technology company described the way he learned to think strategically:

> *I think I had a pretty good education; I went to Harvard for my MBA, studied in France—so that was probably good for basic education. But to be honest, I don't remember much about strategic thinking. (laughter) Maybe I just don't remember specifics—but I've learned the most important things traveling and living in a different country. These are the things that really contribute to enriching your thinking—you know, you get to see all kinds of things and hear things. And most of it doesn't make sense at the time. But that—knowing how to make sense of things—that's what's required, I think, for learning to think strategically.*

His point of sense making reminds us that knowledge is not always the outcome of learning. Rather, the learning outcome is the experience itself and the meaning that individuals give to the experience, as suggested by learning theorists Peter Jarvis[1] and Jack Mezirow.[2] In terms of learning, Mezirow sees learning as:

> *The social process of construing and appropriating a new or revised interpretation of the meaning of one's experience as a guide to action. The learning process, as meaning making, is therefore focused, shaped, and delimited by our frames of references.*[3]

Among the executives interviewed, travel was a dominant theme. Interestingly, they described travel as an influential factor in how they learned to think strategically. For example, when probed about the role that traveling and working in a foreign country contributed to his learning, this same technology executive explained:

> *You're constantly working with mounds of information that seem unrelated, and so much data, and a lot of unknown variables … so it's a game. You're always working with an incomplete entity—it's frustrating, but also exciting in a way. That's what it's like to make strategy!*

The oldest executive in the study, a 61-year-old CEO of a Polish manufacturing company, noted:

As I continue to travel, I learn more about different ways of looking at things, and that's a certain kind of experience too, and it's valuable—I'd say critical to making strategy. Experience, I say, is like the answer book to your new questions. I don't really think that being young or being old is an advantage per se. I'm still learning, and I think experience is probably the best teacher.

> *Learning occurs when our situation is one of imbalance, for learning is the process of seeking balance.*

The connection between travel and experience goes back centuries, as indicated in the following observation from more than a few years back: "Experience, travel—these are an education in themselves" (Euripides, Andromache [c. 426 B.C.]). The experience of travel offers us an environment in which to challenge our own and others' assumptions, to rattle our core belief systems, to expand our perspectives, to test and to imagine new possibilities. When we travel, we see new connections and different relationships between and among objects, people, and values. Sometimes, we are forced to break our comfortable habits and use new patterns—either we adopt something new, adapt, or retain our original frameworks.

Accordingly, the greatest learning occurs when our situation is in a state of imbalance, for learning is the process of seeking balance. As a result, travel is the quintessential metaphor for learning to think strategically. It is when and how we strive to create balance in a highly unfamiliar context that we put ourselves in an optimal state of learning. For example, when we intend to take a trip, we begin by making plans. As plans progress, we may experience imbalance if the ticket gets misprinted, and when we arrive on a stormy night only to find that the hotel reservation has been inadvertently cancelled. The sense of imbalance persists when we get food poisoning, when we address a meeting where our language is not fully understood and our objectives are misinterpreted, and when we assess financial reports that have been "fudged for foreigners." The very success of our travel depends on other people and things we cannot control. The same is true of strategy making as we attempt to seek balance from our imperfect, incomplete, and infinitely complex world.

As discussed in Part I, strategy theorist Henry Mintzberg has made the role of learning explicit in his research, demonstrating the emergent character of much of the real strategy of organizations. In his book, *The Rise and Fall of Strategic Planning*, Mintzberg deciphered the "code" of how strategy is really made. His well-publicized study reported that 90 percent of the projected outcomes in most companies' formal strategic planning processes never actually materialize. Only 10 percent of most companies' actions arise out of their strategic planning (i.e., *realized strategy*).[4] The source of the other 90 percent of what companies do, Mintzberg calls "emergent strategy." This is the accumulation of day-to-day decisions, disjointed initiatives, and actions taken by managers in response to everyday work demands, without any master plan or comprehensive strategic concept to guide them. When everything is taken into account, real strategy can emerge.

So why, then, should we bother to develop strategic thinkers if their strategy is just going to "emerge" anyway? While "chance" strategy or "accidental" strategy will happen—for better or worse—the aim of strategy development is to increase the positive odds, and to decrease happenstance, serendipity, or lucky events. To do this, we must understand what is required, pay attention to what works, and have a process that encourages successful repetition.

Notes

1. Jarvis, *Adult Learning in the Social Context.*
2. Mezirow, *Fostering Critical Reflection in Adulthood.* Jack Mezirow's work was strongly influenced by the work of Jürgen Habermas and is therefore consistent with critical theory.
3. Mezirow, *Fostering Critical Reflection in Adulthood.*
4. Mintzberg, *The Fall and Rise of Strategic Planning.*

7

Context and Learning Transfer as Factors in the Strategic Thinking Process

The role of context as a factor in informal learning cannot be understated or ignored. Context has been found to have a significant influence on the quality of dialogue required for learning to think strategically.[1] A sensitivity to signals from the environment, or context, fosters the ability to deconstruct and reconstruct frameworks and patterns, and to challenge assumptions grounded in past experiences. The importance of context with regard to memory is increasingly discussed within the broad base of cognitive literature.[2]

This role of context with regard to thinking strategically was consistently expressed by the strategic thinkers I interviewed. Particularly inspiring and equally interesting were the passionate reports of executives who consistently and repeatedly credited highly diverse, non-work contexts as influencing their development as strategic thinkers. These strategists tended to "see" sameness in a complex business strategy issue as what they had experienced in a non-work context, such as in an orchestra rehearsal or in the creation of a photo exhibition.[3] Curiously, they reported extensive and expansive use of metaphoric thinking as a means of engaging in strategic thinking. The leaders reportedly used their non-work experience as a metaphor for their business-strategy issue and allowed their metaphor to unravel to a point at which it no longer necessarily applied. At this juncture, their thinking diverged, and they became aware of engaging in critically reflective processes.[4]

The executives' success in vastly different contexts (e.g., painting, auto racing, farming, sculpting, music) prior to successful strategic thinking experiences appeared to actually enhance their learning transfer into a global business context. For example, experiences in an orchestra rehearsal became a metaphor for the strategic problem of a global financial merger. A Swiss financial investor explained:

When I lose myself—totally immersed in the orchestra rehearsal—that is when I am "living" my strategy problem about this new merger. Really, it is a metaphor; and I think to myself like this sometimes. (quiet pause) It is strange, but it is how I see it … I play cello in the orchestra and I am Director of this bank merger. It is good to be in two roles because my metaphor is stronger this way; and so my decisions are better this way. I can understand and see the strategy problem more clearly in this metaphor way.

The executives' learning appeared to be more informed by the experiences to which they are anchored than by who or what was presented at a strategy meeting. Clearly, they were aware of and carefully mitigated the contextual factors that allowed their informal learning process to remain constant, regardless of their context.

The extraordinary range of contexts from which these leaders learned and successfully transferred their strategic thinking calls into question the role of context and the function of transfer in the informal learning process.[5]

The places in which the executives' prior successful life experience occurred (e.g., studio, race track, farm, rehearsal) were strikingly different from the global business environment in which they currently worked, yet the broader context was surprisingly similar. Each non-work context provided executives with opportunities to learn framing, reframing, and meaning making in environments that were incomplete, unpredictable, uncontrollable, and demanding—precisely the kinds of environments in which they are charged to develop global business strategy. This contextual transfer equipped executives to identify broader contextual factors and to trace their similarities, while they interpreted the current situational specifics presented in the learning opportunity. Instant pattern recognition, the ability to reframe, and the ability to transfer relevant segments across contexts are what the executives credit as crucial to their learning of strategic thinking.

> *It is the ability to transfer that allows lessons to transcend context variables such as time, history, place, and people. We "get it" precisely because we are able to transfer learning.*

Metaphor as a Learning Transfer Mechanism

Curiously, the use of metaphor was a consistent theme in the interviews. Executives repeatedly described their strategic problem as a metaphor, sometimes in the form of a parable, a fable, or an allegory.

A metaphor is when something is "like" something else. Metaphor is a mechanism that makes the unfamiliar familiar, and a metaphor has a strong appeal to our senses. For example, this smells like, or looks like, or feels like something we have already experienced. Metaphors and analogies use complex memory functions of comparative ability, content, operational, contextual, and symbolic transfer. Furthermore, metaphor offers a safe way to talk about things that are emotionally charged and also helps to explain complex and conceptual issues such as strategy. Conceptual metaphors refer to the comprehension of one idea in terms of another and are used frequently to convey and explore theories and models.[6] First written about by George Lakoff and Mark Johnson in the 1980s, the use of conceptual metaphor has been explored more recently by Howard Gardner, Daniel Ariely, Daniel Kahneman, Philip Tetlock, and others.

Analogies were another useful and very common tool that successful strategists recalled when reflecting on how they learned to think strategically. An analogy begins with a simple story or situation, but it becomes an analogy when it is compared with something else. Analogies do not have to be long or complicated—a simple action or anecdote may suffice—but for an analogy to be useful, it must be familiar. Something must be happening, a particular process must occur, or the observer must recognize a special kind of relationship in order for an analogy to resonate.

Analogies are vehicles for relationships and processes. These relationships and processes are embodied in actual objects, but they can also be generalized to other situations. Such correlations can be expressed *directly*, in terms of the actual objects involved, or *indirectly*, in terms of the process involved.

Analogies are useful for encouraging thought movement. We can change the analogy to shift the thought direction. For example, "debate is war." Imagine now, "debate as dance." A strategic problem can be translated into an analogy, and then that analogy can be developed or expanded along its own lines. Subsequently, we can translate it back and see what might have happened to the original problem. Convoluted as this may sound in writing, the process is intriguing, in that the executives interviewed made extensive use of metaphoric thinking (including analogies, parables, fables) as a means by which they learned to think strategically. I have been endlessly fascinated by the captivating and animated analogies that successful strategists from various countries share with delight—it is storytelling and imagery in all its glory. This age-old, highly complex cognitive capability has practical application for leaders who allow themselves to play with the language and the imagery of analogies.[7] Using analogies is irrefutably valuable and undeniably relevant for learning to think strategically. Metaphoric thinking requires a complex cluster of cognitive capabilities. Descriptions given by the leaders showed a sequence of:

1. *identifying* a metaphor that works for their strategy;
2. *recognizing* that their strategic issue is "like" a previous experience;
3. *engaging* with the metaphor as far as they can along the progression of the metaphor;
4. *realizing*, at some point, a juncture when the metaphor may no longer apply, and the leaders' thinking about the strategic issue diverges. This *point of divergence* can trigger critical assessment of variables at play, contextual factors, or data against the strategy aim and resources. Questions that typically come up are: "What, about this, is different? What is similar? What variables would need to change to make it similar or different? How do the factors and players in the metaphor react or respond? What could be the consequences of certain choices?"

Figure 7.1 is an example of an actual early stage of a strategy problem that is "drawn" first as a metaphor. A written description of the metaphor follows in Box 7.1, and the process of drawing and writing the strategy metaphor is reflected in Box 7.2. An arts administrator of a prestigious theater organization was struggling with the strategic challenge of an industry issue of how to get theaters to produce new works while not putting their revenue at risk.

When I work with clients on metaphor, I invite them to create thoughtfully the following three steps—*Draw, Describe, Reflect*—on their learning about their own strategic thinking. The description (writing their parable, fable, or whatever metaphoric form they choose) is actually a highly engaging, intensely focused, and very rigorous experience in reflection-on-action. While I distinguish the three steps, leaders are critically reflecting as they go along, often oscillating among the three steps; yet their focus is on constructing symbolic representation and action. They appoint representative symbols and positions, and create and clarify meaning of relationships and action. They challenge their operating and habitual meaning-making schema. Also, they get to "see," revise, and rehearse choices, scenarios, and options—continuously engaging in an iterative and generative (i.e., highly disciplined yet messy) process.

FIGURE 7.1 Metaphor: A Strategist's Castle

BOX 7.1 A STRATEGIST'S METAPHOR: THE STORY OF THE CASTLE AND THE MOAT

Once upon a time, there was an expansive kingdom, perched on the shore of a grand continent. The people lived across the peaceful land, as diverse as the terrain—mountains to the north, desert to the east and south, and a beautiful glistening ocean to the west. In the center of the kingdom there was a castle, high upon a hill overlooking the land. So high was the hill that the citizens of the kingdom had to live some distance from the castle, leaving the lands nearest to the royal family quite barren, and forcing the citizens to travel many miles to reach the castle grounds. The citizens were happy to travel this distance because their time at the castle was always so rewarding.

In past years, the castle was the center of activity, with crowds of denizens coming and going—socializing, learning, interacting, being entertained—all on the steps and grounds of the castle. The castle was where the fine people of the kingdom would distract themselves from the mundane aspects of daily life, and where they would meet new friends, discover new topics of interest, smile, and laugh.

But over the last 20 years, a curious thing happened to the grand castle. The measly moat surrounding the edifice, originally installed to protect the castle and the royal family from danger, started to widen and deepen. For reasons largely unknown to the kingdom's custodians, the moat grew and grew, slowly eroding the earth beneath the grounds. The ocean, thought to be a safe distance away, seemed to burrow cunningly toward the castle, building inlets and streams, reaching its long sapphire arms toward the castle, grabbing at the walls of the moat and pulling them back, stretching them, warping them.

At first this oddity sparked little more than head scratching. "Perhaps it's not such a bad thing," the royal family thought. "Perhaps it's better this way." And yes, perhaps it was, for a while. The widening gap between the castle and the kingdom provided for extra security and allowed no one with ill intentions to upset the throne. Also, the citizens attending castle events, though they might have a slightly more difficult time getting in, were truly invested in being there, and the castle might benefit from this investment. There were fewer people saying "nay" to the castle's entertainment and activities. Fewer people were challenging the castle's programing. Also, the larger moat made the castle appear to be even higher on the hill, and reminded the citizens that the royal family was indeed in charge, and the family's authority was not to be questioned, giving the royal family solace. In fact, the family liked their unquestioned authority so much, that they began trusting the advice only of people who grew up and were educated within the castle walls. This trust ensured that there were no nay-sayers on the staff.

While the first few years of this strange moat expansion seemed inconsequential or even beneficial, slowly, over the decades, some people began to take notice. They feared that the ground beneath the castle was starting to weaken and that this danger could jeopardize the royal family's safety. To solve this problem, the workers erected huge flying buttresses to support the castle walls. The buttresses were anchored deep into the bedrock beyond the moat. The expense was monstrous, and the manpower was colossal, but the custodians of the castle grounds reinforced the castle walls.

Once the work was finished, the royal family realized that the castle itself deserved some attention, so they overhauled the castle, which took many years. All the while, the moat continued slowly to make small gains, each one absorbing just a tiny bit more of the earth.

Finally, the royal family unveiled the new grounds, which were a sight to behold, and devised a grand plan for a festival to showcase the grounds to the citizens. Believing that the castle crowds had waned a bit, they thought: "We'll give them something to see and draw large crowds!" At the festival, only the most popular jesters in the land would perform, presenting games and tricks that everyone knew and loved. The royal family decreed that no killjoys would be allowed at this festival and nothing controversial would be tolerated. If the king and queen felt that a certain game—say *horseshoes*—would offend someone—say, *a horse*—then the game was removed. The same held for all the activities they planned. "We shall have no bellows blowing, as the bellows-mender will not appreciate this game!" the king's council told him.

The royal family, who stayed safely behind the walls of the castle, was sure of the festival's success. What the royal family did not notice was that the moat problem was becoming ever more serious. The long arms of the ocean had thickened and grown, and continued to break apart the earth and carry it away, until finally the inevitable happened.

One afternoon, while all the knaves and knights and peasant workers were stringing lights and building stages, preparing for the festival, a monstrous "crrrrrrrrrr-aaaaaaack" rang through the castle grounds. Everyone froze. Shaken and frightened, the king walked to the drawbridge, followed by his enormous legion of workers, who lowered the bridge and stepped out onto it. Looking down around them, their faces all fell in horror.

Below the bridge—where once the moat sat still and stagnant—was the ocean itself, and the castle now perched on scarcely a scrap of land. What the king saw was a stalagmite sliver poking up precariously through the shaking, shifting water, with the castle balanced on top. The buttresses, thought to be unsinkable, were eaten by the ocean, which smiled up at the king with a sea-foam grin, with the ocean's rhythmic waves making Poseidon's deep belly laugh. Inside, the castle was ready for a grand and festive celebration, but among the family and their enormous coterie, there was no festive spirit whatsoever.

The royal family and their cadre of employees, now marooned on the island that was the castle, and distanced inexorably from the citizens, could do nothing but sit and wait, and hope to someday be reached. With each subtle wind, the royal family and their workers took a collective deep breath, wondering if this was the wind which would capsize the castle.

The castle people hollered and cried for the citizens to save them, begging the citizens to build bridges or move earth back into the moat. The royal family schemed to get a citizen brave or nostalgic enough to come for a visit. Some tried, and a denizen or two would occasionally take a small row boat out, docking near the base of the island cliff and climbing up through the earthworks of the grounds. But when they did so, they would find themselves unimpressed and inconvenienced. The reality of the castle did not match its memory, so they would not return. The royal family and their confidants, perplexed, sad, and convinced that they could not win the battle of the missing moat, remained forever there on the teetering island, simply waiting to topple into the ocean and to be forgotten forever.

As he reflected on the experience of drawing and writing his castle metaphor, the arts administrator described some of his thoughts in Box 7.2.

What matters in the exercise is not the quality of writing or drawing (stick figures work perfectly fine) but, rather, the quality and clarity of thinking that the process invites. The invitation to view and read others' metaphors (parables, fables, allegories) can serve to create and clarify our ideas. We see instantly positions, players, and outcomes regardless of context, as well as points of similarity and difference in our respective strategy issues and those of the metaphor.

While the benefits to a strategic thinker of such a metaphoric exercise are many, three are particularly pronounced. First, the very act of drawing shifts the brain function from an *analytical* process to a *divergent and creative* cognitive process. A basic premise is structured; characters, symbols, a relative scale, weight, and positions are assigned. Second, an emotional detachment from the real strategic problem is required (because we are thinking metaphorically), which allows a certain emotional shield and protection. This safety enables us to imagine more freely different associations and possible movement and can ease the removal of blind spots. Also, metaphor creates a broader perspective and an expanded horizon, allowing for a panoramic view. Third, we can safely test various strategy hypotheses, and can engage in sensitive conversations far more easily within the metaphoric framework, than with real issues. This can be a beneficial approach for dealing with strategic issues such as mergers and acquisitions and other emotionally charged strategic problems.

Learning to interact in ways that succeed over a broad range of situations requires the ability to "see," to diverge, and to critically reflect. Learning theorist Donald Schon's explanation supports this assertion: "It is this entire process of reflection-in-action which is central to the 'art' by which practitioners sometimes deal well with situations of uncertainty, instability, uniqueness, and value conflict."[8]

BOX 7.2 REFLECTIONS ON THE PROCESS OF DRAWING AND WRITING THE STRATEGY METAPHOR: A THEATER ARTS ADMINISTRATOR'S EXPERIENCE WITH METAPHOR

As a theater arts administrator, the metaphor of a castle on a hill was one that I've often used to reflect how I feel about large theater institutions. They [administrators] deem themselves makers of taste and smarter than audiences, and, because of this, they have put a major distance between themselves and their potential ticket buyers. Then they sit back and wonder why the people don't come running to them for their product. It is a major strategy problem in the industry.

What I didn't realize when beginning this metaphor exercise was just how much was going to come out when I began to draw and write. What's left, I think, is a theater which is very good at supporting itself as a company, and very bad at supporting the artist and audience relationship, which it set out to support in the first place. [An institution] that has an enormous administrative staff, but no full-time artists. One that must commit itself to producing profitable work with wide appeal just to attract a tiny sliver of the potential audiences in order to stay afloat. One that teeters scarily on the edge of collapse—each economic wave, a potential kiss of death.

The metaphor grew immensely as I wrote it. Things that I didn't even stop to think could compound the greater problem, I am now certain, are. For example, the fact that these theaters only hire and work with artists and administrators that come from similar educational backgrounds, and the fact that actors are now largely trained in conservatory settings where they are treated like royalty and told they don't need to understand the world, only the training, are making the problem even worse by not opposing the leadership of these organizations.

I can really see how very valuable this exercise is for strategic thinking—to physically draw and write out a parable completely. Through this exercise I am now able to clearly see that this problem is a strategic, complex, and systemic problem. Armed with these new insights, I look forward to asking tough questions and am thrilled to be moving forwards, in hopes of eventually breaking down the castle walls. Or maybe moving the royal family out of the castle altogether!

The ability to transfer across vastly different contexts is what enables us to hear a story, see a play, watch an episode, connect to a cartoon, or relate to an illustration which occurs in a totally different setting than the one we are experiencing and still "get it." We can transfer particulars or generalities across contexts and learn from second-hand or peripheral experiences precisely because we are able to make the transfer. The story or picture makes sense to us, even when the context is changed. This ability to transfer is what allows lessons to transcend variables of context such as time, history, place, and people.

What is required for *contextual transfer* is a degree of reflective processing ability, something that is learnable. Whether we realize it or not, we are capable of making seemingly unrelated connections quite effortlessly, and sometimes playfully, through the use of metaphor. We regularly transfer learning across vastly different contexts in our day-to-day lives, as well as in our business lives. Making this transfer is part of the informal learning process that is essential to strategic thinking.

Notes

1. Sloan, "A Case Study of How Nine Executives Learn Informally to Develop Strategy in a Global Context."
2. Both of these sources are interesting references on the use of metaphors: Baddeley, Eysenck, and Anderson, *Memory*; Woike, Bender, and Besne, "Implicit Motivational States Influence Memory: Evidence for Motive by State-Dependent Learning in Personality."
3. Lakoff and Johnson, *Metaphors We Live By*.
4. Von Ghyczy, "The Fruitful Flaws of Strategy Metaphors."

5. Tetlock, *Expert Political Judgment: How Good Is It? How Can We Know?*; Pink, *A Whole New Mind: Why Right-Brainers Will Rule the Future*; and Gardner, *Five Minds for the Future*, are all works that discuss the role and function of context and metaphor.
6. Lakoff and Johnson, *Metaphors We Live By*.
7. Tetlock, *Expert Political Judgment: How Good Is It? How Can We Know?*; Pink, *A Whole New Mind: Why Right-Brainers Will Rule the Future*; Gardner, *Five Minds for the Future*; Ariely, *The Upside of Irrationality*; and Kahneman, *Thinking, Fast and Slow*, all reference their respective studies on the function of the language and imagery of metaphor.
8. Schon, *The Reflective Practitioner*, 50.

Summary and Questions

The definition of strategic thinking is often confusing because the term is frequently used synonymously with the terms strategic planning and strategic implementation. However, the very intent of strategic thinking is different, as is the underlying cognitive cluster that supports it. The intent of strategic thinking is to suspend problem solving in order to challenge and test the problem, while the purpose of strategic planning is to solve the problem. Strategic thinking is comprised of two key dimensions: divergent thinking and a deep-dive critical reflective process.

No single linear model can effectively portray the complexity and non-linear nature of strategy in today's highly unpredictable and constantly changing strategic environment. The Triad Model of Strategy™ suggests that strategic thinking is but one essential domain to the overall strategy process. It positions strategic thinking within a broader strategy framework, with each domain being equal in importance to the overall process of strategy.

Prolonged and innovative strategic success requires individual and organizational mastery of strategic thinking and further integration of this informal learning process into an organization's functions. Unlike a convergent, rational, logical, linear sequence that leads to a specific product outcome for strategic planning and implementation, strategic thinking is a divergent, continuous, iterative, nonlinear, a-rational learning process.

The contrasting cognitive clusters that support strategic thinking and strategic planning are starkly different. While the cognitive cluster that develops strategic planning is conducive to formal learning, the cluster that supports strategic thinking occurs most often informally. Learning to think strategically requires us to harness this complex cognitive cluster in order to contribute to the unfamiliar, rapidly changing, and complex nature of strategic problems.

What does this process look like in an organizational setting? Repeatedly, the most influential learning occurs informally and often incidentally, and learning to think strategically is no exception. Structuring a strategic problem as a metaphor can facilitate the "messy" strategic thinking process. Metaphor can tap into the more complex cluster of cognitive capabilities and help diverge the thinking about a problem. Literally drawing complex problems and engaging with the problem as a metaphor within a different context allows strategists to imagine associations, relative positions, and movements across boundaries that may not be apparent within a traditional linear, rational context. Furthermore, exploring the strategic problem as a metaphor helps to remove "blind spots," shatter frames, and also helps to objectively and safely deal with emotionally charged issues.

1. How could leaders benefit from differentiating the definition of strategic thinking from strategic planning and strategic implementation?
2. In what ways does strategic thinking strengthen strategic planning and implementation?
3. What are some ways (informally and formally) that you could further develop your own strategic thinking?
4. Which domain is your own strategy strength and preference? Your habit? Your team's strength and habit? Is there a domain that tends to get rewarded in your organization?
5. As you think about your past, what are the most influential learning experiences in your recent history? Were they incidental or intentional? Formal or informal? How could this experience further strengthen your learning to think strategically?
6. How could you enable a more informal learning environment that could support others to learn to think more strategically?

WHAT DOES LEARNING TO THINK STRATEGICALLY LOOK LIKE?

Murky and Miraculous: A Three-Stage Model for Strategic Learning

Experience is not what happens to you; it is what you do with what happens to you.

Aldous Huxley (1894–1963), English author and critic

8

Preparation Stage

Part II of this book discussed informal learning as the way in which we actually learn to think strategically. In Part III, we examine a three-stage informal learning process for thinking strategically. The three stages of the process (Figure 8.1) are:

- Preparation;
- Experience;
- Reevaluation.

Although we are referring to three stages of the informal learning process, in reality the process is iterative; that is, we move back and forth between the stages—creating a "messy" learning process.

The *preparation* stage is difficult to identify because it can happen at any time and place, yet we need to be able to recognize what happens in this stage if we want to facilitate learning to think strategically. The Polish CEO explained how he "begins" to think about strategy:

> *You need a reason to begin. Sometimes the reason is only to survive. Sometimes the reason is to fulfill a dream or an idea you cannot let go of. Sometimes the reason is to avoid a punishment or you are afraid something terrible will happen. But the reason must be a powerful one, or you will not really make strategy; it will only be a simple plan. Planning can be step by step, but strategy is not. You must have a very strong reason. And you must feel and believe this reason deeply. Otherwise, you have no motivation to look for the bigger picture, and the work of thinking and searching will be too exhausting and difficult. So it must be something you feel very strongly about.*
>
> *To build a strategy requires inspiration; you must want something very deeply. If that happens, then you must think carefully to yourself about why this is worth so much trouble, because I tell you—you will lose sleep, and who knows, maybe friends over this!*

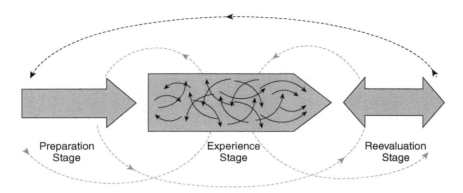

FIGURE 8.1   Three-Stage Model of Informal Learning Process Used for Strategic Thinking[1]

> *You know, I said that strategy is not so simple. But you must continue no matter how tedious or troublesome. Because if you really believe something, it will need to have a strategy—you must see a very broad picture without a frame—it has no limit.*

There are two aspects to the preparation stage: an *affective* component, which is a kind of emotional readiness during which the intensity of a must-win attitude is tested, and a *cognitive* component, during which information is gathered and data are examined. These two components prepare us for action by enabling us to assess a situation, gather information, and initiate a retrieval of past knowledge and skills for adaptation and application in the strategic thinking process. The affective and cognitive components coexist and have a simultaneous interchange during this preparatory phase.

Affective Component

The affective component of the preparation stage is often described by successful strategic thinkers as the starting point, or as a strong urge one cannot disregard. An American technology company executive best articulated this:

> *You have to have a gut-level reason or strong feeling for moving something ahead. I mean, you just don't make strategy for the sake of making it. I had this strong—this unbelievable drive, dreams, and piles and piles of plans about what I thought and really believed needed to happen with software production. I guess I couldn't let go.*

According to the successful strategists I interviewed, the pursuit of strategy starts with a relentless desire to win. The sources of such compulsion can be quite varied, but a must-win attitude, regardless of its origination, is essential. This competitive affect is critical for learning to think strategically. One American financial executive said:

I start with a desire to get things 'right'—to make something happen—to do some-thing or go somewhere with an idea or a problem. Sometimes I suppose you could even have a disaster that gets you going. You don't have a choice but to clear it up.

Another manufacturing executive stated succinctly: "Although I'm an engineer by training, I like the intellectual work of figuring out strategy—it's very emotional—and I like that."

But it was a Japanese executive who offered an even more emotional decree:

Find something in your life that you love to do—and you are not making money on (laughter)—then you know you really love it—and not the money! Then, as I said, you will always want to protect it. This will be the most important lesson in learn-ing to make successful strategy. Because you will be successful because [of] the fear of losing what you love.

An interesting and important part of the strategic thinking equation is how tension manifests itself in the learning process. In the United States, we have long been taught that fun learning is effective learning, and this myth has profoundly influenced our approach to learning to think strategically. Knowing about this myth, our greatest chal-lenge is to confront this deeply held belief and test its validity with those responsible for facilitating strategic thinking. Data from my research shows that strategic learning is rarely the result of enjoyable educational experiences but, rather, the result of perplexing and frustrating situations.

Another point to consider is that challenge can be motivating, even stimulating. Thinking through problems can even produce feelings of pleasure and satisfaction as profound learning occurs. Accepting this affective component of strategic thinking is critical to the process itself. If one can acknowledge his or her negative feelings and expe-riences, there is a greater likelihood that he or she will be capable of deciding what to do with them. This tension needs to be worked with, not against. The benefits surface when one maintains a must-win attitude and commits to a reflective process.

The affective component in the preparation stage is frequently expressed in terms of passion, conviction, and emotion derived from past experience. These expressions are most pronounced at the outset, when we invoke a conscious self-check or a sort of readi-ness assessment to determine if we have the must-win attitude to sustain the strategic thinking process. This emotional component is necessary to ensure that we are ade-quately prepared to move forward with good strategic thinking—not planning. The exec-utives whom I interviewed seem to believe that an absence of this emotional component would lead to a lack of the stamina or drive necessary to pursue a truly effective strategy.

One Swiss executive with whom I was supposed to meet cancelled a meeting not too long ago because of "mind fatigue." He took several days off to rejuvenate at a private mountain retreat because he was literally exhausted from "thinking very hard." Just days after "fixing the strategy in his mind," he knew he had to take some time off, or else he wouldn't be able to continue into the planning phase. This degree of fatigue had hit him several times before when he became so engrossed in thinking that he nearly collapsed. As we talked by phone, he said this is one of the lessons he tries to pass along to junior executives because they need to understand that "truly good strategy is an emotional experience; it is not just an intellectual exercise."

In addition to cognitive constraints, emotions influence how we attend to a situation. The simple decision to mentally bring ourselves into or to remove ourselves from the activities of a group or task is often done tacitly, yet doing so can dramatically impact upon what we learn from a situation. Furthermore, strong emotions and deeply embedded cognitive processes can result in defensive routines that prevent us from learning at all. Without an awareness of our individual tendencies, or time to reflect and learn from events, we cannot generate effective and actionable knowledge from our experience.

Moving from feeling to action is not always easy, nor is this movement a predictable sequence. While a fiercely competitive must-win feeling can be a powerful impetus to the learning process, new information may also provide the impetus. The intersection of affective and cognitive components can be helpful in igniting the informal learning process, though there is no guarantee that what follows will be a linear progression.

> *Traditionally, the role of the affective in strategy development has been viewed either as an inhibitor of learning, due to anxiety and stress, or as something that can be brought into conscious awareness as an "object" for rational analysis.*

All too frequently, corporate and university approaches to strategy development address only the cognitive component: the planning, data-gathering, and analysis piece. Too often, the affective component is either ignored or relegated to an artificial "vision" phase in which contributors are asked to "think passionately about a vision for the next hour," which instantly promotes switching off the affective and prioritizing the cognitive for the sake of planning. While this common exercise may indeed be of noble intent, the assignment is a rather over-simplified and misguided instruction that does little to support learning to think strategically.

Traditionally, the role of the affective in strategy development has been viewed either as an inhibitor of learning, due to anxiety and stress, or as something that can be brought into conscious awareness as an "object" for rational analysis. The former has generated an emphasis on creating safe learning environments for discussion; the latter has led to psychological and therapeutic approaches aimed at dissecting the issue so that strategic thinking can proceed.

Learning theorists David Boud and David Walker have highlighted the role of feelings and emotions in the learning process, noting that they are often treated separately from the action of the task. They propose that in spite of our observation that learning is experienced as a seamless whole, there is a cultural bias toward the cognitive aspects of learning in modern English-speaking societies. The development of affect is inhibited, leading to a lack of emphasis on people as whole persons.[2]

Why are we so overly focused on the cognitive aspect of strategic thinking? Partly because our formal education habitually reinforces the cognitive learning aspect, often at the expense of the affective. The affective is much more the reserve of our informal learning. The cognitive is more easily structured into "teaching" material and a "teachable" approach— the cognitive is definitive, easily measured, linear, and largely instrumental and mechanistic. Although the affective is present, it can feel elusive and ambiguous and is not easily "taught" or articulated. Our formal education often teaches us to ignore or actively remove the affective learning dimension because it can "get in the way" of the cognitive learning.

When learning to think strategically, we must pair the affective component with the cognitive. As mentioned, the former tends to remain invisible. As a result, many leaders lack the confidence and ability to deal with the affective component of strategic thinking and thus tend to ignore it. But it is precisely the affective aspect that inspires the strategic-learning process to be nonlinear, difficult to articulate, and hard to measure. What is "felt" is what propels and intensifies the fierce desire to win.

Researchers David Boud and David Walker emphasize the importance of the affective component within the overall informal learning process:

> *The heart offers more than simply feelings or inchoate impulses. Emotions do more than indicate crudely and vividly that something feels good or bad. A person's feelings can actually help make sense of an issue, give shape to it, and indicate what the stakes really are. In other words, the heart has reasons ... [which] are written in a language different from the formal, explicit, logical one in which our minds operate. Discerning how one's instincts define a situation is a matter of translation. It is an interpretive art, and a difficult one.*[3]

While theorists have long acknowledged the importance of the affective dimension on the learning process, the emphasis of learning within the strategy literature focuses on cognitive change, assimilating information, and acquiring behavioral skills. Increasingly, the emotional aspect of learning is becoming explicitly incorporated into learning theory through research on emotional intelligence, but this emotional aspect remains absent from most strategy literature.

Cognitive Component

The cognitive aspect (see Figure 4.1) is also present in the preparation stage of the informal learning process, primarily in the form of information gathering and analysis. Of course, thinking strategically requires that we have specific information and clear analyses, and data needs to be gathered and tested on a continuous basis. This is the linear and quantitative part of the strategic thinking process with which many are most familiar and comfortable. The cognitive aspect is extremely important, but it must be paired with the affective in order to be effective over the long haul.

Within a strategic thinking process, information gathering is regarded as intentional learning and has four purposes:

1. To generate new possibilities.
2. To verify an existing belief.
3. To provide a new perspective within the framework of making strategy.
4. To test other information.

So what kind of information is it important to gather when thinking strategically? This information can range from highly analytical and quantitative to more qualitative data gathered through conversations with other people. Interestingly, the executives interviewed indicated that they used conventional sources of data (e.g., reports, statistics, newsletters, publications, conferences), but relied on unconventional sources (e.g., talking to fellow airline passengers, listening to university students, coffee shop conversations, discussions with people outside the industry) to verify the data received from conventional sources. Some voiced humor and skepticism when talking about conventional methods of information gathering. For example, an American technology company executive said:

Of course I read the same data everybody else does (laughter) … everybody reads the same things! But you know, one of the advantages to traveling is that you hear from people first-hand. We need to get out there and talk to people and think about things, and think about different things—what it could mean for us. Talking to people is kind of a check. Actually, it gives perspective and meaning to data, when everybody's reading the same stuff. It's just what I have to do—reading and going to places to hear other people, and I talk to a lot of people to see what they're thinking and learning. I think a big part of being able to make really good strategy is to constantly know what's going on all over the world.

Another technology company executive concurred:

And that's what I really like about strategy—you kind of bring everything into it. I mean, you need to know what's happening with federal regulations, state laws and what's happening with international laws, trademarks, patents, property rights—you need to keep up to speed with inventions and distribution and all the laws around these.
And then there's economics, and how U.S. events and policies matter to what's happening in other places. It's not enough to just pay attention to forecasts and projections—anybody can print those things! We can't rely on other people's numbers; we need to run our own. And the only way to do that is to keep on top of things— all kinds of things.

One of the financial executives from Japan stated:

I read economic forecasts and financial market newsletters, but it's data people get paid to print! I think traveling is a good way to check on this data and make a test of it. Otherwise, it might not be true. And then your strategy won't work and you've been fooled! (laughter) It's your own fault!

As we can see, the preparation stage relies on both affective and cognitive learning components. The affective is most pronounced when we become aware of a compelling must-win attitude. This emotional drive propels our learning process to a sometimes overwhelming degree, until our desire is satisfied.

Notes

1. Sloan, "A Case Study of How Nine Executives Learn Informally to Develop Strategy in a Global Context."
2. Boud and Walker, "Barriers to Reflection on Experience."
3. Boud and Walker, "Barriers to Reflection on Experience," 72.

9

Experience Stage

Our individual experience most strongly influences our ability to learn to think strategically. We tend to draw on two kinds of experience: current experience and prior successful life experience. But how do we go from having an experience to learning to think strategically? In short, we engage in critical reflection and critical inquiry, and dialogue critically with others about our situations, such that learning and transfer occur. (See Chapters 6 and 7.)

> *Successful strategists learn to think strategically through informal learning, primarily from their own experience.*

The particular focus of this chapter is *experiential learning* because it is the area of informal learning considered most relevant to learning to think strategically. We will discuss the application of prior experience to new situations, as well as the role reflection plays in drawing meaning from our experiences.

The American philosopher and education reformer John Dewey first spoke about the relationship between learning and experience, and his assertions informed many of the subsequent learning theorists, including Chris Argryis, Donald Schon, Edgar Schein, Peter Jarvis, and Jack Mezirow, among others. According to Dewey, the impulse of experience gives ideas their moving force, and learning is the process of transforming concrete experience—converting our interaction with our environment—to purposeful action.[1]

Dewey proposed that we learn by confronting an error or a problem, by observing surrounding conditions, by developing and testing hypotheses about the problem through reflection, and, finally, taking action. For Marsick and Watkins, learning from experience meant how people make sense of situations in their daily lives. And learning theorist David Kolb outlined the process of experience transformation as a four-stage learning cycle and insisted that it is the foundation of all human adaptation.[2]

As we embark on a new strategy-making experience, we start with a conscious and compelling must-win attitude, proceed to information gathering, and then immediately move into an experiential learning mode during which we draw on either our current or our prior experience as a means of creating a challenge–test–reflection–refinement cycle. At this stage of the informal learning process we make sense of our feelings and thoughts by integrating them into a perspective. By accessing our current experience, or prior successful life experience, we semiconsciously engage in a form of action–reflection in which appropriate recent or prior experience is recalled—either intentionally or intuitively—and serves as a pattern for transferring the learning to a new situation.

Current Experience

Current experiences come from many areas of life and can directly or indirectly influence our strategic thinking. By perceiving and responding to a situation, we draw on our previous experience and knowledge and attempt to frame or make sense of the situation in terms that we already know and feel.

Prior Successful Life Experience

There is a point at which we choose a current experience or a prior successful life experience against which to test our new experience. Sometimes we may vacillate between the two; this flexible process allows us to compare and test pattern validity. Often, we initially draw on and engage in a current experience and later tap into a prior successful life experience as another "check" or reference point for transferring learning. Referring to a prior successful life experience provides us with both a familiar standard for acting and a place from which we can diverge in our thinking and acting.

As discussed in Chapter 7, we very often use the prior experience as a metaphor for the current experience. Clients say things such as: "This is like when I prepare for a photo exhibition," or, in the case of my husband: "This is like when I pilot a balloon in a race," or "This feels like what happens when I'm in the middle of a sonata and my string breaks—I have to figure it out on the spot." Metaphors by their very nature are sensory, and metaphors appeal to the affect. This metaphoric thinking is a widely reported phenomenon, yet a generally overlooked part of learning to think strategically.

How does this comparative "test" happen? First, a quick reflection occurs during which we assess the similarities and differences of the new situation as compared to our old experiences. The second stage of reflection occurs when we decide on a course of action. And the third stage of reflection occurs after the fact and enables a full reevaluation of the learning.

A prior successful life experience appears to be, according to the data in my research, the foundation on which we learn to make good strategy. This foundation is the accumulation of experience that eventually becomes our "tacit" knowledge or our "autopilot" setting. Although the time, place, people, and circumstances can be very different in each prior successful life experience, the learning experience can transfer to a business context and continue to transfer to other contexts over the course of time.

Interestingly, a prior successful life experience was identified and described by each of the executives interviewed. The prior successful life experience that all executives described occurred in a non-business context and was different for each executive.

The executives often referenced a current experience first and then reflected back on a particular earlier life experience to test against. Surprisingly, in each case the earlier life experience was not work related, but simply success related. What is important to acknowledge is that these experiences were rarely standalone events, but instead "life interest" experiences that became anchors for subsequent learning. This is striking because it attests to the ability to transfer learning from one context to another, something we often have great difficulty in trusting.

One of the American financial company executives explained:

When I was thinking about whether to include consolidation of our new equities divisions, I bounced back to this experience about a year ago—looking for clues and troubleshooting problems. And then I—after a while—I thought I'd run it past my old days, about my farming—you know, I do that a lot when I'm thinking.

The Japanese CFO mentioned that he uses a similar pattern to test his thinking, but by first referring to a prior successful experience of painting and then, later, to a current experience: "So it seems I always have a habit to check with my way of painting first." When asked to explain why this pattern contributes to strategic thinking, he continued:

It's because I see and know that my thinking is good then. And then I must examine it (laughter)—because I must try to find weak points in my thinking, and so I will next think about a recent experience—well, really, it's a little back and forth to make sure it's really a good way to think.

These executives created their own models of strategy making according to their prior successful life experiences. Each compared and contrasted his or her model against itself by continuously testing the model using an informal "ritual" of reflective processes. The American finance executive, who explained the similarities between farming and learning to make strategy, said that farming has become his model for thinking strategically. Similarly, the Japanese executive continually referred to painting as his model for thinking strategically. Although their prior successful life experiences were very different, their learning processes were basically similar, and congruent with our three-stage process.

On the one hand, the prior successful life experience serves to intensify and solidify our commitment to a particular belief or way of thinking; this experience reinforces our frame of reference. On the other hand, the successful life experience creates a curiosity and confidence that allows us to test and try new ways of thinking and acting.

*We often reference a prior successful life experience
in our "dress rehearsal" routine—playing through
numerous scenarios before selecting one to act on.*

Theorists Marsick and Watkins[3] developed an eight-phase model for learning through experience that begins with individuals facing a new experience:

1. Framing the experience based on past experiences.
2. Diagnosing the new experience.
3. Interpreting the context.
4. Deciding on a solution.
5. Drawing on or developing skills.
6. Producing a solution.
7. Assessing consequences.
8. Drawing further conclusions.

As noted, prior successful life experience anchors present thinking. Various testing methods, which include dialogue, debate, storytelling, and discussion, allow us to diverge in the safety of our mind before testing in real life. An example of this is the German CFO who explained that every few months her executive group has debates and arguments about what various scenarios may mean to them; she referred to this as a type of "dress rehearsal" before making a decision to act.

We often reference a prior successful life experience in our "dress rehearsal" routine—playing through numerous scenarios before selecting one to act on. This can occur instantly and intuitively, or in slow, deliberate motion over the course of weeks or even months—all the while interrupted by more data, more dialogue, and more analysis. Drawing on a prior successful life experience is critical to our learning to make meaning in a new and different context.

When learning to think strategically, it is necessary to be aware of the importance of a prior successful life experience and to use it as a reference point from which to construct future successes. For example, the American banker continually made metaphoric reference to his farming experience when describing how he learned to make good strategy. In response to a question about how he fit strategy making into his farming experience, this executive said:

> *It's just the same thing. Making strategy is not limited to corporations—sometimes I think it's narrowly presented that way. I mean people have made strategy forever— in all kinds of different settings. I never knew the word until I got my MBA, but I knew strategy making! I'd say probably better than just about anybody, and it came from my farming background. I'd been doing it for years—so I knew it.*
> *Well, of course I've tried a lot of different things and made a lot of mistakes in business, but I think where I've learned the most has been from applying what I've*

*learned from my farming experience to a business setting. That [farming] experi-
ence has been the toughest teacher, and just invaluable to me. It's exactly the same
as making corporate strategy, only the context is different.*

*You've got to have some successful life experiences to draw from—these are the
most important places to learn from anyhow. You know, when we encounter new
challenges, we have to learn somehow—and so we draw on these experiences. It's
how we learn. Farming is a business, and you've got to figure out how to make
damn good strategy, or you'll never survive. There's no better teacher—you learn.
Period.*

A technology company CEO said:

*I think it's important to have these life experiences outside of a business context if
you're going to be successful within a business setting. What I mean is, you need to
have some successes—that's the experience that is so valuable for making really
good strategy. And you're probably not going to get it in any company. They just
don't give you the chance to learn. You'll get the boot.*

This same CEO recalled his prior successful life experience as a sculptor and credited
it with influencing his strategy learning: "I've studied sculpture. I think art is a good way
for thinking about strategy." When asked to talk about how that is, he said:

*You know, when you think, it's easy for your ideas to slip away. But when you're
doing art, any kind, you record those ideas—sometimes in forms that only you recognize. But you can then go back to them and redo them, add on or change them
or whatever. That's like making strategy, and I think that's why I like it.*

He explained how his sculpting experience related to learning strategic thinking by
continuing:

*Maybe I've learned from my experience with art, sculpture, working with the clay. I
think, for me, maybe, that's where I've learned the most. I think the most practical
and valuable things we learn in real life, not in business. And like sculpture, most
people would probably never think it relates to running a software company or anything (laughter), but it does for me! It's just not that different really, only the context
is different—you know, the people, the product, and the business. But the thinking
and being able to see things and work with things differently, that's the art part.*

Curiously, when probed, all of the executives resisted the notion that their learning
stemmed from previous strategy-making experiences per se. Instead, they "skipped back"
over time and linked their new strategy-making experiences to prior successful life experiences. Such a pattern suggests a strong conviction on the part of the executives that
successful experience in early life is most valuable. A Japanese financial executive
explained:

I've learned to make good strategy mostly from unrelated experiences. Like I said before, when I [auto] race, I like to win. And I learned from my junior high school days that I could not just sit in my car and keep racing. I never really took any lessons or [had] a teacher who showed me how to race—it was just something I really wanted to do. And I learned by listening to older racers talk before and after races, and watched them on the television, and then just tried very hard. I think it is necessary to have early experience—a good experience. Then you learn to make strategy. Then you just do the same thing in a company. For me it was auto racing—and I just learned by practicing it.

Application of Prior Experience to New Situations

One way to apply past experience to new situations is to assess the gap between what we think we know, and what is unknown. By evaluating the gap between prior learning and the unknown, we are able to construe a learning process to fill that gap. Past experience brings technical expertise, understanding of people, and knowledge of processes. It also brings a diagnostic capability to understand new situations more readily by asking the right questions and assessing against appropriate criteria. As one of the Japanese banking executives explained:

I think it's most important to have one experience—anything—early in life that you are successful with. And then you just keep building on it for other situations. It's the foundation for learning something new. You must find something you enjoy very much to be inspired to think. And this is my painting experience—it is so good for me; it is exactly how I learned about making good strategy.

Further illustrating the importance of a prior successful life experience on present strategic situations, he explained:

I learned to love to paint, so I think it's natural that I take what I learned and had good enjoyment [with it] and use it when I make strategy. And [I] just keep doing it in other areas of my life, not just banking. My painting background was very important to prepare me to make strategy. It was everything.

When asked how it helped him think strategically, he explained:

It taught me to be curious, and also that we will have many limitations in our thinking—so we must constantly acquire, add ideas. It's exactly the same as making corporate strategy, only the place and names are different. Everything else—it's the same.

Another financial executive described a similar belief:

You know, strategy making is not at all like we're taught. In fact, I don't really know about all these courses and methodologies. You really need to find something you really care about, really love doing in your life—and you'll start to learn strategy from that. Because you don't ever want to give up something you care about, so you'll just naturally work on developing strategies to hold on to it because it's that important. That's why being a kid and finding out what you really enjoy and care about is important. You carry all that over into your life and will always draw on those experiences.

Echoing the importance of a prior successful life experience, yet another executive noted:

You do not begin to make strategy as an adult. It is a failure that way. You must continue to make strategy according to how you do it in another area of your life, for example, a hobby or some other sincere passion you have. Making strategy will come to you if you have a strong will to win at something. And then you do it the same way for business. It's exactly the same.

Certain aspects of an experience capture our attention and influence our focus, because our existing knowledge base shapes what patterns we see in a situation.

Our cumulative experience provides us with an ever-evolving source of self-reliance, self-confidence, skills, knowledge, and practice for employing various conscious and unconscious reflective processes. Our remembered successful experience is a powerful and integral experience to which we automatically refer, and we use it as an anchor for subsequent strategy making, time and time again. This foundation brings consistency to our strategy making because we tend to use a similar thinking process each time; yet we differentiate each experience, due to context, and refine the reflective process each time.

What we learn from an experience is subjective and can often be fundamentally different from one person to another, even when each person experiences the same event. Certain aspects of an experience capture our attention and influence our focus, because our existing knowledge base shapes what patterns we see in a situation. Furthermore, our interpretation of that same experience changes over time.

Role of Reflection in the Three-Stage Informal Learning Process

Critical reflection is one of the essential abilities for transforming experience into learning, and it is utilized in all three stages of the informal learning process. The literature is filled with references to reflection as an essential part of the learning process.

Dewey's concept of reflection is set within the context of hypothetical-deductive problem solving.[4] Dewey defines reflective thought as "active persistent and careful consideration of any belief or supposed form of knowledge in the light of the grounds that support it and further conclusion to which it tends."[5]

The myriad terminology used to describe nuances of reflection can sometimes be confusing. Descriptions of what Chris Argyris calls *triple* and *double loop learning*,[6] what Donald Schon has named *reflection-in-action*,[7] and what Jack Mezirow refers to as *critical reflective learning*,[8] may provide some clarity as we attempt to learn from our experiences, first-hand or second-hand, current or past. Put simply, reflection-on-action is merely reflection after the fact—looking back on an action or experience, as opposed to reflection *during* an action or experience.

For Mezirow, reflection plays a key role in learning. It is the process of "critically assessing the content, process and premises of our effort to interpret and give meaning to our experiences."[9] The central function of reflection is validation of prior learning, or attending to the justification for our beliefs. Reflection may be used to examine the content or the description of a problem (*content reflection*), to question the problem itself (*process reflection*), or to look at the belief systems or meaning schemes on which the problem is founded (*premise reflection*).

Critical reflection assists in the ability to question presuppositions, routines, and patterns. A description provided by one of the Japanese financial company executives implied reflection when he explained:

> I've just learned [strategic thinking] from myself, just from experience and thinking and doing something and rethinking—and then I discuss matters with other people and I try, or test something I've been doing one way—it's good to do this, because you learn.

When asked to elaborate on how he learns from this, he continued:

> I learn because I have a habit that is good for me. I do something a certain way, and always somebody debates with me, or tells me I'm wrong, or to try it another way—and so I do. And then I must think, sometimes for a long time and in a serious way, about why did it work or not. And then I have more discussions or arguments (laughter) and I must think and try another new way—you know, it's a very good way to learn.

Adult educator Stephen Brookfield notes that critical reflection "is the process to engage the learner in a continuous and alternating process of investigation and exploration, followed by action grounded in this exploration, followed by reflection on this action, followed by further action, and so on."[10]

Such an iterative and dynamic form of informal learning was described in Marsick and Watkins' *Informal and Incidental Learning in the Workplace*:

> Reflection is key to this learning, but it must be combined with action, else it becomes speculative. Through action, managers test out insights, but they also

invite public examination of the problem, which leads to dialogue among them-
selves and the stakeholders of the problem. Action and reflection are not separate
phases, although at times, managers may be doing more of one than the other.
Action and reflection take place simultaneously or concurrently.[11]

The old adage that past success is a predictor of future success may hold partially true for learning to think strategically. Executives who can use reflective processes to connect a past experience to a future challenge are likely to be successful at strategic thinking. And yet there remains a divergent aspect of learning to think strategically—a reflective exercise that broadens our perspective, activates our imagination, and ultimately inspires us to think in ways that result in truly competitive strategy making.

Notes

1. Dewey, *Experience and Education.*
2. Kolb, *Experiential Learning: Experience as the Source of Learning and Development.*
3. Marsick and Watkins, *Informal and Incidental Learning in the Workplace.*
4. Dewey, *Experience and Education*; Brookfield, *Understanding and Facilitating Adult Learning,* 91.
5. Dewey, quoted in Mezirow, *Transformative Dimensions of Adult Learning,* 100.
6. Argyris, Putnam, and McLain Smith, *Action Science.*
7. Schon, *Educating the Reflective Practitioner.*
8. Mezirow, "A Transformative Theory of Adult Learning."
9. Mezirow, *Transformative Dimensions of Adult Learning,* 104.
10. Brookfield, *Understanding and Facilitating Adult Learning,* 91.
11. Marsick and Watkins, *Informal and Incidental Learning in the Workplace,* 74.

10

Reevaluation Stage

The third stage is, quite simply, a reevaluation of an overall experience. Reflection, as we have mentioned, is a critical element of learning to think strategically, and reflection is utilized in all three stages of the informal learning process. Yet reflection plays a particular role at the end of the three-stage informal learning process: to validate prior learning or justify our beliefs. Reflection in this third stage is critical and evaluative in nature, and it is used to "review" actions and decisions and to provide the rationale for those decisions. In essence, it "checks" our strategic decisions.

To be clear, one's reflective capacity has nothing to do with "going soft." Rather, reflection is an essential ability for strategic thinking, in that our reflective capacity can help us to realize that not everything can be solved, measured, or controlled. Reflection reminds us that sometimes we must trust and simply provide support—in the form of time, listening, critical questioning, and critical reflection.

The reflective processes used in this reevaluation stage allow us to interpret and reinterpret experience by opening up different lines of thinking. The reevaluation stage is a combination of an act–think–talk–think–act loop. Such an iterative cycle allows us a strategic opportunity to experiment, imagine, refine, and then decide.

The reevaluation stage is where new perspectives about priorities and relevance are generated. The earlier testing and validation of ideas, expectations, and assumptions formulated during the experience stage can be leveraged as "current experience" against which this new, reevaluative practice of critical inquiry can be tested. Values are confirmed or reassessed during this process. Successful strategists incorporate reevaluation consciously, yet informally, into their strategic thinking process.

The executives with whom I spoke consciously and deliberately cited steps of reevaluation even after they made a decision and took action. After the CEO of the financial company decided on a first phase of his strategy, but before the actual delegation for implementation began, he consciously and critically examined this phase within the larger strategic context for "things he should do differently." He requested not only that his senior executive team "retest" the idea and its underlying assumptions, but that the junior executives responsible for the implementation do so as well. Furthermore, he booked a four-stop flight, rather than his usual direct flight, to Europe in order to make time to "talk to a lot of totally uninformed strangers" about his first phase. He engaged consciously in an informal and intentional repetitive process of challenge–reflection–refinement in this reevaluation phase.

Interestingly, the executives interviewed were comfortable with not having a finite task completion in the "cycle" of making strategy, because they believed that making strategy was a generative, iterative, and continuous process. Not too dissimilar from the ancient Greek notion of strategy, their statements expressed a clear expectation that there will always be incomplete and inaccurate information, contradictions, and things that cannot be rationalized. The ideas of *metos* and *cosmos* described in Part I are as central to strategic thinking today as they were in pre-modern times.

> *Emotions are vital facilitators to informal learning and they are integral to the reflection process.*

The post-reflection stage of reevaluation promotes learning through communication as well as reflection and introspection, for the enhancement of understanding and the expansion of meaning. Reflection during the reevaluation stage occurs when we resurrect the perspective that we held when we embarked on the strategy-making process, and compare this initial perspective to the perspective that emerged from the experience.

As highlighted earlier, emotions are vital facilitators to informal learning and they are integral to the reflection process. Attending to feelings and reevaluating the experience need not be placed at the end of the process; rather, these emotions appear and can be acknowledged in each stage. Reevaluation occurs in an iterative way—eventually connecting to the preparation stage, where the learning process recycles.

Figure 10.1 shows the three-stage model of informal learning used for thinking strategically, and the model includes the affective component in each stage.[1] The executives interviewed recalled strong emotions as they experienced each of the three stages. They mentioned fear as the predominant feeling present in the preparation stage, followed by a wide range and combination of emotions throughout the strategic thinking process.

Understanding and mastering this three-stage cycle is imperative if we wish to develop innovative strategy in very different contexts. Being informed about this informal strategic thinking learning cycle supports a disciplined approach to developing new habits of learning for strategic thinking. By understanding and diligently practicing such a learning cycle, we can develop a sustainable pipeline of strategic thinkers capable of making meaning in the complex, unpredictable, ambivalent, and high-stakes global business environment.

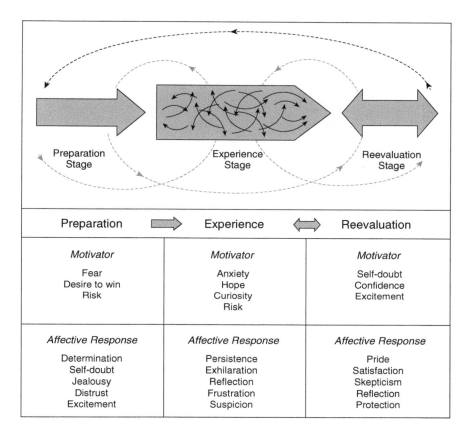

FIGURE 10.1   Affective Role within the Three-Stage Model of Strategic Thinking

Note

1. Sloan, "A Case Study of How Nine Executives Learn Informally to Develop Strategy in a Global Context."

Summary and Questions

Strategic thinking occurs as a highly iterative and generative process—it is "messy" by nature. Movement among the three stages of Preparation, Experience, and Reevaluation occurs in a fluid, oscillating, and non-linear manner. Contrary to common belief, emotions or intuitions are typically what launch our journey toward strategic thinking; this often inspires the conviction to begin thinking about a strategic problem in a new and different way. Grasping and leveraging the intensity of emotions around a complex and paradoxical strategic issue can enable us to more deeply understand and to diverge a strategic problem. It also galvanizes a desire to win in the strategic thinking process. Avoiding engagement with the affective dimension of strategic thinking may yield a less messy process, but it is not likely to result in an innovative, genuine, and expansive strategic thinking process.

It is our collective experiences from across business, personal, and leisure activities that serve the informal learning process that underlies strategic thinking. Critical reflection on these experiences helps us to expose their broader meaning and deeper assumptions. Specifically, success in any context can readily transfer to a strategy context and enable us to think metaphorically about a complex issue. While reflection occurs in each of the three stages of the iterative strategic thinking process, it is most critical at the end of the process. Critical reflection in this stage allows us to look back at our learning process to validate our findings, conclusions, or breakthroughs. Moreover, it enables us to make meaning, or create new meaning, from the strategic process as a whole.

1. What are some cues that might indicate that you are ready to begin the strategic thinking process?
2. When you consider a recent strategy that you have been involved with, what did you notice about your emotional response as you embarked on the challenging strategic issue? What was your intuitive response to your challenging strategic issue? Was there anything that restricted or constrained you? Anything that excited you?

3. How could leaders within an organization limit awareness, acceptance, and communication of the affective component of strategic thinking? How could they increase these?

4. Reflect on a time that you felt successful outside of your professional environment. Describe a metaphor that illustrates how that experience was like an experience in your current professional environment. What were the common factors? What factors were different? At what point did the experiences diverge? How might you transfer what you learned within one context into another context?

HOW CAN WE GET STARTED?

Go Exploring!: The Surf and Dive Domains of Learning

Though this be madness, yet there is method in it.

William Shakespeare (1564–1616), English dramatist and poet

11

Overview of Learning Domains Used for Strategic Thinking

In the course of my observation and facilitation of high-level strategy meetings in corporations, governments, and international agencies, one observation has become consistently apparent, and that is that the processes of questioning, responding, and interacting often use less complex levels of cognition than we might imagine. Although the position of the executives may be high level, the levels of questions and quality of the conversations I have found are variable at best. Many of these meetings consist of an exchange of summary findings, reports, analytic data, rapid-fire question–answer segments, and perhaps a brief brainstorming session to decide on a solution. Sometimes, there is debate about the analysis, but this inevitably concludes with recommendations for a future course of action. Rarely do I encounter meaningful critical dialogue.

Over time, the absence of critical dialogue and deep, dive-level questions can result in personal and organizational same-frame thinking or, worse, frames that are frozen entirely. Such rigidity and staid habits of mind can have a tremendously negative impact on the quality of the strategy made. Some of what is missing, of course, has to do with political posturing and power games for which such meetings provide a forum, but much of it has to do with a lack of common understanding and a collective confusion about what strategic thinking is, how to develop it, and responsibility for the consequences of not having the courage to engage in it.

Part IV consists of two chapters. The key concepts presented in this part are learning domains—specifically, as the domains relate to thinking strategically. The first chapter serves to differentiate between data, information, and knowledge and offers an overview of these learning domains. The second chapter discusses two specific domains of learning that are essential for facilitating strategic thinking. These two domains will be referred to throughout this book as the *surf* domain and the *dive* domain.

By understanding the learning domains required for strategic thinking, we can greatly expand and enrich our own learning. These domains bring focus to our questions and responses. Working with clients in my consulting practice, I find that they quickly benefit from information about learning domains in order to choose the domain most suited for their particular strategic situation.

The dynamic process that is used to convert information into knowledge is learning.

While there are many definitions of learning, the fundamental characteristic is that it involves some kind of change that is a reaction to an encounter, not just a function of a natural maturation process. This change can occur in domains of motor skills, intellectual skills, knowledge content, cognitive strategies, awareness, affect, or attitude.[1] The term *domain* refers here to an area of learning influence, similar to a taxonomy of learning activity.

Data, Information, and Knowledge

A starting point in any discussion about learning and strategic thinking is to distinguish between data, information, and knowledge. For the sake of simplicity, this book considers *data* to be neutral, static, and meaningless. *Information* is derived from data and is given meaning through the interpretation of facts or statistics. The aim of information is to construct knowledge using the surface domain of learning. *Knowledge* is information that is framed according to our (mostly) implicit belief systems. And the dynamic process used to convert information into knowledge is *learning*.

An example of data is: A half million American adults living in nine states are not enrolled in any health insurance program.

Information derived from this data might be:

- The incomes of these adults rank in the lowest quartile and the states represent the nine poorest states; or …
- This segment of the population is comprised of 75 percent non-native English speakers; or …
- These states have governors who rank near the bottom of an annual peer-review poll.

Knowledge gleaned from this information could include:

- Our social and medical systems are at risk; or …
- Our political system is failing us; or …
- The insurance business is an industry at fault.

Knowledge is the result of how the information has been interpreted within a context and the meaning it has been given. "The purpose of knowledge is to appreciate wonders even more," proclaimed Richard Feynman in his renowned 1964 lecture entitled "What Is and What Should Be the Role of Scientific Culture in Modern Society," which was about the role of scientific culture in modern society.[2]

Knowledge is most often tacit and is embedded within individuals and groups. It requires reflective learning, or what I refer to as the deeper, dive-level of learning. As John Dewey noted, the aim of knowledge is to reconstruct and make meaning, processes that are inextricably linked to social interaction, dialogue, and critical inquiry.

In order to leverage knowledge into the learning required to make innovative, sustainable, competitive strategy, we must "convert" the information and knowledge into strategic learning experiences through transfer.

Knowledge-creation pioneers Ikujiro Nonaka and Hirotaka Takeuchi regard knowledge as a dynamic human process of justifying personal belief toward the truth. "Knowledge is about beliefs and commitments, ... action and meaning."[3] Accordingly, information is a flow of messages, whereas knowledge is created by that very flow of information, and distilled by the beliefs of the holder.

The distinction between information and knowledge is important for any discussion about learning to think strategically, because one of the fundamental requirements is that the information flow be consciously and routinely interrupted, and that the knowledge base be challenged and rigorously tested against our beliefs or anchors.

> *Strategists must be willing to seek out facts that*
> *might disconfirm a generally held belief and be*
> *willing to explore other possibilities.*

Although knowledge and learning are sometimes difficult to express, strategists should be encouraged to pursue an awareness and explicit means of expression of both knowledge and learning. Knowledge and learning are essential to being able to challenge beliefs and assumptions; and this challenge is fundamental to strengthening our capacity to think strategically.

When data, information, and knowledge interact with critical reflective processes (critical inquiry, critical dialogue, critical reflection, critical thinking), the result is *insight*. The iterative process of a synthesis of knowledge, insights, and ideas develops improved judgment, which is a critical output of the strategic thinking process. This improved judgment, in turn, informs the development of strategies within the organization's strategic planning processes, which ultimately make the organization more competitive. The insights generated must be continually challenged and diverged with an expectation that things are constantly changing. Strategic thinking serves this role by using a cognitive cluster that supports divergent thought and deep, dive-level questions to continuously test.

Strategists must be willing to seek out facts that might disconfirm a generally held belief and be willing to explore other possibilities. Knowledge benefits strategic thinking when the perspectives of multiple sources, information, experiences, reflective processes, creative thought, dialogue, and supporting technologies are fully integrated and embedded within an organization. Those responsible for strategic thinking should be continuously encouraged to seek new knowledge and to habitually challenge and be challenged.

As a means to developing strategic thinking, knowledge sharing is best facilitated through critical dialogue; however, information technology can support this dialogue as well. While information technology can only record and store explicit knowledge, such systems do enable easy transfer of information that can later be interpreted and challenged in context by those responsible for making sense of the data and who bring their own knowledge from past experiences.

SCENARIO

Margot, the CEO of a midsize software firm, panicked because her three-year winning strategy was failing. Her stockholders were complaining, the board was on her case, competition was on the rise, and her neck was on the line. Instead of opening up, she surrounded herself with people whom she considered to be loyalists, those who were like-minded and knew "where the lines were drawn." She fired her two top "antagonists" and refused to hire "outsiders" because they wouldn't know the company way and would bog down the process. She insisted that her global executive committee relocate back to Seattle for convenience and to help with "continuity" for some time. Fearful of shattering frames, Margot locked into her existing frames of reference, hoping to revive her strategy by simply extending what she already knew and doing more of what did not work! Her experience reminds us that there are times when we must pursue what is counterintuitive and break out if we want to survive.

Three Predecessors of the Surf and Dive Learning Domains

In strategy-making seminars, I often hear executives conclude that they have either a lot or a little "knowledge about" a certain topic. They tend to distinguish between what they "know of" and what they "really know." As we will see in this section, theorists have differentiated these same domains of learning using various models and terminology. Prior to a discussion of what this book refers to as the surf and dive learning domains, it will be useful to have some background on the arguments of several earlier theorists about learning domains.

Knowledge About and Knowledge of Acquaintance

The distinction between the domains of practical and abstract knowledge was first made by the philosopher William James at the turn of the twentieth century. He made reference to these domains as *knowledge about* and *knowledge of acquaintance.* To learn knowledge about requires that we effectively transfer information and integrate that information into conceptual models and frameworks. With regard to strategy making, we commonly learn this way through instructional workshops, videos, lectures, reading, seminars, web-based programs, and other direct instruction methods designed for teaching various models of information and analysis. The meaning of such information is interpreted through the learners' frames of reference, through the rationale or framework of a particular theorist, professor, trainer, consulting firm, or school.

As content becomes more complex, contradictory, or controversial, the ability to interact with others and to critically question is required. This is what James referred to as knowledge of acquaintance.[4] Knowledge of acquaintance is learned through personal experience, and the essence of such knowledge is embedded in one's decisions and actions—in a person's tacit knowledge. Knowledge of acquaintance can only be acquired through first-hand experience of an issue or situation in question—through practice, reflection, challenge, testing, and reaction. This knowledge can be learned through informal learning, incidentally through experience, and through structured activities, such as action-learning initiatives.

While the technical difference between knowledge about and knowledge of acquaintance is distinct, it is helpful to understand the relationship between the two kinds of knowledge for strategic thinking. Knowledge about provides a framework against which practical experience can be tested. This framework can then be modified in practice and ultimately becomes knowledge of acquaintance. This conversion takes place when we apply analytical models, interpret complex content, and make decisions about the implications of a discussion in order to make informed strategic decisions.

P and Q Types of Learning

Various authors have differentiated structured and unstructured problems within different domains of learning. Learning theorist Reg Revans refers to *P* and *Q* learning types, which he classified according to two different problem structures. P learning refers to programed learning or knowledge that has been codified in books, lectures, or analytical techniques. P learning is often used to describe "puzzles," or problems for which a correct solution exists, even if the answer is hard to find. An example of P learning would be finding the best way to reduce the time or cost of some specific manufacturing operation. P learning is commonly used for addressing problems of operational effectiveness, and discussion or debate is commonly employed when using P learning.

By contrast, Q learning typically represents "quandaries," difficulties, or opportunities to which no solution clearly exists. A common example would be determining the direction a company will take after a merger. Q learning can be supported through coaching individual executives and facilitating group meetings. Q learning requires executives to reinterpret the meaning of current decisions and emerging trends, to challenge their assumptions, and to reframe their experience. Action-learning programs, future search methods, lateral thinking, scenario planning, and introducing critical dialogue at all levels of the organization are ways of facilitating the Q domain of strategic learning. In relation to learning theorist Karl Weick's terminology, P learning correlates to problems of uncertainty, whereas Q learning is equivalent to ambiguous problems that require judgment.

Clearly, strategic thinking involves both P and Q learning domains, but strategists may find it easy to get stuck using the P learning domain because it is far easier to structure, it moves more quickly, it is convenient to track, is often habitual, is far less risky, and has an end solution. Q learning involves questioning insight, but, before that can occur, we must gain strategic insight by asking discriminating questions and then reconciling data analysis with past experience and intuitive judgment to answer those questions. Each strategic decision requires a different combination of analysis, experience, and judgment. Obviously, there is no formula, because the variables in each situation are different.

Four Types of Learning

Another way that strategic thinking can be perceived is according to the theory put forth by yet another learning theorist, Edward Cell. His model distinguishes learning by classifying it into four domains: response learning, situation learning, trans-situation learning, and transcendent learning.

Response learning refers to a change in the way we respond in a particular situation; we respond with a prepared set of answers or techniques when handling a specific situation.[5] Response learning is studied by behaviorists in psychology and includes rote learning and what Skinner called "operant conditioning."

This kind of learning can also require the learner to apply a sequence of skills or to match responses to options of varying complexity in situations, such as selecting the best negotiating tactic from among many possibilities, while in the midst of a contentious debate. For example, a country manager learns to offer a set of appropriate responses when questioned by auditors investigating the profit picture. This manager's experience of repetitive learning is effective for problems that involve low-level learning transfer and ensures that the skill becomes an automatic baseline response. But in circumstances with less predictable outcomes, such as security training, a different type of learning is required.

Presenting strategic thinking as something that can be easily taught and learned through a prescriptive model, a formula, or a structured sequence is highly tempting. We are all too familiar with this learning approach and, unfortunately, many of us have come to think of it as the best way to learn everything. Not every problem or decision can be, or should be, solved in such a linear, instrumental manner. When confronted with the complex issues involved in strategy, this learning method just doesn't pass the test.

Cell's second kind of learning, *situation learning*, involves a change in how we organize our understanding of a situation. He notes that response learning is dependent on situation learning, since it is how we interpret a situation that shapes our response to it.

Trans-situation learning, Cell's third kind of learning, is learning how to change our interpretations of a situation. This is often called "learning to learn." This kind of learning involves reflecting on the learning process and identifying and questioning the assumptions and attributions we are making about a situation, by using reflective inquiry for critical self-reflection.

Cell's final kind of learning, *transcendent learning,* requires that we modify or create whole new concepts. This kind of learning is generative and provides new possibilities and new tools for interpreting individual situations. Transcendent learning is sometimes referred to as transformational learning.

If we understand the learning domains presented here, we will assist ourselves, our teams, and our organizations as we move toward strategic problems. The ability to identify the appropriate domain(s) is a first step to understanding the nature of a strategic issue.

Notes

1. Hilgard and Bower, *Theories of Learning.*
2. Feynman, *The Pleasure of Finding Things Out: The Best Short Works of Richard Feynman.*
3. Nonaka and Takeuchi, *The Knowledge-Creating Company: How Japanese Companies Create the Dynamics of Innovation*, 58–9.
4. James, *Pragmatism.*
5. Cell, *Learning to Learn from Experience.*

12

The Surf and Dive Learning Domains

The complex, unpredictable, and paradoxical nature of the global strategy environment in which traditional transaction-oriented, linear, controlling executives now find themselves requires that they pursue a broader range of, and more agile, thinking in order to make sustainable and innovative strategy. A board member of a British investment bank with whom I was working coined the terms *surf* and *dive* after we had been collaborating on strategic thinking issues for several days. The surf domain is a metaphor for surfing—the kind of learning that happens on the surface. Surf learning is easy to understand, has answers, is instrumental, transactional, and is relatively safe. We can make sense of things through transacting with information and events, creating a series of responses, and taking new actions.

On the other hand, the much deeper and more complex level of learning requires us to dive beneath the surface in order to make meaning of data, information, experiences, and situations. This learning domain is about exploring the unknown and the unfamiliar, lacks apparent answers, has no boundaries, and can be very risky; dive learning is difficult to describe in words and is heavily reliant on past and present experience.

I have since borrowed these terms because the imagery really works, and it conveys the concept quickly. The colloquial terminology makes sense and runs parallel with other terms, such as *single*, *double*, and *triple loop* (Schon), *model I* and *model II* (Schein), and *instrumental* and *communicative* (Mezirow).

> *Frequently, executives are hammered for*
> *not being good strategic thinkers, but rarely do they*
> *(or their bosses) know how to improve.*

Once clients have some knowledge about learning domains, I find the strategic thinking process accelerates considerably. Executives are often defined by perpetual activity:

doing deals, running meetings, and conducting transactions. If executives are to be successful strategists, they must get things done, but they must also take time to understand why they are doing what they are doing and thinking what they are thinking. Taking a deep dive requires the capability to reflect critically, ask tough questions, and employ divergent thinking. Dive learning is no longer an option or an indulgence; it is a necessity.

Not surprisingly, strategic thinking can be a sensitive subject. Frequently, executives are hammered for not being good strategic thinkers, but rarely do they (or their bosses) know how to improve. Therefore, those involved in strategy generally feel vulnerable, defensive, or resistant. By offering a bit of information about the learning domains, executives gain a renewed sense of control over their own learning because this learning gives them a concept, a vocabulary, a process, and a choice. They can choose to be responsible for the learning level required for various aspects of strategy making.

Consequently, we can choose which learning domain to employ at a given point in the strategic thinking process. What we call the learning domain is not important, but what *is* important is developing the cognitive cluster necessary for each domain in order to support the requirements of our strategic situation. Also, understanding the learning domains can help us keep track of where we are in the strategic thinking process and facilitate our own learning, as well as that of others. Table 12.1 shows the necessary learning domains when learning to think strategically. The domains of learning and implications for thinking strategically will be presented later.

The model on which the surf and dive domains of learning are based is what theorist Jack Mezirow calls instrumental, communicative, and transformative domains.[1] While Mezirow draws on Edward Cell's work, as well as on the thinking of John Dewey and William James, his work is grounded in the critical social theory of Jürgen Habermas.

Mezirow's critical pragmatism defines learning as the process of using a prior interpretation to construe a new or revised interpretation of one's experience in order to guide future action.[2] For Mezirow, "Action is an indispensable phase of the process of adult learning. But action can mean making a decision, being critically reflective, or transforming a meaning structure as well as a change in behavior."[3]

The Surf Domain

The surf learning domain is premised on the notion that learning "what" and "how" will accomplish tasks or solve problems because we control our environment by acting on it. Surf learning is essentially an instrumental, mechanical, response kind of learning. In strategy, this domain is the one in which meaning is attached to day-to-day, transactional kinds of actions. Learning in this domain is primarily about determining cause–effect relationships and learning through task-oriented problem solving. The surf domain uses a kind of learning that "involves predictions about observable events which can be proven correct, determining cause–effect relationships and task-oriented problem solving. The logic of instrumental learning is hypothetically deductive."[4]

TABLE 12.1   The Surf and Dive Learning Domains

Domains of Learning	Description of Learning	Common Meaning-Making Techniques	Significance to Strategic Thinking
Surf domain	Linear Sequential Progressive Mechanistic Predictable Transactional Instrumental Routine Instructional Informational Avoid surprises "What" "How-to"	Analysis Tactical reasoning Logical reasoning Identifying "correct" and "incorrect" answers Exchanging data and information Reporting Feasibility studies Problem solving Decision making Debate Discussion	Convergence oriented Positions formulated and defended Opponents and proponents identified Competitive data collection Analysis Closure
Dive domain	Nonlinear Intuitive Logical or a-rational Strong affective component Invite surprises "My opinion" "My beliefs" "My values" "My conviction" "My principle" "Why" "What else"	Critical reflection Dialectic thinking Metaphoric speech Analogic thinking Storytelling Collaborative inquiry Critical questioning Imagining Improvising Experimenting Expanding perspectives Testing Challenging Creating Critical dialogue	Divergence oriented Is "messy" Continuously changing Open to exploring new ideas and perspectives Imaginative Surprising
Transformative domain (can occur in surf or dive domains)	Triggered by disorientation or catastrophe "Why" "How" "What next" "What else" "Why not" "What if"	Critical reflection Critical dialogue	Transformative Dramatic shift Unpredictable Shatter frames Reveal assumptions Test premise Expand assumptions

Source: Based on the model of instrumental, communicative, and transformative domains by Jack Mezirow[1].
[1]Mezirow, "A Transformative Theory of Adult Learning," 58.

Many senior executives and those responsible for the development of strategic thinking often try their best to simplify and reduce strategic thinking to a "how-to" model—conforming to the familiar and habitual. Ultimately, this effort restricts their learning techniques to the surf domain and only reinforces planning.

Most traditional, formal, and behavioral programs directed at improving strategy performance are stuck in the surf domain. For example, surf learning occurs through strategic planning replication models, analytical model simulations, and prescriptive models. Many leadership-development approaches to strategic thinking are based on some variation of such "how-to" models and imply a fill-in-the-blank type of solution. Surf learning is an effective learning domain for facilitating the development of strategic planning, but less than ideal for improving strategic thinking.

The Dive Domain

The domain of dive learning is about making sense—learning to understand what others mean and learning to challenge and make our deeper selves understood. This domain of learning is key for developing strategic thinking. Critical reflection (detailed in Part VI) is heavily dependent upon critical dialogue, which is central to this dive domain of learning. The dive domain draws on Mezirow's communicative domain of learning, which emphasizes the use of communication and interaction (language and nonverbal, cognitive and affective) in order to anticipate the actions of others and delve deeper into our own actions and decisions.

Mezirow describes this learning domain as follows: "It involves understanding values, ideals, feelings, and normative concepts like freedom, autonomy, love, [and] justice. It identifies and clarifies the known through a process whereby each step suggests the next."[5] This form of situational learning requires that we expand or change our frame of reference and provides the contextual framing for strategic thinking initiatives. For example, leaders of strategic discussions announce frequently that diverse opinions are sought, and later see those opinions shot down prematurely because someone declares: "We can't do that here because…" or "That won't work these days because…"

The dive learning domain serves as a counter to such reductionist and elimination discussions in that it invites us to identify, test, challenge, refine, and possibly alter our frames of reference in the interest of strategic thinking. The result may be a frame change of varying degree. Minimally, we may change the way we see patterns and specific situations. Maximally, we may experience a total transformation, a truly life-altering or business-altering experience. Too often, we jump to solutions in strategy meetings without critically examining, identifying, stretching, and challenging the real problem. Suggesting premature solutions tends to reinforce same-frame thinking and disregards creative or divergent thought.

Dive learning requires critical dialogue, critical inquiry, and critical reflection, and often integrates experience in order to construct meaning within a social context. Also, dive learning may consist of some discussion and debate, which can further enrich dive-level learning if they expose the underlying position and premise of arguments.

Dissent, contrariness, and opposition can be particularly useful triggers to dive learning because they invite critical reflection, critical inquiry, and critical dialogue. We learn tacitly which frames are acceptable and unacceptable for use within our respective organizations, and through critical reflection and critical dialogue we can challenge frames and strengthen strategic thinking.

Frames

Having mentioned frames in the above discussion of dive-level learning, within a strategic thinking context, a frame is a way of categorizing or compartmentalizing patterns and perceptions of data, decisions, and behaviors. Frames bring specific topics or perspectives into focus, and play a central role in learning to think strategically. What we frame is that perspective to which we pay attention. For example, a particular frame might be regarded as "functional," and actions and decisions would be judged according to their definition and degree of functionality. Another frame may be economic, where all actions and decisions would be evaluated according to their cost and financial value to the business.

We all bring a stack of frames (personal and professional) with us; these frames can include an "age" frame, a "job title" frame, a "Mom" frame, or a "political" frame. Moreover, organizations have frames that are taught, reinforced, rewarded, and applied to strategy meetings both formally and informally. Frames such as a "profit" frame, an "innovation" frame, a "harmony" frame, a "survival-of-the-fittest" frame, or a "seniority" frame tend to drive strategy priorities and decisions.

Understanding which frames are used in strategy meetings and within an organizational culture is critical. Equally essential is establishing permission and a process to challenge, test, revise, and reframe our thinking to develop a pipeline of strategic thinkers and winning strategy.

More simply put, a frame of reference is a perspective organized by the assumptions and expectations that influence how we see the world. Our frames have two dimensions: *habits of mind*, consisting of a set of assumptions and broad, generalized predispositions that guide our interpretations of events and experience—a mindset; and *points of view*, which consist of clusters of beliefs, feelings, attitudes, and judgments that are specific expressions of our broader habit of mind—in other words, an opinion. These dimensions tend to operate outside of our awareness most of the time, but we need to understand that every aspect of our thinking is influenced by our frames.

The current business goals to which we are committed, as well as the overall business climate and our personal belief systems, shape the frames we use to discuss, determine, and decide strategic issues. Frames are passed on in organizations through stories, protocol, policy, and conversation channels, and they contribute to the subjective interpretation of strategic events. Because our frames influence our interpretation of strategic events, we must continuously include a broad diversification of frames and points of view regarding all strategic issues, and invite challenge as a means to support innovative thinking and to ensure that our strategy is consistently aligned with our values. Strategic thinking thrives on frame change as a means to divergent thinking and deep, dive questions.

A frame is a belief schema or an organized cognitive way of perceiving a complex set of behavioral patterns and decisions. Consider for a moment the problem of obesity among children in the most economically developed countries. A business executive may frame the issue as one of market potential for new lines of food and clothing, but an educator may frame it as a problem of learning deficits, behavioral disorders, and long-term development issues. A scientist may frame the obesity problem as a population-growth rate that has outstripped agricultural activity, and a sociologist might frame the problem as inadequate family and social structures. An economist may frame the same problem in terms of insufficient purchasing power or the inequitable distribution of agricultural commodities. Each of us frames our strategic problem according to our own experience and what we

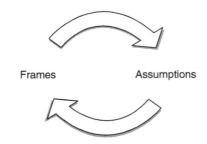

FIGURE 12.1   Frames and Assumptions

"know." Accordingly, we proceed to make assumptions that inform and influence our decision making. Figure 12.1 illustrates this dynamic cycle.

From a strategic thinking point of view, a beneficial practice is to include as much diversity of thinking as possible in the early stages of strategy conversations. Why? Without coaxing, our frames accompany us to strategy meetings. The intent and challenge of strategic thinking is to get everyone to see the others' perspectives, as a means of generating more questions and alternative thoughts, rearranging patterns, shifting and shattering frames, and possibly constructing a new frame.

Repeated rounds of asking key questions about data, positions, and recommendations regarding the strategy problem and attentive listening, followed by further inquiry, can be useful to identify and make explicit hidden frames and underlying assumptions. But beware that our tendency is to gather data that fits neatly into our existing or habitual frames—which only perpetuates same-frame thinking.

Our frames of reference outline the categories of patterns. For example, if we use the frame of "honesty" when we encounter certain circumstances and observe specific behaviors, we then place the observations within the framework we call "honesty" to define patterns. If, for example, a supplier is supposed to deliver a product according to specs at a certain cost on a certain date, but pockets a healthy 3 percent off the records, I might frame that behavior as dishonest. Someone with different cultural insight, however, may frame the same action as a loss-of-face or a "shame" frame.

Same-Frame Thinking

The influence of corporate culture can sometimes supersede that of a national culture, particularly in companies that have invested heavily in creating and teaching a distinct corporate culture. If the strategic learning process is not monitored, this learning can inadvertently lead to a "group-think" mentality—that is, when collective critical inquiry ability is allowed to atrophy and executives from everywhere in the world begin to develop same-frame mindsets and to think in the corporate way.

Readily, I acknowledge that this "group-think" mentality can be a highly efficient and lucrative environment in which to manage, but it can also be detrimental to strategic thinking because everybody shares the same frame and no one wants to "rock the boat" or take the risk of challenging frames. In these environments, employees, managers, and executives at all levels and in all locations fail to realize that their individual frames bear a strategic value. In fact, the more different, the more valuable. For too long, they have been encouraged to seek rewards for contributing as good corporate players. As companies approach globalization in a variety of ways, and as corporate culture assimilation and acculturation are increasingly influential forms of incidental learning, companies must keep tabs on their approaches and periodically test for same-frame thinking so that the corporate culture doesn't become an impediment to their own survival.

Three Common Framing Mistakes

Three common strategic thinking framing mistakes that I have noticed countless executives make are:

1. Unintentionally (or intentionally) restricting the tip of the triangle to a familiar small strategy group.
2. Surrounding themselves with loyalists and like-minded thinkers.
3. False frame change.

All three mistakes can result in the exclusion of contrary opinion, ignorance of and immunity from opposing data, minimized opportunity for divergent thinking, and avoidance of controversial dialogue. In essence, these mistakes cancel the very processes required to learn strategic thinking.

The unintentional learning that occurs as the result of these three mistakes makes us think about strategy in terms of using same frames. The incidental learning that results from such inclusion and exclusion is that expressing contrary views, challenging authority, or testing tradition is punished, while conformity of thinking is rewarded. Yet challenge and testing are essential for shifting and shattering frames and for learning to think in innovative and adaptive ways.

Restricting strategy to a small, select group flirts with the temptation of creating same-frame thinkers and excluding those whose frames may be dramatically different and desperately needed for diverging thought, testing, and challenging. Whose frames are habitually included in strategy meetings? What other frames could be valuable, but are excluded? Often, shifting or shattering some organizational or individual frames is required in order to expand the range of frames.

Loyalty should, of course, be rewarded. But loyalty itself needs to be challenged as a criterion that supports quality strategic thinking. If loyalty to a person, a product, a brand, or an organization leads to or reinforces same-frame thinking, this loyalty can negatively impact upon strategic thinking by reinforcing habits of thought. Such loyalty can all too easily prevent the examination of new or different frames, distort patterns, and ensure that shattering or reframing does not occur. I have observed this narrowing of perspective, particularly in times of urgency and desperation, when strategy is deteriorating and executives are frantically seeking a new strategy. Well-intentioned but blind loyalty can quickly undermine strategic thinking.

A false frame change is when we believe that a frame change has occurred, but instead, only an illusion of change has been created. Sometimes we become so enthralled with "active participation" in strategy meetings that we don't pay attention to the range of frames or to the level of genuine engagement. For example, in a meeting in Dubai an executive proudly stated that his team was using dive learning and that it had shattered its frames. But actually, the team was surfing and still perpetuating same-frame thinking under the guise of compliant behavior according to the established corporate frames. In other words, the team was faking it in order to be perceived as being politically correct and loyal.

> *Executives may "act" in accordance with compli-*
> *ance requirements while their beliefs, blind spots,*
> *and biases remain unchanged.*

The strategic decisions we make are strongly influenced by the national, ethnic, cultural, gender, religious, and sexual-orientation frames we hold. Executives may modify their behavior (i.e., actions and words) after taking courses; they may role-play, watch videos, and internalize feedback in order to conform to the corporate cultural norms so as to avoid disciplinary action, or to be rewarded. Executives may "act" in accordance with compliance requirements while their beliefs, blind spots, and biases remain unchanged. In other words, response learning follows the training experience, but fundamental frames of reference do not change. The underlying beliefs that these executives hold are what keep their strategic decisions bound within the same frames. Such inflexible perspectives and frozen frames impede strategic thinking because frames do not shift or shatter—they are merely disguised.

The following are several suggestions that I have found helpful for fostering frame change within strategy meetings.

- Vary the usual composition of strategy groups to increase exposure to new frames.
- Change the location of strategy meetings. Create an element of surprise.
- Invite provocative conversations and presentations with "outsiders," including those outside a functional group, a product group, an industry sector, or a particular level of management.
- Establish interactions with non-experts, academics, politicians, consultants, professionals from various fields, children, teenagers, young adults, middle-age and mature adults, religious leaders, people from an extreme range of economic backgrounds, and those of diverse cultural and ethnic backgrounds.
- Volunteer to be part of an action-learning team to solve a problem for tasks that are outside of familiar functional or product areas.
- Join conversations, discussions, and meetings where your frame is an outlier.

- Participate in high-level strategy-making meetings and code the frames represented as points of view are expressed.
- Note any frame omissions that could bring value.

Frame Change and Dive Learning

The good news is that frame change can result from learning in the dive domain.

> *The ability to change a frame of reference is a hallmark of successful strategists; in order to do this, strategists need to be able to shift or shatter perspectives and create new ways of looking at situations.*

Both the surf and the dive learning domains have their own standards of validity. Surf learning holds to validity tests of facts, measurements, and outcomes; something is true or false, accurate or inaccurate. The validity test is seen in concrete experience—something either happens or it does not; there is a result or there is not. This kind of testing is typical and familiar in strategy discussions and debates. Meanwhile, dive learning has more nuanced validity tests, including the assessment that others make of our own (and each other's) authenticity, truthfulness, and qualifications. Dive learning is heavily influenced by and, in turn, shapes or transforms the cultural context in which we act. We can easily draw erroneous conclusions from reflection alone on the content of our experience, leading to a closed cycle of non-learning. Therefore, practices such as reflecting on the foundations of our beliefs (premise reflection) and publicly testing our conclusions with others are effective validity tests within this domain of dive learning.

Shattering existing frames of reference may sound easy enough, but it is extremely challenging in practice. The ability to change a frame of reference is a hallmark of successful strategists; in order to do this, strategists need to be able to shift or shatter perspectives and create new ways of looking at situations. This effort is easier to articulate than it is to carry out—as many worthwhile things are.

SCENARIO

For example, Tyson, an American executive based in Detroit, who fundamentally believed numbers tell the truth and nothing but the truth, was unaware of how his strategic decisions impacted upon others in the global rollout of several plans. Reflecting on his assumption—numbers are facts, and facts equal the truth—he extended an existing meaning frame when he decided to hire an external consulting firm to analyze the data and the findings against additional information to which his company did not have access. His basic frame did not change; he simply extended it.

After moving to an office in Paris, Tyson began to have regular, long lunch conversations with colleagues and other business associates that sometimes grew into heated arguments. This was something new for him. His colleagues questioned his every action, didn't accept his numbers at face value, and demanded to know the "why" behind every decision he made. They challenged the very decisions that had successfully opened markets in 21 countries. As much as Tyson found them irritating, he noticed that they seemed to enjoy this lunchtime exchange. After months of stress, he began to treat the conversations as daily workouts. Gradually, he realized the significance and expanded meaning that the story behind the numbers offered in terms of how the decisions he made affected customers, shareholders, and employees around the world. Slowly, he began to invite more challenge about the numbers he had once considered sacred.

Developing the Dive Learning Domain

Strategic situations can, according to learning theorist Jack Mezirow, be reinterpreted in one of four ways:

- *Extend* or develop an existing frame of reference.
- *Learn* a new frame of reference and adopt it.
- *Change* viewpoints (create new patterns for certain situations or issues).
- *Transform* frames (construct new belief systems and adopt new values).

One of the key objectives of strengthening our ability to use the dive domain of learning is to enlarge the scope and depth of our strategic thinking by modifying or dramatically changing our frames of reference. Our frames of reference shape our understanding of both the surf and dive domains of our experience. In other words, even neutral data and information are interpreted by our frames, often unconsciously or instantaneously.

Purposeful critical dialogue enables reframing of perspectives. In the absence of critical dialogue, we make judgments about the validity of the message, based on our assessment of the trustworthiness of the source. Reflective processes and capabilities are necessary for deep, dive learning to occur. Playing the "devil's advocate" and intentionally testing assumptions through direct and open inquiry are two potent methods of validity testing.

Some learning is basically additive in nature, as when we elaborate or extend an existing frame of reference or add a new frame of reference without changing the beliefs and presuppositions of existing ones. There is nothing wrong with this, but in the strategic thinking process we must remain aware of the learning domain that is required for the situation, so that we can choose the appropriate level of questions and responses accordingly.

In my consulting practice, I am astounded by the number of global executives who have developed or are developing business in emerging markets and lack even a rudimentary knowledge of, or interest in, frames that are historical, cultural, humanitarian, social, military, and political in nature. Not only do these business leaders not seek out these frames, they often dismiss such frames as being irrelevant, superfluous, and time consuming. Including diverse data, points of view, and perspectives in a strategic dialogue is essential to maintaining a competitive strategic edge. The implication of these missing frames is the emergence of blind spots, and their impact on long-term business strategy is the writing on the wall.

SCENARIO

From the very beginning, it seemed like a great business idea: an American automobile company selling Russians a stripped-down, locally assembled version of an American SUV at a premium price. The research confirmed that the demand was there, as well as the purchasing power. With the seemingly low labor costs and the tax breaks negotiated with government authorities, the financials looked very promising.

The problem, which did not appear on the radar of the American strategic planners, was that most of the Russians in their market segment and price range viewed a Russian car as a contradiction in terms, and they applied the same attitude to any car assembled by Russian workers in a Russian–American joint venture. (The fact that Russia is one of very few car manufacturing countries where the head of state does not use a locally manufactured limo as his official car attests to the prevalence of this attitude. As the saying goes, if you want to buy Russian, stick to vodka!)

As soon as the prospective Russian clients realized that several thousand dollars more would get them the same SUV—a slightly used standard American model (and here is the deal breaker) made in the U.S. by American workers—the future of the project was doomed. The U.S. corporate strategists and CEO had concentrated only on the economic and financial research, at the expense of cultural, social, and political information and data. Shortly thereafter, the U.S. corporate strategists and CEO faced the realities of the market and began lobbying the Russian authorities to raise custom duties for the import of used American SUVs to Russia.

This automobile scenario illustrates why developing a capacity to use dive learning is an essential part of any strategic thinking approach. A competitive strategy does not result from brilliant analysis or brilliant people alone. Critical reflection, critical inquiry, and critical dialogue must be woven into the strategic thinking process. Risk-management models do generate excellent analysis, and this analysis provides an excellent starting point for dialogue, but this analysis is no substitute for critical reflection, critical inquiry, and critical dialogue. Knowing this is essential for those who facilitate strategic thinking because a frame-shifting, shattering, and reframing of situations is a key intent of strategic thinking.

Transformative Learning

When a fundamentally disconfirming experience or disorienting dilemma challenges our frame of reference, we are presented with an opportunity to dive to the deepest levels of learning and draw meaning from the trauma. So powerful is this kind of learning that Mezirow described it as "emancipation from libidinal, linguistic, epistemic, institutional, or environmental forces that limit our options and our rational control over our lives, but have been taken for granted or seen as beyond human control."[6] Such experience can lead us to critically reflect on our beliefs and presuppositions, resulting in either a new mode of pattern recognition or, at the deepest level, a fully transformed framework.

Although this kind of transformative learning can occur in either the surf or the dive domain, critical reflection, critical inquiry, critical dialogue, and critical thinking are necessary to make new meaning. This experience can be epochal in nature, such as an abrupt, "blinding light" kind of instinctual experience, or it can be incremental in nature, as the result of gradual accumulation of experiences.

Fear can be a powerful impetus
for strategic thinking.

While a frame change of this degree is hardly an everyday experience for most strategists, it does occasionally occur. These dramatic frame transformations typically result in major overhauls in the way a company does business. Such deep and transformational learning can even lead to a dramatic change in strategic thinking because everything appears differently and we either reject or no longer recognize our old patterns and frames.

Truly innovative strategy can emerge from these kinds of experiences. While the experience itself may be frightening, painful, even destructive, it is within the critical reflective learning process that transformation occurs. This metamorphosis can result in a remarkable, miraculous, positive outcome and can be attributed to turning a nightmare experience into a constructive one. Truly transformational learning requires that we experience situations that put us totally outside of our known zone, well beyond the realm of familiarity and control—so much so that our world feels mangled or turned upside down.

Clients with whom I have worked have occasionally experienced this kind of intense, life-redefining frame change as a result of major loss—both expected or unexpected—such as a corporate takeover, the death of a partner, spouse, or child, or the diagnosis of a critical disease, to name just a few. An intense transformational learning experience can also result from a gain, such as the realization that over the years their income has ballooned to substantially more than that of their parents, a successful corporate takeover, the birth of a child, recovery from a critical illness, or adjusting to living in a different country. Executives who have experienced learning in these circumstances sometimes claim to feel "enlightened" or to have become a "new person."

The CFO of a pharmaceutical company with which I was working experienced such traumatic frame change due to a facility bombing in southern Thailand that killed his best friend and two co-workers. He referred to it as an emotional "earthquake"—one thing happened, and after the initial shock and ruinous aftermath, other changes were triggered in every aspect of his business and personal life. After a year or so of "soul searching," he described these changes as a "total rearrangement of my life."

Although it generally takes a catastrophe or a disorienting dilemma for us to experience learning of this magnitude, we need to remember that experiencing a catastrophe is no guarantee that we will experience learning. To ensure that learning results from the experience, or to at least facilitate the likelihood of a learning outcome, we must critically reflect on the experience and test new action that can be incorporated into a new frame. Interestingly, and fortunately, fear can be a powerful impetus for strategic thinking. When we consider the volatile, unpredictable world in which we make strategy, this becomes all the more relevant to those responsible for making and facilitating strategy.

Knowledge of the surf and dive learning domains can facilitate learning from experience. When strategy works well, executives rarely focus on improving their strategic thinking, which is taken for granted. Only when problems creep up and the company's profit, revenue, market share, or reputation is at risk do the sirens blare.

The integration of surf and dive learning domains, with an emphasis on critical reflective processes, should be a perpetual goal of strategic thinking programs. An ability to pursue both surf and dive learning domains profoundly differentiates successful strategic thinkers. The capacity to move from one domain to the other is an internal resource available to each of us, available for everyday access.

By developing the dive domain, we can ensure that the organizational and individual strategic capacities are addressed. Innovative, sustainable, and adaptable strategy becomes possible because the dive domain of learning allows for renewal and the re-creation of strategy. This is the domain of learning that "involves identifying ideas, values, beliefs, and feelings, critically examining the assumptions upon which they are based, testing their justification through rational discourse, and making decisions predicated upon the resulting opinion."[7]

> *Executives who are incessantly connected to the*
> *muddle of other people's voices have difficulty*
> *hearing their own voice.*

The ability to think strategically is compromised if we live our lives without moments of solitude and silence. Executives who are incessantly connected to the muddle of other people's voices have difficulty hearing their own voice.

Within the frame of strategic thinking, successful strategy is always perceived as past tense; it never happens the same way twice. A strategic win is merely a one-time historical business event in need of continuous divergence and deep-dive challenge. In order for wins to reoccur, learning initiatives must be guided by strategic thinking processes and integrated into important business initiatives via formal and informal means.

Notes

1. Mezirow, *Learning as Transformation: Critical Perspectives on a Theory in Progress*.
2. Mezirow, "A Transformative Theory of Adult Learning," 49.
3. Mezirow, "A Transformative Theory of Adult Learning," 49.
4. Mezirow, "A Transformative Theory of Adult Learning," 49.
5. Mezirow, "A Transformative Theory of Adult Learning," 87.
6. Mezirow, "A Transformative Theory of Adult Learning," 49.
7. Mezirow, "A Transformative Theory of Adult Learning," 49.

IV

Summary and Questions

Exploring and understanding the rudiments of learning domains can be beneficial to gaining insight about a strategic problem because one of the fundamental requirements of strategic thinking is that we consciously and regularly interrupt what we "know of" and what we "know about." Strategic thinking deliberately aims to challenge this knowledge base and rigorously test our beliefs and anchors.

Insightful critical reflection on the data, information, and knowledge is essential to exposing our assumptions and beliefs about the premise of a strategic problem. Reflective learning is required for developing innovative, sustainable, and competitive strategic thinking. Assessing your own and your organization's learning habits through the surf and dive domains is an important aspect of understanding the nature of a strategic issue. The surf domain explores the surface level of an issue by understanding the cause–effect relationship of the problem. Surf learning employs "how-to" models and is more effective for strategic planning than for fostering strategic thinking. By contrast, the dive learning domain involves challenging deeply held beliefs and assumptions while critically examining the true nature of a strategic problem. We accomplish this through critical dialogue, critical inquiry, critical thinking, and critical reflection.

Mental frames of reference are belief schema, an organized cognitive way of perceiving a complex set of patterns and decisions. Business goals, belief systems, and the external environment collectively shape our individual and our organization's frames of reference and our perception of a strategic problem. By inviting a broad range of diverse frames and points of view we can cultivate frame change, divergent thinking, and deep-dive questioning. Engaging in the dive domain expands frames of reference and can lead to frame shifting, shattering, and reframing. Dramatic transformational experiences that shatter our frame of reference, often provoking fear as they transport us far outside our comfort zone, may provide a catalyst for strategic thinking and present an opportunity to dive to the deepest level of learning.

1. Are there circumstances where you notice surf or dive questions being routinely asked? Consider a familiar organization. Are there situations where either the

surf or dive domain tends to get rewarded in strategy meetings? Why might this be?

2. What are some common same-frame thinking patterns that occur in your organization's strategy meetings? What might be the origins of these same-frame thinking patterns? Who benefits from this same-frame thinking? How could this same-frame thinking be detrimental to the stated strategic intentions?

3. How could the inclusion of additional frames and new frames be supportive of the stated strategic intentions?

4. What are some of your own "blind spots" that might inhibit frame change that is required of strategic thinking?

5. How do you seek out facts and information to challenge your own assumptions and disconfirm deeply held beliefs?

6. Think of a truly transformational incident that your organization (or another familiar organization) experienced. What frames were shattered? How did this happen? What frame changes ultimately occurred? What was the short-term impact? The long-term impact?

HOW CAN WE TALK ABOUT ALL OF THIS?

Dialogue: An Essential Part of Learning to Think Strategically

The greatest problem with communication is the illusion that it has been accomplished.

George Bernard Shaw (1856–1950), British playwright

13

The Role of Dialogue in the Strategic Thinking Process

When we think of dialogue within a strategy context, we often have an image of people getting together to talk. But that is far too general and far too obvious. We tend not to differentiate the various ways of structuring talk to support strategic thinking, nor do we regularly tend to think about the purpose of the talk.

Most of us have forgotten or were never taught how beneficial dialogue is to the creative and cognitive learning process, and how essential dialogue is for learning to think strategically. Debate and discussion have fallen into favor during the last century as learning methods of the technical rational era. As we move toward a strategic thinking framework, it is necessary to (re)familiarize ourselves with dialogue. Part V takes a closer look at the role of dialogue as it relates to learning to think strategically. The focus here, is on critical dialogue as an essential tool for communication and exploration of the deeper, dive domain of learning as it supports the strategic learning process.

This part consists of two chapters. Chapter 13 compares dialogue, discussion, and debate within a strategic thinking process. These three communication practices are distinguishable and their differences should be understood to support strategic thinking—not merely to split hairs. Thereafter, the focus is solely on dialogue. Chapter 14 presents critical inquiry as an integral part of critical dialogue and outlines seven strategy dimensions that are beneficial for enriching a strategic dialogue. The last section of the chapter looks at how critical dialogue is learned and used in the three-stage informal learning process.

To start with, some good news—dialogue has been around forever, and is learnable. Some aspects of dialogue are skill-based and can be taught in a conventional formal learning setting. Other, less familiar aspects of critical dialogue are experience-based and require critical reflection, which is typically learned informally. The bad news is that critical dialogue requires substantial time, discipline, and a commitment to practice in order to benefit the strategic thinking mindset. These three aspects of dialogue are not about efficiency or brevity but, rather, about the practice of embedding critical dialogue into organizations to ensure sustainability and adaptability for long-term strategic thinking development. Critical dialogue is not necessarily data or fact driven. It can draw from intuition, imagination, and experience, and is enriched by deep, dive questions.

*Most corporate and university executive programs
teach strategic thinking as if time were the most
important aspect of judgment, rather than investing
in developing the habit of critical dialogue, which
leads to trusted experience.*

From political leaders, to media coverage of international organizational proceedings, to corporate meetings, there is a dearth of positive role models who demonstrate constructive and collaborative discourse, dialogue, or even good debate. Our commercial business world is eager to provide shortcuts to rescue our tuckered-out minds. Bullet points and sound bites have replaced critical dialogue, discussion, and debate—especially when it comes to strategy issues. We expect and accept sound bites as the mode for giving and receiving information in meetings, texts, e-mails, phone calls, and conference calls. "Get to the point" takes precedence over a dialogic thinking process that is generative, adaptive, and innovative. Sadly, we have convinced ourselves that we need only the succinct facts to think strategically, as we assume that brevity represents facts, and facts represent "close enough to truth." As a result, abbreviated thinking is frequently mistaken for sound conclusions.

At the opposite end of the spectrum are strategy meetings conducted using so-called "diplomatic" discourse—in which the intent is deliberately diluted and the message can be so convoluted that it lacks authenticity or relevance. Both ends of the dialogue spectrum lack critical reflective practices.

Ironically, companies claim to be desperate for strategic thinkers, but many ignore or actively resist the inclusion of critical dialogue in the process of learning to think strategically. Quite often, I find that many of my corporate and government clients have no personal memory of critical dialogue for use as a reference point in strategic thinking.

Furthermore, most corporate and university executive programs teach strategic thinking as if time were the most important aspect of judgment, rather than investing in developing the habit of critical dialogue, which leads to trusted experience. This outmoded frame—the one that has established time as being paramount to anything else—is begging to be shattered. Purposeful critical dialogue is essential for making meaning and framing habits of thinking.

Comparison of Dialogue, Discussion, and Debate

Dialogue is a versatile, vital, and trustworthy capability in a global strategy-making environment where many things are uncertain, constantly changing, and beyond our control. The terms *dialogue, discussion,* and *debate* are often used synonymously when referring to the nature of the talk in strategy meetings. Though dialogue is a word that is commonly batted about, it is often used quite generically. Critical dialogue is the most essential communication technique for use in supporting the strategic learning process, but discussion and debate also have a place—each can and should be used to enrich the strategic thinking process.

Discussion and debate are most useful in strategic thinking as focused testing techniques for the specific ideas that are generated as a result of the dialogue process. Discussion and debate can serve to highlight and challenge gaps, omissions, or inconsistencies in both the content and process generated by dialogue, which need to be addressed. Discussion and debate can be a useful means of directing and guiding strategy conversations toward critical dialogue.

Discussion and debate, when applied to conflicting frames of reference, depend on data. When we hold conflicting frames, we pay attention to different facts and make different meaning of the data we notice. Debate and discussion (both of which use convergent, mechanical, instrumental, and sequential learning for problem solving) do not allow us to convert situational discrepancies into well-formed strategic perspectives. Rather, it is through shattering our existing frames and reframing through critical dialogue that strategic thinking becomes valuable. When there is conflict, critical dialogue within the deeper, dive domain of learning is imperative.

Dialogue

Before proceeding, we should take a moment to look at what dialogue is and what it is not. Originating from Greek roots, the word *dialogue* consists of two parts, *dia* and *logos*, or "meaning flowing through."[1] Dialogue is not about unbridled chatting or about people arguing, hoping to defend their positions against one another. Rather, dialogue occurs between and among people. Dialogue is conscious and deliberate, and requires discipline and practice.

In differentiating debate and discussion from dialogue, William Isaacs, of MIT's Leadership Center, notes:

> *Dialogue seeks to have people learn how to think together—not just in the sense of analyzing a shared problem, but in the sense of surfacing fundamental assumptions and gaining insight into why they arise. Dialogue can thus produce an environment where people are consciously participating in the creation of shared meaning.*[2]

As we have discussed, strategy making is a high-stakes endeavor occurring in a very unpredictable and highly competitive environment. Gangbuster executives find slowing down long enough to engage in critical dialogue extremely difficult, even though critical dialogue ultimately allows them to speed up. Acknowledging this paradox is essential for learning to think strategically.

> *Dialogue acknowledges that each person, no matter how brilliant or able, still sees the world from a particular perspective and that there are other credible and legitimate perspectives that can inform that view.*

In an article for a Center for Creative Leadership publication, N. M. Dixon explains the importance of the relationship in a dialogue and the idea that "through the interaction of dialogue, people acknowledge the entirety, not just the utility, of others."[3]

Dialogue is a unique form of communication in which listening and learning take precedence over talking and persuading. Dialogue requires the suspension of criticism and opinion, which in turn facilitates exploration of issues and problems. Critical dialogue promotes collective and collaborative thinking through a balance of inquiry, listening, reflecting, and talking. Unlike discussion and debate, critical dialogue uses divergent thinking.

An important point to highlight, particularly within an ego-driven, high-pressure strategy environment, is that dialogue acknowledges that each person, no matter how brilliant or able, still sees the world from a particular perspective, and that there are other credible and legitimate perspectives that can inform that view. As I have mentioned, for most executives, critical dialogue is not part of their experience, so some fundamental skills may be begging to be developed. Such practice takes time and commitment, but once executives see critical dialogue, hear it, do it, and reflect on it, the quality of their contribution to the strategy process reaches an entirely new level.

Discussion

The roots of the word *discussion* come from the Latin *discussus*, meaning "to investigate by reasoning or argument."[4] Also, discussion implies a linear progression to a sequential and resolute end. Discussion, as differentiated from dialogue and debate, focuses on problem solving. Like debate, discussion uses convergent thinking. Generally, discussions do not have the intent of exploring or altering underlying patterns of meaning, and discussions are generally used most effectively for analysis that is primarily conclusive.

Debate

By contrast, the word *debate* has Latin origins of *de* and *battuere*, which means "to beat." Debate is defined in the dictionary as "a contention by words or arguments; a regulated discussion of a proposition between two matched sides."[5] Debate can constructively be used in the strategic thinking process to identify weak spots in our thinking and to expose baseline assumptions that need to be challenged. Habitual and historical patterns of thought and practices are often revealed through debate. Prior to or after debate, however, we find that engaging in critical dialogue can be useful to test and validate the data, and to diverge and broaden perspectives. Participating in critical dialogue after a debate can further challenge and test assumptions highlighted during the debate. Alternatively, engaging in dialogue prior to debate can make the underlying assumptions explicit and enhance the quality of that debate. With both discussion and debate, we strive to articulate our position with persuasion and argument. Critical dialogue aims to explore and search.

Strengthening dialogue, discussion, and debate can serve as a support and a source for enriched communicative learning within the strategic thinking process (Table 13.1). In real life, there is no "correct" linear progression or sequence suggesting when to engage in dialogue, discussion, or debate. What matters is being prepared with the skills and agility to engage in all three, and knowing which one is most appropriate and constructive at any point in the strategy process.

The global head of engineering for a medical equipment company offered the metaphor of a water faucet to illustrate how we can assess which of these three communication techniques (dialogue, discussion, debate) is needed during the strategic thinking process. He claims that the image helps him to keep track of where he and his global team are at any given time. Drawing from his metaphor, if we want to expand our thinking and need a rush of ideas or divergent thinking, then we need to "open the faucet" and practice critical dialogue. On the other hand, if we have thoroughly explored ideas, have listened, tested opinions, invited contrary positions, and have a wide range of people involved, then we may need to gradually converge and "close the faucet" by defining a problem

TABLE 13.1 Dialogue, Discussion, and Debate: Intent of Three Communicative Learning Techniques

Technique	Definition	Direction	Graphic Representation
Dialogue	To explore and search Share and grow by listening to and learning from different perspectives Create individual and collective meaning through expression and empathetic listening Suspend opinions Inquiry and disclosure Partner is an equal to be understood	Divergent Emerging proposition Nonlinear process	
Discussion	To establish or fix Find a solution to a problem. Investigate and examine Present and convince in detail a predetermined meaning Give answers and explanations according to a predetermined agenda or position Aim is single agreement or conclusion Partner is an equal to be convinced	Convergent Push–pull proposition Linear process	
Debate	To defend or argue Win by persuading opponent. Contention by argument Convictions already held Judgmental, competitive, and combative Partner is a rival to be defeated	Convergent Win–lose proposition Linear process	

through discussion. In order to make a decision and draw conclusions, eventually, we may want to use debate to "turn off" the faucet and stop the flow.

Dialogue encourages win-win scenarios and does not try to convince or convert others. Rather, the emphasis is on a cycle of asking good questions and using focused listening. Critical dialogue emphasizes the creation of shared meaning rather than imposing or pushing the meaning of any one person or any single frame, and dialogue supports the learning process by enabling us to see things more truly and honestly. The role of critical dialogue in learning to think strategically is to pose dive-level questions for the purpose of diverging thought, challenging premises, and making assumptions explicit, rather than generating answers. Critical dialogue is divergent by nature; therefore, it includes an inherent quality of uncertainty and change. Critical dialogue is intended to induce an element of surprise.

Three Factors of a Good Strategic Thinking Dialogue

I always smile at the reactions of executives with whom I work when they hear the word *dialogue* within the context of strategic thinking. They cringe and roll their eyes, certain that dialogue will create a bottleneck in their strategic thinking process. They fear an endless spewing of pointless garble, and they are reticent to open a can of worms that they may be unable to contain or control. I remind them that a good critical dialogue is something different; it is informed, risky, and critical. Isaacs notes: "Dialogue is a discipline of collective thinking and inquiry, a process for transforming the quality of conversation and, in particular, the thinking that lies beneath it."[6]

> *A good strategic thinking dialogue is informed,*
> *risky, and critical.*

Speaking, listening, and critically reflecting are three parts of a good strategy dialogue. The three are inseparable when practicing good dialogue. Some degree of trial and error occurs through the use of critical dialogue as we react to others' questions and comments on our recent or past actions, decisions, and thoughts. The reflection in action, it seems, frequently occurs when executives engage and respond to counter-questions, deep, dive questions, or criticisms. Some enjoy the dynamics of a verbal and intellectual joust and a test of opposing wills. Many are taken aback, either by hearing themselves say something or by the unexpected response of a listener.

For the executives with whom I have spoken, critical dialogue became a conscious habit through practice. These strategists have developed a routine for testing and validating their assumptions against prior successful life experiences, which included various forms of dialogue with a wide variety of people. These strategists came to enthusiastically anticipate and deliberately incorporate a rigorous dialogue as a learning method. Their comments indicated that challenge, often encountered through the use of dialogue, was a vital experience for learning to think strategically.

For example, the Hong Kong executive recommended that aspiring strategists:

Talk to many people and read everything, and insist that others ask you questions. We must think about what we don't know. I think that I talk to so many different people and bring our different ideas and opinions together—and that's very good. Sometimes maybe it looks like we spend a lot of time talking about things that are not related to economics or technology, but everything is connected when you're trying to put together a big puzzle—so why not? It's the most helpful thing.

One of the American technology company executives said that he thrives on

smart people to talk to and bounce ideas off of. We have a lot of really smart people here—and egos are in check. And we all are really focused and want to make things work, so it's good. That's a good learning space—where ideas are tossed around and you can try things—and then toss them around some more.

When starting to practice critical dialogue about strategic issues, as a means of testing and diverging information that is assumed to be known or understood, I find it useful to incorporate the following seven questions:

1. Why?
2. Why not?
3. What else?
4. Who else?
5. Where else?
6. When else?
7. How else?

Generally, I find it tends to take at least six rounds of these questions before executives start to hit on something—that something may be beliefs, assumptions, new creative thoughts, or a new appreciation for the possibility of different frames and assumptions. With practice, this simple dive-level drill becomes a thinking habit leading to critical reflection, and eventually it can contribute to generating meaningful strategic dialogue.

If we are to learn strategic thinking, we must be able to take part in dialogue, and we must make strategy to some degree in order truly to participate in the dialogue.

Critical dialogue is an essential part of the deeper, dive domain of learning, and it requires commitment and practice to master to any extent. Regardless of how awkwardly or mechanically we carry out these initial dialogues, we must begin somewhere in order to learn what it feels like and to experience the new elements these dialogues bring to strategic decision making. We learn the meaning of the actions by performing them, just as we practice riding a bicycle, skiing, or driving a car.

In order for strategists to begin to see the collective patterns of their dialogues, strategists must take some time after meetings to pay attention and reflect on the dialogue, discussion, or debate. Reviewing records, coding, mapping, or notes can provide data to identify emerging or entrenched patterns of exclusion, limited breadth, or premature decisions.

Good Strategy Dialogue Is Informed

Good critical dialogue is informed, in the sense that the partners have substantive knowledge and engage from a position of curiosity in wanting to understand the other person(s). Starting with intent, the purpose of an informed strategy dialogue is to stretch the parameters of current thinking, deepen our knowledge base, introduce new data, expand information and ideas, and allow us to listen and think in different ways. When practiced with regularity and in a disciplined and trusting manner, critical dialogue can lead us to new possibilities.

> *The human ability to convert data into information*
> *should drive the data-gathering effort in the*
> *strategic dialogue process, not the reverse.*

Prior to having a meaningful critical dialogue we need some degree of instrumental learning and a certain amount of content knowledge. In other words, we need to know what we are talking about. The surf domain of learning is generally how we acquire a broad range of data and information. We analyze in order to have valid information as part of an informed dialogue. Having valid information allows us to enter a dialogue with something other than our untested feelings; we have the data and information to bring to the table to establish shared knowledge. As we see in Figure 13.1, data are useful for informing good dialogue, but it is critical dialogue that enables us to extrapolate new meaning from that data.

The ease with which we can gather data today is extremely seductive. Unfortunately, the focus is too often on more data rather than good data. The task of filtering, filing, cross-referencing, and categorizing data can easily take on a life of its own. Converting all of these data into information requires reasoning, interpretation, and judgment—all human mental functions that are slower processes than those used by technology. As a result, our technical ability to generate vast amounts of data has far surpassed our human

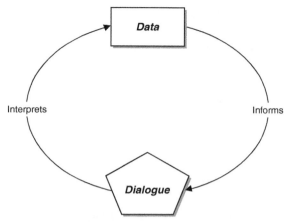

FIGURE 13.1   The Data–Dialogue Cycle: The Role of Dialogue in the Strategic Thinking Process

ability to convert it into meaningful information. The human ability to convert data into information should drive the data-gathering effort in the strategic dialogue process, not the reverse.

> *Dialogue partners must agree that a dialogue will emerge and go places that a discussion or debate would not, because dialogue is divergent. There is always an element of surprise and uncertainty in a good dialogue.*

A truly informed critical dialogue should not prioritize data dumping but, rather, should revolve around three issues. First, we need to deal with the substantive problems of the task. We must describe in whatever way is available to us—questioning, describing, or explaining—the problem as we see it. Second, we must keep our descriptions and examples particular. Descriptions should be linked to the immediate questions, confusions, difficulties, or potentials. And third, dialogue partners must agree that a dialogue will emerge and go places that a discussion or debate would or could not, because dialogue is divergent. To be sure, some find this intimidating and exasperating, but the element of surprise and uncertainty is the most vital and valuable part of good critical dialogue.

Good Strategic Dialogue Is Risky

A good strategic dialogue is risky because it requires challenging and testing the underlying assumptions and beliefs of our information and thinking—an emotional hotwire, to be sure. In strategy, critical dialogue exposes our flaws in thinking and can touch raw nerves that are deeply embedded in our thinking process and belief system. Critical dialogue demands that we become vulnerable and open about what we tout and test as our "truths," even though these questions are difficult to ask, and equally difficult to answer. Without this testing of data and information, there is a danger that we might miss constructive strategic dialogue and default to meaningless or familiar talk that simply perpetuates our current frames of reference. We end up using our communication efforts to defend untested information and possibly to sever relationships. Defending does little to further strategic thinking. It keeps us locked in the same frames and allows us only to persuade, convince, pressure, or coerce others to accept our frameworks—a trap that defeats the very aim of learning to think strategically.

The affective dimension of cognition rears its head when we take the risk of engaging in critical dialogue. I find that apprehension and frustration are two common responses of executives who engage in strategic thinking dialogue early on. This dialogue process includes a large learning component, which creates a state of imbalance and tension. This lack of balance causes a natural tension, a feeling of uncertainty, a lack of control, and vulnerability.

In contrast, discussion and debate are convergent by nature, and there is some comfort in knowing that an endpoint exists and the tension is relieved. But critical dialogue is divergent and requires creating a shared meaning, which requires figuring out a rhythm with our dialogue partner(s), who may have a different pace of reflecting and a different style of expressing and responding. The endpoint is unpredictable.

Meaningful strategic dialogue requires honesty and authenticity.

In an effort to reduce the risk and enhance our ability to speak, listen, and reflect optimally, we need to have the confidence to speak—a skill that can be greatly enhanced by experience and practice. Also, we need to have something specific and valid to say, and we need to trust that those in the immediate and greater environment are willing to listen. Retribution, ridicule, interruptions, and having ideas nipped or robbed can all be inhibitors to meaningful dialogue, as can an environment that does not reward collaboration. Furthermore, we need to trust the intention and skills of the partners with whom we are in dialogue. Meaningful strategic dialogue requires honesty and authenticity. Language and articulation sometimes interfere, but these are minor issues if the intent of the critical dialogue is genuine and true.

A Polish executive explained:

It's necessary to have other people, especially people who are younger or from a different industry, to talk to and get their ideas and opinions. And we must talk to each other often—but I don't mean in an organized way necessarily—you know, I think it makes most people uncomfortable and they cannot think in a good way if it

is too organized. That's why coffee shops will never be out of fashion (laughter)—
they are necessary for good business! It is the only place people really think! (more
laughter)

Actively seeking out critical dialogue with colleagues, other professionals, and strangers is risky, but essential to broadening our perspective, stimulating our imagination, identifying factors we can and cannot control, and increasing the level and quality of thinking—for the sake of a winning strategy.

Good Strategy Dialogue Is Critical

The purpose of critical dialogue is to bring strategy partners to a juncture of thinking and acting through challenge and divergence. A critical dialogue is not intended for the purpose of attacking or beating the opponent, as in debate, or for the purpose of convincing, as with discussion. A critical dialogue intends to diverge thinking as a means to expand and test strategic possibilities. The element of listening is closely tied to thinking and speaking, and is held to a higher level than talking or persuading.

Furthermore, critical dialogue involves an honest exchange of probes as a means to reflection, and it involves variant perspectives on the dialogue topic at hand. Reflecting and responding to questions enable dialogue partners to become aware of inconsistencies as well as consistencies in their ideas and opinions. The process of critical dialogue causes us to think aloud, thereby creating clarity and insights not possible when our thoughts and feelings are internal.

A critical dialogue includes reflecting on our own decisions and actions. During strategy dialogues, executives routinely ask themselves: "What are my solutions and evaluations right now?" "What do I habitually and spontaneously do in this situation?" "Why?" "Who would see this differently?" "Why?" "Who would object to this?" "Why?" "Who else could potentially benefit?" "Why?" I encourage executives to jot down their responses, which allows them to pause, suspend their judgments, and more accurately describe and revise the actions they offer to others. Writing without speaking can be a useful reflective exercise because it allows us to acknowledge thoughts and feelings, and frees us to listen openly, suspend judgment, and explore. The practice also makes our thoughts and feelings easier to retain or retrieve.

Critical dialogue is informed, risky, and critical. A purposeful critical dialogue requires some affective and cognitive readiness on the part of both parties, including an attitude of curiosity. It takes a disciplined and courageous leader to commit to, consciously pay attention to, learn, and engage in critical dialogue.

Notes

1. *Merriam-Webster's Collegiate Dictionary, Tenth Edition.*
2. Isaacs, "Taking Flight: Dialogue, Collective Thinking, and Organizational Learning," 235.

3. Dixon, *Perspectives on Dialogue.*
4. *Merriam-Webster's Collegiate Dictionary, Tenth Edition.*
5. *Merriam-Webster's Collegiate Dictionary, Tenth Edition.*
6. Isaacs, "Taking Flight: Dialogue, Collective Thinking, and Organizational Learning," 232.

14

What Is the Role of Inquiry in Critical Dialogue?

Inquiry serves many purposes for learning to think strategically. Inquiry supports a critical dialogue, forces us to think deeper and more broadly, and enables us to clarify, to understand, and to seek answers. Also, questions provide a springboard for divergent thinking and for generating new ideas, and insights for strategic decisions. According to the research of William Isaacs:

> The central purpose [of dialogue] is to establish a field of genuine meeting and inquiry—a setting in which people can allow a free flow of meaning and vigorous exploration of the collective background of their thoughts, their personal predispositions, the nature of their shared attention, and the rigid features of their individual and collective assumptions.[1]

Inquiry Supports Good Strategy Dialogue

Within a strategic thinking context, questions are an effective means of gathering information. Asking and responding to questions helps us to analyze a situation and to broaden our perspective. Additionally, inquiry strengthens strategic thinking by helping us to identify and challenge assumptions. A Japanese financial executive forthrightly commented:

> (smiling) You know very well, that I like to ask many questions!
>   (laughter) So, I have always tried to do my best, and for me that is to try many new things and watch other people and ask questions, many questions. Then I read and talk to people—especially people who are different from me, and then I ask new questions! (laughter)

*Interestingly, it is nearly impossible for any one
person to dominate within a good dialogue, when
everyone is expected to focus on questioning.*

Inquiry is a particularly appropriate form of communication for learning to think strategically, because there is no need for any dialogue partner to defer to another, based on hierarchy or expertise. Everyone must be able to inquire of everyone else in order fully to benefit from the dialogue process. Interestingly, it is nearly impossible for any one person to dominate within a good dialogue, when everyone is expected to focus on questioning. When inquiry is paired with reflection, the mind is encouraged to open and to diverge. Questions require us to listen attentively, which in turn generates a need to reflect. This leads to subsequent questioning that requires more careful listening and reflection, and so a cycle is set into motion.

Critical inquiry is essential for probing deeper to understand patterns and predict strategic opportunities. In fact, inquiry is probably the easiest way to predict patterns and trends. Why? When we become comfortable with a pattern, we tend to become complacent in assuming that this pattern will remain static, so we fail to look at the potential for variation or innovation. Inquiry can help us project where a pattern or trend is headed by explicitly testing assumptions, as well as generating alternatives.

Encouraging inquiry is essential if meaningful strategic thinking is to occur. With few exceptions, critical reflection does not come easily, as there must be space and time to step back and examine the deep, dive questions and responses that have challenged our basic assumptions and beliefs. Critical reflection involves more than recalling and dissecting. It involves thinking about and paying attention to feelings, and making sense of and attempting to understand what supports an opinion, an idea, or a belief. Good questions are often the impetus to meaningful reflection.

In certain realms, science may explain some things, yet it will never explain everything. In the case of strategic thinking, for every question answered, a mass of new ones are generated. And these questions are usually far more perplexing and more challenging than the prior problem. This was brilliantly stated by the British geneticist J. B. S. Haldane early in the twentieth century: "Life is not only stranger than we imagine, it is stranger than we can imagine."[2]

In my practice, I find that no two executives hold the same standard with regard to the time and space needed for inquiry and reflection. Some require periods of several weeks or months away from the place, people, and the topic at hand in order to reflect. Others need to pull away mentally and retreat to the quiet shade of a tree or different room for only a short while, and then reengage intermittently in dialogue.

Often, executives comment that when they are responsible for asking good questions of themselves and their strategy teams, this responsibility reduces the pressure of solving the strategic problem. They tend to trust the process of inquiry, knowing that it ultimately produces better strategic solutions. When the process of inquiry is a collective responsibility, the executives feel less defensive and are able to think more openly.

The search for answers becomes an exploration of ideas, and generation of alternatives is a responsibility shared by all the dialogue partners.

Inquiry builds on the knowledge that partners bring into a dialogue group; at the same time, inquiry constructs new knowledge, fosters learning, and develops shared meaning. Questions enable us to remove the layers around a problem and uncover the core issues necessary to discover the solution. Isaacs points out:

> *Unlike most forms of inquiry, the inquiry in dialogue is one that places primacy on the whole. Dialogue's aim is to take into account the impact one speaker has on the overall system, giving consideration to the timing of comments, their relative strength, their sequence, and their meaning to others. Dialogue seeks to unveil the ways in which collective patterns of thinking unfold—both as conditioned, mechanistic reflexes, and potentially as fluid, dynamically creative exchanges.*[3]

An American technology executive explained his appreciation for strategy dialogue:

> *We kind of realized that we'd never have all the answers to all our questions. You know how it is—once you find one answer, you suddenly have a thousand more questions. (Talks faster, raises voice, gestures with hands on tabletop) At some point, you just realize it's part of the process.*
>
> *And it's kind of a gamble. You never know exactly which questions you need to pay attention to at that moment. I don't want to say it's hit or miss, but you do the best you can. You read everything, you look at what other people are doing all over the world—and you plug in every imaginable number. (Leans forward, moves toward researcher) You spot trends across all kinds of industries—and then I think there's an element of luck. I don't know, it's probably just me, but at some point you just have to put it [strategy] into orbit.*

Good Dialogue Questions

As any strategist knows, asking the right questions is not easy, especially when grappling with a serious or complex problem. The ability to ask good questions in an environment of risk, constant change, confusion, and uncertainty is, however, a competitive strategic advantage. In these circumstances, a "right" answer very often does not exist, only an answer that is "good enough for the time being"—one that propels the next question.

Also, keeping in mind that the beginning of an answer most often lies in the questions we ask, a focus on the best kind of questions rather than on the right answers is crucial. For some, this requires a big leap of faith, but I have seen, time and again, how asking good questions eventually does lead to the best solution. The better the questions, the more attentive the listening, the richer the reflection, the better the solutions, and the deeper is the learning.

*Questions are more powerful than statements when
attempting to solve difficult strategy problems.*

So what makes a good question? As you might expect, there is no single answer to this question. Yet, there are several key characteristics of good questions. Good questions take courage to ask and cause us to stretch and squirm. They help us to unveil truer perspectives or beliefs, and challenge assumptions that prevent us from taking a new and different action. Good questions prompt us to reflect deeply and inspire us to become more insightful before we take action. Furthermore, good questions are:

- offered with a caring and sharing intent;
- presented as selfless and not asked to "show off" the knowledge or wit of the questioner;
- asked with courage and are difficult to answer;
- supported with good listening;
- followed through with time for reflection.

Often, the most obvious way to start a good question is to build on the foundation of a previous question. Another way is to ask a question based on the response that was just given. Also, selecting from the "who–what–when–where–why–how" is good for starters. Another option is to ask a question from an opposing point of view or to ask: "Why not?" or "How else?" Draw questions from both the surf and the dive domains of learning, but keep in mind that dive-level questions are bound to cause stretching, squirming, and deeper reflection, as they often shed light on a true belief. Also, remembering that questions are far more powerful than statements when attempting to solve difficult strategy problems is worthwhile.

Seven Strategy Dimensions for Critical Dialogue

There are seven dimensions of strategy (Figure 14.1) that I consider necessary topics for strategic thinking. While strategy meetings are sometimes limited to a discussion of data, metrics, and analysis drawn primarily from the finance dimension, with other dimensions randomly appearing if time permits, a broader, more diverse, and ultimately more competitive strategy perspective can evolve by bringing all seven dimensions to the table for rigorous rounds of critical dialogue. The influence and consequences of the seven dimensions should be included at every stage of the strategic dialogue because they are critically important to strategy success—they constitute a more comprehensive approach to strategy. Figure 14.1 illustrates these seven dimensions.

Outer Ring:

- Finance (economics, budget, profit/loss, investment).
- Risk assessment (financial security, physical security, intellectual property).

FIGURE 14.1 Seven Strategic Thinking Dimensions

- Technology (hardware, software, integration).
- Integrity (authenticity, truth, honesty).

Inner Ring:

- Business value (stakeholder, customers, products, services, expansion, improvement).
- Individual development (learning as investment, satisfaction, knowledge/thinking/creative capability).
- Social contribution (environment, human rights, arts, health, politics, community development).

The four dimensions in the outer ring (finance, risk assessment, technology, integrity) influence what, how, and why we think and believe as we do about the three dimensions in the inner ring (business value, individual development, social contribution). Critical questions from inside and outside the organization should essentially center on: How will this decision promote or prevent the strategic intent, and the corporate mission and values? What impact will this decision have on individual development (business value/social contribution)? Where do our competitors stand on each of these issues? Who might see this very differently? Why? Who gains and who loses from this decision? By how much? For how long? Who cares (now and later)? Why?

The underlying assumptions and beliefs about these dimensions and their impact on and relation to one another beg to be challenged on an individual, business unit, geographic, generational, and corporate level.

*If we genuinely consider "human capital" as a
valuable asset, these dimensions are imperative to
strategic thinking.*

By inviting contrarian opinions and provocative ideas to each of the seven dimensions, executives can encourage critical reflection that challenges and refines their strategy decisions to become more adaptive, innovative, and competitive.

Structuring strategy dialogue according to these seven dimensions highlights potential risks, offers new perspectives, and invites new data immediately. As a result, I find that strategic priorities are often shuffled, new connections are forged, and the impact and consequences can be disclosed in the initial thinking stage rather than in the implementation stage of strategy.

Nothing fundamentally unique is required to use these dimensions in constructing a strategy dialogue. Framing the conventional strategy categories (shareholders, products, services, customers, employees, and industry sector) within these seven dimensions simply, but not easily, expands the dialogue by bringing in new players, posing additional questions, and connecting the data differently. Various analytical models and metrics can be introduced to support and challenge each dimension, which further enriches the dialogue.

The interplay and infinite connections between and among these dimensions serve to test, check, balance, build, refine, and strengthen the overall strategic thinking process. Interestingly, I find that when these seven dimensions are included as part of the strategic thinking process, issues of integrity, core competencies, values, and hidden agendas tend to surface early and candidly. The critical dialogue process tends to illuminate potential incongruence, inconsistency, or misalignment.

Learning to Dialogue

The dialogue process lends itself well to informal learning. Dialogue can happen constructively anywhere and at any time. A young technology executive said:

> *I just draw on my own experience, and I've also tried to learn from others' [experience]. I guess I'm just curious, for better or worse (laughter), and it's so important to talk to a lot of people—learn from them this way. People are happy to tell you their experiences. Nobody taught me, I just learned things, you know ... my life experiences were all I ever had.*

More structured and formal approaches to facilitating dialogue can also be useful. In structuring a strategic dialogue, there are several small details that I find helpful for ensuring that the critical dialogue process takes root. Care needs to be given to keeping a record of strategic dialogues in order to identify and track who has and has not been included, on what issues, and on what date. This effort can take many forms. The important thing is to record and collect this information in a simple way that makes sense to everyone involved. Time needs to be allocated to reflect collectively on the dialogue itself. What insights did the dialogue generate? Which areas require more knowledge? Why were certain ideas abandoned for others? Was participation sufficiently broad? Were ideas amply diverged?

Two excellent processes to incorporate in strategy meetings as a means of keeping track of dialogue and uncovering surprise are coding of surf- and dive-level questions, and the after-action review (AAR),[4] a process developed by the U.S. Army to identify lessons learned.

Coding of surf- and dive-level questions is a relatively straightforward and highly insightful means of identifying the current cognitive status of questioning habits within strategy meetings. I have found that executives tend to believe they model and encourage dive-level questions far more than they actually do.

To get a sense of where your current questions stand, select several non-meeting participants to serve as "coders" during the strategy meeting. Simply have them divide a paper into two columns: one column for surf and the other for dive. As the meeting proceeds, coders record all of the questions in one or the other of the columns. Afterwards, the leader and the coders sit down together and look through the questions with an eye toward intent and surf- or dive-level of questions recorded. Questions may include:

- What questions were asked?
- Has a pattern of questions emerged?
- What might have been the intention of asking each question?
- What was your immediate (unspoken) response or reaction generated by each question?
- Were there surf questions? How could they be changed into dive questions?
- What were the content questions?
- What were the process questions?
- Were there any premise questions?
- Were there any thought-provoking or puzzling questions?
- Were there any questions which provoked further questions (upon reading and reflecting) as a result of recording and reviewing them?

Follow-up questions and reflections are infinite, and can be insightful. When repeated within strategy meetings, this coding exercise can hone dive questions, focus reflection, embed critical reflective processes, and help to diverge thinking—all of which serve to strengthen strategic thinking.

The AAR technique can be useful after a major decision has been taken, after a surprise outcome has been caused by our action, or as a routine meeting process. While the AAR is based primarily on the surf domain of learning, it offers room to move into the deeper learning domain by inviting strategists to capture their learning from experiences.

In the U.S. Army, an AAR is conducted immediately after a decision or a major action is taken and generally includes at least three leadership levels and others who were involved in the action. A trained facilitator monitors the dialogue process to ensure that the review is honest and candid and that members respect each other. The AAR is not an open-ended brainstorming session, but a straightforward process of experiential learning structured around five questions:

1. What was the intent? What was the strategy at the time the action began? What was the desired outcome? How was the strategy expected to be achieved?
2. What actually happened? What were the actual events as they occurred within a specific timeframe? Who did what? Where? How? When? Reactions? Blame is not ascribed but, rather, a factual chronology is collaboratively pieced together.
3. Why did it happen? This is the diagnostic portion. Commentary is offered about possible reasons why the specific outcome was not the intended strategic intent, or about reasons for success.
4. How can we do better? What was learned?
5. What do we do now?

Lessons learned from the events of each action are identified in order to enable others to carry out actions that will more precisely achieve the strategic intent.

We return now to critical dialogue. Prior to a strategy meeting, and again at the beginning of the meeting, all partners need to be explicitly informed as to the talk mode that will be used. A quick mention of, "We'll be using dialogue for part A and debate for part B of the meeting," should suffice. Equally important is that all partners consciously develop the skills and confidence to participate in dialogue, discussion, and debate. Strategy meetings are like preparing for a triathlon. Explicitly stating expectations and systematically preparing allows participants to do their best. Triathletes need to know that the first part requires running, the second part requires swimming, and the third part is cycling. Otherwise, a well-intentioned strategy meeting can end up feeling like a sumo wrestling match or a free-for-all.

Good critical dialogue requires that all partners take responsibility for ensuring that the other(s) have what they need to fully express their perceptions, perspectives, ideas, feelings, and thoughts. Also, the successful strategists whom I interviewed reported that having an expectation to learn is critical, for this becomes a self-fulfilling prophecy. If we enter a strategy dialogue expecting to learn, we are more likely to diverge our thinking and deepen our reflection.

We could learn new information from a different perspective, or we may learn from having our long-held belief shattered. We may be jolted into questioning our conviction of an idea we hold simply by hearing ourselves talk and by saying it aloud. The very act of speaking an incomplete thought aloud can be a new learning. Another learning may be the sheer exhilaration of being questioned—and having others listen to us. Critical dialogue is an excellent technique for clarifying thoughts, testing convictions, and building confidence.

Surrounding ourselves with people who can and will challenge, test, and engage in meaningful critical dialogue is easier said than done. We all tend to like people who reinforce our perspectives and echo our opinions. I cannot count the number of "monkey-say-monkey-do" strategy meetings I have observed. In such meetings, anyone who attempts to challenge an existing frame is blackballed, and the bearers of bad news are thrown into the den with those who persistently question the way things are done. The resulting strategy is anything but innovative, adaptive, or competitive because the very elements required for strategic thinking have been squelched or expelled.

In order to develop a pipeline of strategic thinkers, critical dialogue that is initiated and modeled by senior leaders is helpful. Such modeling establishes implicit permission and stakes out the real parameters of challenging and testing norms of thinking. Connections must be made with diverse knowledge sources both inside and outside the company, and a vast range of professional relationships must be cultivated and rewarded. Then, these relationships must be given adequate attention to support meaningful dialogue and challenge. Creating a culture where learning is valued, knowledge is shared, and critical dialogue is practiced is among the most challenging issues facing conscientious executives and those responsible for supporting strategic thinking.

Critical Dialogue in the Three-Stage Informal Learning Process of Strategic Thinking

Critical dialogue is important in all three informal learning stages: preparation, experience, and reevaluation. As noted in Part III, the three stages of the informal learning process are not distinct from one another, nor are the levels-of-learning domains (surf and dive), but, rather, they are iterative in nature. The challenge becomes to discern one stage from the next, for we tend to vacillate between the preparation, experience, and reevaluation stages, continuously gathering information, and engaging in dialogue, discussion, and debate as a means of testing our thinking.

Preparation Stage
In the preparation stage, dialogue guarantees that the data and information are substantiated and validated, and serves as a means of information gathering as we consciously seek out different opinions, different data, ideas, and new interpretations of regulations, procedures, and information. Also, dialogue in this stage of strategic thinking can greatly enrich the quality of analysis by testing the intent of the source and relevance of data and information.

Experience Stage
In the experience stage, dialogue serves as a means of testing and challenging. This dialogue is regarded as a critical part of learning from experience and was commonly described in the executive interviews with words such as *exciting, intellectually stimulating*, and *invigorating*. Critical dialogue with total strangers from diverse age, industrial, cultural, and educational backgrounds can serve to test our ideas and thinking and reveal underlying assumptions. Also, in the experience stage, dialogue leads us to different

perspectives, tests assumptions and underlying opinions, and challenges ideas. Dialogue in this stage serves to stimulate our imagination. As one of the financial executives indicated:

> I'd say I'm heavily influenced and dependent on listening to many different people. I look to economists, forecasters, politicians, journalists, experts in many fields, let's see—associates sometimes (laughter), friends, books, even neighbors, my children, and strangers—and lots of other people I talk to. I'm constantly talking to people in all kinds of fields to see what they know and what they're thinking—this is so important. You can't just rely on the experts. Everybody sees something different, and it all needs to be considered.

A Chinese executive explained:

> We spend a lot of time hanging out, talking about things. We just spend a lot of time talking about different possibilities, we draw pictures, tell 'what if' stories. This probably doesn't sound too organized (laughter); it isn't! But it's fun, a good time. You just keep repeating it.

Critical dialogue in the experience stage is an essential part of learning in action and learning on action, both of which are essential for learning to think strategically. The difference between learning *in* action and learning *on* action is tense: "in" action is present tense, and "on" action is past tense. We learn in action and on action through critical dialogue with our experiences, colleagues, professional associates, casual acquaintances, and strangers in both work and non-work places.

The German manufacturing executive described what happens when she is involved in thinking strategically:

> Every few months we seem to have some debates—you might even call them arguments—about what's happening in the industry or with economy trends. And then we discuss different scenarios about what it may mean for us. Do we need to change something? Do we need to stop doing something? And I always calculate from a financial perspective—it's my job, and he [CEO] usually disagrees. (laughter) He [the CEO] likes to disagree, and so do I, because it makes you think of other questions … and in a different way. And then he [CEO] talks to other people. I do the same thing. And then we sit down and talk again. And this is how it happens, over and over.

When asked what the advantage of this kind of dialogue and disagreement pattern was, she replied:

> Oh, I think it's the most important reason our company is so successful! And he [CEO] is very successful and well respected in the industry.
> It's just his ways are a little different from the ordinary, usual theory. I've learned so much from him—he thinks that he needs to ask questions to get clear in

his own mind—so he talks to everybody he can, not just in textiles or manufacturing. He likes to debate because he never believes anything anybody tells him; so he always says that debate is a way to test and purify ideas. (laughter)

So you can imagine it's a very good way to make high-level thinking—which I think is important to making good strategy. I suppose this doesn't make sense as the way I explain it, but it's much better than a model with some artificial, detailed rationale and charts. (laughter)

Critical dialogue, critical reflection, critical inquiry, and challenge are recurring learning themes within the experience stage.

Reevaluation Stage

During the reevaluation stage of learning, dialogue serves as a means of critical reflection and assessment. The very nature of recalling an experience that is no longer current, and verbally articulating the experience to another, moves us into the stage of reevaluation. In this stage of informal learning we use dialogue to test and to challenge comprehensive frameworks and to retest and refine belief systems and assumptions. Critical dialogue is used to deliberately escalate thinking and refine ideas in order to continue to move the decision-making process forward. Strategic thinking requires dialogue to direct attention away from producing results and, instead, to focus on uncovering assumptions through the process of critical inquiry and critical reflection.

Dialogue is a versatile, dynamic, iterative, and trustworthy process that can be enormously beneficial in a global strategy-making environment of uncertainty, volatility, and unpredictability. Serious strategists know they must take the time and discipline to develop the habit of engaging in critical dialogue in order to create competitive and new possibilities. Critical dialogue is fundamental to the cognitive and creative processes that are essential for learning to think strategically.

Notes

1. Isaacs, "Taking Flight: Dialogue, Collective Thinking, and Organizational Learning," 233.
2. A modified version of the quotation by Haldane, *Possible Worlds: And Other Essays*.
3. Isaacs, "Taking Flight: Dialogue, Collective Thinking, and Organizational Learning," 234.
4. Bender, *Operation Excellence: Succeeding in Business and Life—The U.S. Military Way*.

V

Summary and Questions

Critical dialogue is an essential tool for the exploration of the dive domain and for strategic thinking to occur. Yet all too often, critical dialogue is sacrificed or cut short for the expediency of bullet points and sound bites. Engaging in critical dialogue requires suspending judgment and acknowledging that there are other credible and legitimate perspectives that weigh upon a strategic issue. Effective critical dialogue uses divergent thinking, poses deep, dive level questions that challenge premises, and exposes implicit assumptions. Utilizing a critical dialogue partner can help keep strategists honest and authentic and can serve as an effective means to developing strategic thinking and "sharpening the saw."

Critical inquiry should be encouraged and practiced by leaders during the process of strategic thinking. It requires appropriate space and time for divergent and deep, dive questioning, and for critical reflection and critical dialogue to occur. Good questioning that instigates critical reflection is often far more enlightening than proposing solutions to a problem. As a social process, critical inquiry can reduce the pressure on the leader to solve the strategy problem alone. Focused critical dialogue identifies new potential risks, shapes new perspectives, and highlights new frames and data.

Critical dialogue can cultivate informal learning. Two effective techniques to track and learn from critical dialogue include coding the questions that are asked and performing an after action review at the end of the session. Priming your team for critical dialogue and critical inquiry prior to a strategy meeting encourages new learning, deep reflection, and divergent thinking. Strategic thinkers can model critical dialogue by intentionally surrounding themselves with others who purposefully challenge their thinking and assumptions.

1. How could engaging in critical dialogue bring new value to your strategy sessions?
2. Who, within your organization, could you invite as your critical dialogue partner(s)? Anyone from outside your organization?

3. Why is critical inquiry such an important aspect of critical dialogue?
4. How can leaders share in diverging and deep diving into strategic problems with colleagues in different functions and locations across the organization? How could this ultimately strengthen the strategic direction?

WHY DOES SOME OF THIS FEEL SO FAMILIAR?

We Just "Know": Intuition as an Outgrowth of Experience

The intuitive mind is a sacred gift and the rational mind is a faithful servant. We have created a society that honors the servant and has forgotten the gift.

Albert Einstein (1879–1955), scientist and Nobel Prize winner

15

Intuition as a Must-Have for Learning to Think Strategically

Anton is a hedge fund whiz. At just 25 years of age, he has such a feel for numbers that big names from all over the financial world want to run their ideas by him. Once they get Anton's nod, they move forward with a plan. In spite of enormous amounts of data, he knows precisely what to focus on. He can sift and filter volumes of information and figure out what is relevant, highlight key points, and prioritize in minutes. Although he dropped out of graduate school, he had lots of experience in analyzing numbers while helping his dad and uncle run a small investment business and while working as a trader for two years. He has learned to trust his gut to such a high degree that he can listen to analytic reports and in 15 to 30 minutes "know" his decision. No need for detailed explanations. His experience allows him to see what he needs, interpret, and decide in a flash. This makes Anton seem almost supernatural to his colleagues. He relies on his judgment, and everyone else envies it. His bets are on, and he rarely loses.

With strategy, everything hinges on decision making. Since we are often not fully aware of how our experience influences our ability to learn to think strategically, or fully aware of how we learn informally, a closer look at intuition in strategic decision making is necessary.

Part VI is divided into four chapters. Chapter 15 focuses on tacit knowledge and how intuition is imperative for strategic decision making. Chapter 16 looks at the strong influence of intuition on pattern recognition and framing, and the effect intuition has on strategic decision making. Chapter 17 considers the role of critical reflective processes in shattering frames of reference. And Chapter 18 discusses reframing.

There are two premises underlying this part on intuition. The first is that intuition guides strategic thinking—although this does run counter to what traditional strategy development approaches teach. The second is that intuition and analysis are complementary in the strategic thinking process, which is similar to the more expansive notion of strategy making offered by the ancient Greeks.

In my practice, I often notice that merely uttering the word *intuition* can make strategic planners grimace and unseasoned strategists squirm, because the term seems to conjure images of some kind of mystical daydream or worse. But among successful strategic thinkers, intuition is a familiar and comfortable concept, though it is an experience that is rarely articulated. Bringing intuition into the strategic thinking process simply requires paying attention to another way of knowing that can facilitate learning to think strategically.

Intuition is a natural outgrowth of experience and a vital component for learning to think strategically. Intuition researcher Gary Klein formulated a theory of intuitive decision making called the recognition-primed decision (RPD) model, based on his extensive research on decisions made by firefighters and medical providers. In *The Power of Intuition*, Klein notes that, "The evidence is growing that those who do not or cannot trust their intuitions are less effective decision makers, and that as long as they reject their intuitions, they are destined to remain less effective."[1]

While we may mistrust intuition, in the belief that it springs from emotion as opposed to reason, intuition does not come from emotion.[2] It is a highly complex process based on thorough understanding of a situation. Intuition draws from a vast reservoir of knowledge in our subconscious and is rooted in past experience—it is not an irrational process.

There are several areas of strategic thinking that are particularly relevant to intuition. I am advocating the type of *deliberative rationality* that Bert and Stuart Dreyfus described in their book *Mind Over Machine*:

> *The ... split between the mystical and the analytic will not do ... for neither pole of that often misleading dualism names the ordinary, non-mystical intuition that we believe is the core of human intelligence and skill. ... Analysis and intuition work together in the human mind.*[3]

Among the executives with whom I work, I have found that while intuition is a driver, analytic thinking is also a necessity for anyone learning a new skill. Bert and Stuart Dreyfus also contend that analytic thinking is good for scrutinizing data and information for validity, reliability, and accuracy. "It is also useful at the highest levels of expertise, where it can sharpen and clarify intuitive insight. ... Detached deliberation and intuition need not be viewed as [opposite] alternatives, as is all too often [the case] in simplistic treatments."[4] In the strategic thinking process, intuition and analytic thinking are very much complementary parts of the whole. As Carl Jung noted: "Intuition does not denote something contrary to reason, but something outside the province of reason."[5] This concept is as the ancient Greeks defined strategy, not as competing parts, but as a whole.

Often, I find that corporate strategists are overwhelmed by strategic decision making, which involves constantly changing information, uncertainty, incomplete data, and things they cannot control. Experienced strategists, as well as those beginning to participate in strategy, know from their experience that there are limits to the rational linear approach when dealing with human endeavors such as strategy. As a consequence, strategists also seem to tacitly know about the iterative and generative process that is fundamental to strategic thinking. Good strategic decision makers notice and think while they are in the process of managing complex and high-stakes situations—they register subtle cues without even realizing it. Decisions are made subconsciously, before they even begin their analysis. What explains this, and how can this process be used to facilitate strategic thinking?

> *Our intuition is based on accumulated and compiled experience.*

Strategic thinking includes continuous decision making; therefore, learning to think strategically can be enhanced by understanding how our intuition influences our ability to make choices. Daniel Kahneman's research has led him to an explanation about how this occurs, as he notes that, "a tentative plan comes to mind by an automatic function of associative memory ... The next phase is a deliberate process in which the plan is mentally simulated to check if it will work."[6] Our intuition is based on accumulated and compiled experiences. Solid intuition is like solid data—it is neutral and free of interpretation or evaluation.

In learning to think strategically, we should not blindly follow our intuition, because intuition can be unreliable and requires monitoring. Yet, we should not suppress our intuition either, because it is essential to our decision making and cannot be supplanted by analysis or procedures. We rely on intuition to make all kinds of judgments related to strategy. Thus, a highly competitive option is to strengthen intuition so that it becomes more accurate and provides us with better insights.

One Japanese finance executive whom I interviewed insisted:

> *Thinking about strategy is not a "task"—it is about what you think and feel and believe and how you react ... and don't try to separate your feelings from your thinking—I don't understand how that helps anyone because it is not possible to do. But many people try only to think [without feeling] when they make strategy. It's a mistake.*

As any strategist knows, there is a big difference between an informed and uninformed gut feeling.[7] We want to avoid impulsive actions and make decisions based on informed intuition. Luckily, skillful intuitive decision making can be learned. Intuition skills can be acquired and expanded by building a richer experience base and putting the skills to better use. We are not born with good judgment skills, just as we are not born good skiers, skaters, or swimmers. Similarly, the kinds of know-how and judgments that successful, seasoned strategists make also require tremendous energy and work. Such strategists have to build up an experience base that lets them accurately size up situations and know how to respond. The better we understand situations and the more expansive our experience base, the more polished our intuitive skills become.[8]

Know-How: Our Tacit Knowledge

When we are engaged in the spontaneous, intuitive thinking of strategy in everyday life, we demonstrate our knowledge in a particular way. But when we try to describe it, we often find ourselves at a loss. Our knowing is often tacit, implicit in our patterns of action and in our feel for the stuff with which we are dealing. Our knowing is in our action. The role that tacit knowledge plays in strategic thinking is often underestimated and ignored.

The term *tacit knowledge* connotes knowing in action, or what is commonly called *know-how*. The tacit knowledge of a prima ballerina, for example, is embedded in and revealed by the way she glides across the stage—her knowing is demonstrated in her graceful action. Similarly, a tennis pro's tacit knowledge is in directing his serve to an opponent's weakness, or rapidly changing his pace.

Tacit knowledge is not about the know-how in the rules or detailed plans of the action that we entertain in our mind prior to action; tacit knowledge is a kind of knowing in the action. Tacit knowledge is not to be confused with either luck or some "gift." Tacit knowledge comes from accumulated and acquired success experience, disciplined skills, knowledge, and extraordinary amounts of focused practice. The fact that tacit knowledge becomes spontaneous, like a sixth sense, deceptively, makes it appear to happen easily.

Although sometimes we think before acting or deciding, spontaneous decision making does reveal a kind of knowing that does not stem from a prior intellectual operation. This decision making comes from a tacit knowledge that we accumulate through successful repetition. Tacit knowing is partly intuitive and is triggered by our feelings and affective responses. Also, tacit knowing draws from exceptional mastery of disciplined techniques that have become automated.

When a tennis pro has a "feel for the ball," this knowing lets her repeat the exact same tactic she used previously that proved successful. Her repetition is her acknowledgment that she has been doing something right, and her "feeling" allows her to do that same thing over again. This process requires reflection on her own patterns of action and on the situations in which she is performing. She may reflect *on* action and occasionally *in* action. Numerous theorists point out the limitations of technical rationality and explain how we think on our feet, or just know what to do, based on our tacit knowledge and habits of acting.

Learning theorist Donald Schon notes:

> We learn to execute such complex performances as walking, skipping, riding a bicycle, skiing without being able to give a verbal description even roughly adequate to our actual performance. Indeed, if we are asked to say how we do such things, we tend to give wrong answers, which, if we were to act according to them, would get us into trouble.[9]

*Every competent strategist can recognize groups of
"normal" patterns associated with a specific market,
peculiarities of a certain kind of organizational
structure, or irregular patterns of data—for which
he cannot give a reasonably accurate or complete
description.*

Good strategic thinking requires an awareness of tacit knowledge. Every competent strategist can recognize groups of "normal" patterns associated with a specific market, peculiarities of a certain kind of organizational structure, or irregular patterns of data—for which he cannot give a reasonably accurate or complete description. Amidst day-to-day operations, a strategist makes innumerable decisions, but cannot state specific criteria used in those decisions. A seasoned, successful strategist demonstrates skills for which he cannot state the rules and procedures. Even when making conscious use of research-based theories and techniques, seasoned strategists rely on tacit recognitions, judgments, and skillful past experiences. In other words, the strategist operates automatically because of trusted intuition, due to a vast repertoire of successful experience; but she also has the capacity to pause and critically reflect.

Tacit knowledge can be a source of sustainable competitive advantage because it is impossible for competitors to imitate and difficult to substitute. For that very reason, it is incredibly valuable. As T. S. Elliot once heeded: "Talent imitates, genius steals."

Notes

1. Klein, *The Power of Intuition*, 5.
2. The following three interesting articles are directly related to intuition and decision making: Agor, "The Logic of Intuitive Decisionmaking: An Agenda for Future Research"; Ray and Myers, "The Role of Intuition in Strategic Decision Making"; Vaughan, "Varieties of Intuitive Experience."
3. Dreyfus and Dreyfus, *Mind Over Machine: The Power of Human Intuitive Expertise in the Era of the Computer*, xiv.
4. Dreyfus and Dreyfus, *Mind Over Machine: The Power of Human Intuitive Expertise in the Era of the Computer*, xiv.
5. Jung, *Modern Man in Search of a Soul*.
6. Kahneman, *Thinking, Fast and Slow*, 236.
7. Ariely, *The Upside of Irrationality*.
8. Duggan, *Strategic Intuition*.
9. Schon, *Educating the Reflective Practitioner*, 24.

16

Framing and the Intuition Factor

So what role does intuition play in how we make strategic thinking decisions? Intuition is what allows us to recognize patterns and frames that we use as part of strategic decision making. Interestingly, we recognize patterns primarily through a process based on intuition.

A pattern is a set of cues, which usually appear together, so when we see a few of the cues, automatically, we expect to find the others. In other words, a pattern is any repeatable concept, thought, or image whose repetitions together make up an approach to a problem, a way of looking at things. A pattern is a repeatable sequence of neural activity.

A particular viewpoint may develop gradually over time. An idea that was beneficial at one time, however, may not be useful today, and yet the current idea will have developed directly from the outdated idea. A pattern may develop in a specific way because the pattern was derived from the combination of other patterns. In organizations, we tend to form patterns based on partial, inaccurate, or incomplete information—snapshots of our condition. However, if all the information had been available at one time, the pattern would probably appear quite differently.

Patterns persist because their sequences are useful and sufficient to our frames; but if we allow ourselves to pause and step back from the sequence, we might be able to imagine a restructuring of that pattern and create something quite different or even better. Once experienced intuitive strategists see a pattern, any decision they have to make is usually obvious. Following patterns can be enormously useful when we are dealing with day-to-day decisions that occur in rapid succession, when we are under pressure, or when we are dealing with scenarios that include a lot of inconclusive, uncertain, and incomplete information, which makes finding patterns difficult. We need to be able to filter and sift rapidly. Intuitive pattern recognition is how we do this.[1]

Pattern recognition can take place in a split second and without conscious thought. Because this process is rapid and not conscious, we are rarely aware of how we arrived at an intuitive judgment, which is precisely why it seems mysterious to us. Even if the situation is not identical to what we have seen before, we can recognize similarities with past events and automatically "know" what to do, without deliberately having to think through the options. When we recognize a pattern, we familiarize ourselves with a situation. We have a "feel" for what will work and what will not. Basically, at this point our decision making becomes intuitive.

Formal analysis can be valuable to supplement intuition, but it cannot substitute for intuition when it comes to complex strategic decisions.

Very large repertoires of patterns that have been acquired over years of practice enable successful strategists to make good decisions using intuition. Without these patterns and without this experience base, strategists would be paralyzed as strategic decision makers. The formal methods of analysis are not enough, even when applying the fastest and most advanced computers to crunch all the numbers. Strategic analysis serves to generate testing, challenging, reflecting, and acting on the intuitive hunch. Formal analysis can be valuable to supplement intuition, but it cannot substitute for intuition when it comes to complex strategic decisions.

When we think strategically, we need to be mindful of pattern recognition as an automatic process of making sense. However, problems emerge when we expect to see a certain pattern and are blinded from seeing anything else. We must judiciously monitor ourselves by making sure we can and do switch off our autopilot from time to time, and deliberately set out to test and challenge the patterns we notice and the meanings we attribute to these patterns. This monitoring is our strategic thinking advantage. An inability to recognize our patterns can get us locked into constructing strategy based on false or irrelevant assumptions.

We know intuitively what cues are going to be important and need to be monitored. We "know" what types of results we "should" be able to accomplish. We have a sense of what to expect next because of our patterns and frames of reference. So detailed and habitual are our patterns that they include routines for responding and *action scripts*. If we recognize a situation as typical, we can recall the typical ways to react. These nearly instantaneous recollections are our hunches about what is really going on and how we determine what we should do about it.[2]

Figure 16.1 illustrates the process of intuitive pattern recognition and framing that we typically and automatically use in strategic thinking.

Just as we see a new problem as a variation on patterns in the old one, so our new problem-solving actions and decisions are a variation on the old. Just as we are unable at first to articulate the relevant similarities and differences of the situations, we struggle to articulate the similarities and differences of our problem-solving procedures. Indeed, the whole process of "seeing as" before and "doing as" before may continue without conscious verbal articulation.

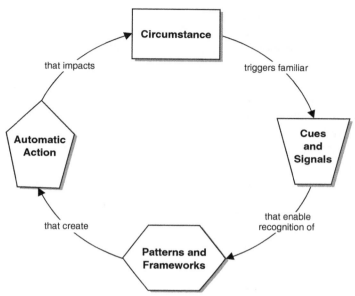

FIGURE 16.1 Intuitive Pattern Recognition and Framing Process that Occurs in Strategic Thinking

> *It is our capacity to see unfamiliar situations as familiar ones and to decide and act in unfamiliar situations as we have done in familiar situations that enables us to bring our past experience to bear on a unique situation.*

It is our capacity to see unfamiliar situations as familiar ones and to decide and act in unfamiliar situations as we have done in familiar situations that enables us to bring our past experience to bear on a unique situation. Our capacity to "see as" and "do as" allows us to have a "feel" for problems that do not fit existing rules. This capacity rests on the range and variety of the repertoire that we bring to unfamiliar situations. Because we are able to see these new and unfamiliar situations as elements of our repertoire, we are able to make sense of the uniqueness of unfamiliar situations and need not reduce them to instances of standard categories.

Intuition is the way we translate our experiences into judgments and decisions. Intuition is our ability to make decisions by using patterns to recognize what is going on in a situation and to access the typical way to react.[3] We use our experience to recognize and determine what to do and how to respond.

When strategists fail to recognize or respond to patterns in value conflicts, violate their own ethical standards, fall short of self-created expectations, or ignore public problems they have helped to create, increasingly, they are subject to expressions of disapproval, failure, and ineffectiveness. These important areas of strategic thinking stretch beyond the conventional boundaries of rationality, logic, and analysis. They call on us to draw on a "feel" or a "sense" about the problem that doesn't fit our existing rules. Our a-rational processing becomes eminently important. This processing includes the skillful judgments, decisions, and actions we make tacitly and intuitively, without being able to state the procedures or rules that we follow.

The successful executives whom I interviewed spoke of vacillating back and forth between rational and a-rational thoughts without any concern. Each had a well-developed intuitive sense of the situational appropriateness required for using rational and a-rational thinking. This is a characteristic that comes from successful intuitive practice.

Noticing "Red Flags"

What makes us tune in to the alarm bells or recognize the red flags waving in front of our faces? Our intuition. Built up through repeated experiences which we have linked together unconsciously to form a pattern, our intuition endows us with a sense of familiarity—"Yes, I've seen that before!" Pattern recognition explains how we can make effective decisions without conducting a deliberate analysis. Regardless of the business or functional area in which we make strategy, we accumulate experiences and build up a repertoire of recognized patterns. The more patterns we learn, the easier it is to match a new situation to one of the patterns in our repertoire. When a new situation occurs, we recognize the situation as familiar by matching it to a pattern we have encountered in the past.

For example, at a quarterly meeting in Jakarta, Tobo, a lifetime Indonesian, hears the global strategy team suggest trucking the company's product across the country. Quickly, Tobo sees a *red flag* waving as a cue that there could be problems with security. By transferring his knowledge from previous logistical efforts in the country, and assessing the variables therein (e.g., time, place, people), Tobo "gets it." Without pausing or thinking, he grimaces and abruptly redirects the conversation to alternative transport options because he "knows" the danger signs.

> *Pattern recognition explains how we can make effective decisions without conducting a deliberate analysis.*

SCENARIO

While scouting for a new and more economical plant facility, Nicholas reviews the demographic data of a fairly desolate region of Romania, and zooms in on its 70 percent unemployment rate among 18 to 50 year olds in eight surrounding villages. Also, he notes that the average education level is fourth grade. A warning light flashes in his mind, and within minutes he dismisses this region outright as a potential site for a new commercial container assembly plant because he can read the writing on the wall—disaster!

As the global chief operating officer of a commercial container manufacturing company, his gut feeling is that operating costs will be sky high. Expats will have to be cajoled to join his team as supervisors and as top management, local staff training will nibble chunks out of the budget, and equipment replacement costs will be exorbitant because everything will "grow legs" and walk away. He knows that a bribe cache will need to be replenished constantly to appease the local government officials, not to mention that there will be drugs, crime, theft, lack of loyalty, and a deplorable work ethic. Nicholas "knows" the rest of the story because he grew up in Romania and witnessed four similar assembly plant mistakes (against his advice) as chief operating officer of his previous company. He sees the data, recognizes a familiar pattern, and makes a negative judgment in a matter of minutes.

Across the table from Nicholas sits Chiho, who cannot believe what she is hearing. These same data make her salivate! She had championed the company in its business development initiatives with tremendous success in Vietnam. She has scrutinized these data, not just zoomed in on a couple of points. The region looks like a dream to her—no competitors, a captive recruitment ground, eager and appreciative employees, no distractions from work, no labor unions, rock-bottom operating costs, and an opportunity to contribute to the future of the region.

The company heeded Nicholas's gut feeling and decided to postpone a decision while it studied other options. Within months, a competitor set up shop, only to find itself involved in a nightmare of expenses and crime. The operation closed up shop one year later.

This scenario reminds us that executives from different countries and industries recognize very different patterns, as a result of their unique repertoires of experience, culture, and education. Needless to say, these differing viewpoints can complicate strategy sessions when people see the same data in different patterns, different patterns from the same data, or the same patterns from different data. Although a certain pattern may be a red flag to one person, the pattern itself may not even register with another. Knowing that patterns may be understood differently requires us to identify and explicitly articulate the patterns we see, as well as the assumptions we make about them, through critical reflection and dialogue. Bringing people from other socio-national, functional, and corporate cultures into strategy making ensures that we get some degree of variation in the interpretation of data because, unconsciously, all bring along their patterns and frames.

Even the most experienced executives can make the mistake of assuming that their colleagues see the patterns that are so obvious to them. The ability to detect patterns is simple and, as such, is easy to take for granted and difficult to learn. Therefore, it is critical that we challenge ourselves as much as we challenge others to carefully describe, listen, and see patterns. Differences in pattern recognition can be as important as similarities when creating winning strategies.

Notes

1. Ariely, *The Upside of Irrationality.*
2. Glöckner and Witteman, "Beyond Dual-Process Models: A Categorization of Processes Underlying Intuitive Judgment and Decision Making," 1–25.
3. Hilbig, Scholl, and Pohl, "Think or Blink—Is the Recognition Heuristic an 'Intuitive' Strategy?"

17

Shattering Frames

Once we have collected patterns and automatically put them into frames, our patterns and frames become compatible and help us to make meaning quickly. But when our intention is to create an innovative, sustainable, winning strategy, we must slow down and turn off this instant pattern recognition and deliberately challenge the very process that has served us in the past. The rearrangement and innovative arrangement of patterns created by consciously choosing to escape from the fixed patterns that have been established by experience provides the basis of what I call *shattering* frames.

> *Truly innovative strategic thinking is not about playing out new patterns in existing frameworks but, rather, about creating new frameworks and different patterns within these new frameworks.*

As we recall from Part II, strategic thinking has both a divergent and a deep, dive component (or a creative and a critical aspect). In an effort to serve both, we need to be able to switch off our old habits of mind and to experiment with forming new habits of mind. In order to do this, we must consciously seek out, explore, and create totally new combinations of patterns and frames, test existing frames, and experiment with reframing. Having an understanding of pattern and frame construction, an appreciation for how we make decisions, and the ability to shatter frames is essential to being able to think strategically.

This chapter consists of five sections. This first section looks at shattering frames of reference, while the second discusses critical reflection as a technique for shattering frames. The third section examines reflection *in* action and reflection *on* action in terms of learning to think strategically. The fourth section presents the element of *surprise* in the critical reflection process, and the fifth section looks at three specific kinds of critical reflection.

Research studies show that executives use intuitive pattern recognition to create mental simulations in order to imagine how a scenario might play out. In order to recognize the framework in which we are playing out our scenarios, we need to learn to stop the automatic process.[1] Truly innovative strategic thinking is not about playing out new patterns in existing frameworks but, rather, about creating new frameworks and different patterns within these new frameworks. Daniel Kahneman's research has led him to conclude that it is "far easier said than done, [as] our mind tends to make up narratives about the past as a way of making meaning."[2] These narratives are placed within frames that can stubbornly resist shifting and shattering.

Rational linear thinking is selection by exclusion. We work within a frame of reference, and toss out what is not relevant. With a-rational lateral thinking, we realize that a pattern cannot be rearranged from within itself, but only as a result of some external influence. Part of the shattering process is to invite outside influences and embrace their provocation.

I find many of the techniques developed by the originator of the concept of lateral thinking, Edward De Bono, to be helpful for expanding perspectives as well as for identifying dominant ideas and giving vague ideas definition. Without bringing dominant themes into focus, good strategic ideas remain stuck, tangled, or oblivious within patterns secured in old frames.

Good intent itself, however, cannot generate possibilities and options; we need to develop ways of generating alternatives. The technique of lateral thinking can increase the chances for rearranging a pattern, which may in turn generate a strategic insight or innovative ideas. De Bono reminds us: "The more irrelevant such influences are, the more chance there is of altering the established pattern. To look only for things that are relevant means perpetuating the current pattern."[3]

The differences between *rational linear thinking* and *a-rational lateral thinking* are fundamental. The processes are quite distinct. One process is not more effective than the other for learning to think strategically, but, rather, both are necessary, and we must realize their differences in order to be able to use both effectively. Developmentally, there may be situations that require an emphasis on strengthening the rational linear thinking process, while other situations may call for a focused approach to learning a-rational lateral thinking. Strategists need to be aware of and adept at shattering and recreating patterns and frames in order to be generative and innovative.

Critical Reflection as a Tool for Shattering Frames

With few exceptions, I find that seasoned strategists are disturbed often to discover that they cannot account for processes they have come to see as central to strategic thinking. They find describing and teaching what actually happens difficult, when they make sense of uncertainty or make difficult high-risk choices. Their real processes seem mysterious in the light of prevailing strategic knowledge.

Less-experienced strategists often recognize that what they are doing is not creating a winning strategy, and become frustrated by their lack of vocabulary and process.

They do not want another model—they want something they can do on their own and use wherever they may be confronted with unpredictable circumstances. Contrived as it may sound, critical reflection is one of the best-kept strategic thinking secrets.

As we have mentioned, critical reflective processes are central for learning to think strategically and require a high degree of both the affective and cognitive dimensions of learning. Critical reflection, which can be triggered through critical inquiry, critical dialogue, and critical thinking, is what we use to test beliefs, challenge assumptions, broaden perspectives, and imagine possibilities—the very things that allow us to make strategy that is generative, innovative, adaptive, sustainable, and, ultimately, winning.

Critical reflection is not synonymous with retrospective thinking or hindsight. Critical reflection is a broad and a deep process. "The form of inquiry in critical reflection is appraisive rather than prescriptive or designative,"[4] writes learning theorist Jack Mezirow. The components of critical reflection are identifying and challenging assumptions, imagining and exploring alternatives, analyzing, and, ultimately, taking action. Critical reflection consists of two interrelated processes: learning to question and then reframing or replacing an assumption that is accepted by majority opinion as common sense. Critical reflection is the primary tool for shattering frames of reference—an essential process for every serious strategist to master. A relatively awkward concept to describe, shattering is perhaps the most difficult yet most important process to enact and to develop for strategic thinking.

Figure 17.1 shows the process of shattering, which is a deliberate interruption of our intuitive pattern-recognition process. The pauses may be momentary, or they may take weeks or months. During this pause period, however long, strategists must engage in critical dialogue and exercise critical reflection.

Critical reflection must be understood as essential to the strategic thinking process and involves more than cognitive skills, such as logical reasoning or deconstructing arguments for assertions that are unsupported by empirical evidence. Critical reflection involves our recognition of the assumptions underlying our beliefs and behaviors.

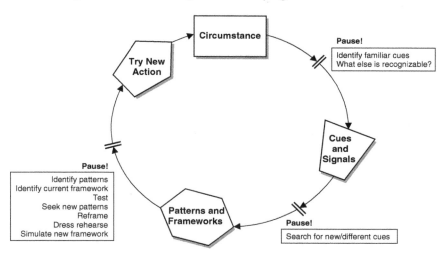

FIGURE 17.1 Shattering and Reframing that Can Occur in Strategic Thinking

Challenging through Reflection in Action and Reflection on Action

What distinguishes reflection *in* action from other kinds of reflection is its immediate and perceivable impact. When we define the scope and breadth of strategy, we choose the focus of our attention and we name the things we will notice. Generally, what we do when we examine strategic situations is to repeat the familiar patterns and frames we have acquired through our experience. Reflection in action requires that by naming and framing we select things for attention and organize these things in the moment; doing this can alter meaning and suggest a new direction.

Reflection in action, based on Donald Schon's work on reflective practice, is a process consisting of "on-the-spot surfacing, criticizing, restructuring, and testing of intuitive understandings of experienced phenomena."[5] Learning takes place when action is informed by reflection. Action and reflection are considered not as separate concepts, but as parts of a single process by which we become aware of our underlying assumptions, reflect on our initial understanding of the problem, and develop new ways of defining problems. Reflection in action implies that we learn as we define and implement new strategic decisions and action.

As Schon sees it:

> When someone reflects-in-action ... [h]e does not keep means and ends separate, but defines them interactively as he frames a problematic situation. ... [H]is experimenting is a kind of action, implementation is built into inquiry. [Therefore] reflection in action can proceed, even in situations of uncertainty or uniqueness, because it is not bound by the dichotomies of technical rationality.[6]

> *If we can place technical, analytical*
> *traditional problem solving within*
> *a broader context of reflective inquiry,*
> *strategic thinking will be enriched greatly.*

With regard to strategic thinking, reflection in action has a critical function in questioning and identifying the assumptions underlying our tacit knowledge or knowing in action. In other words, we think critically about the thinking that got us into a predicament or presented us with an opportunity. In the process, we may restructure a sequence of action, recreate the meaning, or devise a new way of framing problems. We begin to ask: "What else could I do?" or "How else could I see this?"

Through reflection in action, we can slow down or suspend the process and actively diverge our patterns and frames. We can broaden and deepen our views and intentionally distort the familiar in order to explore and create, because we frame strategic problems in different ways according to various perspectives.

For these reasons, the process of reflection in action is critically important when facilitating the learning of strategic thinkers. Questions about the legitimacy of reflective capacity and its relevance to strategy may dissipate once we understand how reflective capacity balances the analytical dimension of learning. If we can place technical, analytical traditional problem solving within a broader context of reflective inquiry, strategic thinking will be enriched greatly.

Strategic problems are interconnected in complex ways. Indeterminate factors, such as uncertainty, uniqueness, contradictions, and value conflict, defy the basic tenets of technical rationality. What is necessary when making strategic decisions involving these factors is not only the analytic techniques, which have been traditional in strategic development, but the reflective action abilities. Reflection in action and reflection on action involve the natural process of learning decision making and problem solving in a way that fuses the cognitive and the affective dimensions of learning. As we can clearly see, reflection in action and reflection on action require extensive use of the deeper, dive domain of learning.

A further complication of reflection *on* action is that everything makes sense in hindsight. In his insightful book, *The Black Swan*, Nassim Taleb pointed out that

> *our tendency to construct and believe coherent narratives of the past makes it difficult for us to accept the limits of our forecasting ability … The illusion that we understand the past fosters overconfidence in our ability to predict the future.*[7]

And in his book *Thinking, Fast and Slow*, researcher and Nobel Prize winner Daniel Kahneman says: "A general limitation of the human mind is its imperfect ability to reconstruct past states of knowledge, or beliefs that have changed. Once you adopt a new view of the world (or of any part of it), you immediately lose much of your ability to recall what you used to believe before your mind changed."[8]

The process of reflection in action is essential to dealing well with situations of uncertainty, instability, uniqueness, and value conflict. Western historical and cultural bias toward rational thinking blinds us to the a-rational process that is omnipresent in developing critical reflective capability. Our ability to learn to think strategically can therefore be thwarted if we do not learn to pay attention to the affective dimension of learning and to appreciate how this dimension impacts upon strategic thinking.

Phrases like "thinking on your feet," "keeping your wits about you," and "learning by doing" all suggest that we can, and sometimes actually do, think about what we are doing while we are doing it—when we reflect in action.

The Element of Surprise

Much reflection in action hinges on the experience of *surprise*. When intuitive, spontaneous performance yields nothing more than the results we expect, we tend not to think about it. But when an intuitive decision leads to surprises, whether promising or unwanted, we may respond by reflecting in action. Until this moment of surprise, we have been deciding and acting via autopilot. After the moment of surprise, we focus on what we have unintentionally created. In such processes, reflection tends to focus on the outcomes of action, the action itself, and the intuitive knowing implicit in the action. Very often, due to a surprise, and the inherent tension it brings, we are propelled to reflect on the understandings that have been implicit in our decision or thinking process or pattern. Due to the surprise, we are able to uncover assumptions, criticize, restructure, and reframe for further critical action.

Strategists often do think consciously about what they are doing—sometimes, even while doing it. Particularly when struck by surprise, they reflect back on action and on the knowing that is implicit in their decisions. For example, they may ask themselves: "What features do I notice when I recognize this incident as being familiar or dubious?" "What are the criteria by which I make this judgment?" "How am I framing the problem that I am trying to solve?" Generally, the aftermath of a surprise is when we look reflectively and introspectively on these opportune moments in an attempt to describe the tacit knowledge behind our action. Our descriptions of the surprise may vary, depending on our purpose and the language of descriptions available to us. We may refer, for example, to the sequence of operations and procedures that we execute or to the clues we observe and the rules we follow, or the values, hunches, and assumptions that underlie our reasons for action.

The sequence involved in the process of reflection in action resembles a breakdown outlined by learning theorist Donald Schon. Initially, we are involved in a situation where we take action spontaneously and routinely—using our autopilot response. This action reveals our tacit knowledge and is our way of framing a problem appropriate to the situation. This knowing in action is spontaneously delivered without conscious deliberation. This sequence of pattern recognition works, providing intended outcomes, so long as the situation falls within the boundaries of what we have learned to treat as normal.[9]

Next, a routine response produces an unexpected outcome—pleasant or unpleasant—that is incongruent with the categories of our tacit knowledge. This incongruence or surprise is what gets our attention, and our autopilot is interrupted. The attention we pay has significant implications for our ability to choose the focus of our critical reflection in strategic decision making.

Surprise provokes the final step, which is reflection in or on the present action. Reflection is, to some degree, conscious, although it need not be conveyed with words. We ask ourselves, "What is this?" or "What's happening?" and at the same time ask, "How have I been thinking about it?" Our thought turns back to the surprising incident and, at the same time, includes our present thinking and feeling.

Honing our reflective capacity is essential because reflection serves as an important corrective technique—one that halts over-learning, interrupts complacency, and reduces overreliance on our autopilot. Through critical reflection, a strategist can recognize and greet surprises as an opportunity to reveal and critique the tacit understanding that has developed around repetitive experiences of expertise and familiar habits of mind. Looking at surprises in this way can create a chance to make new sense of the situation and to look differently at uncertainty or uniqueness, which is an inevitable part of a global strategy environment.

Pseudo Frame Change

An increasingly common global strategy problem is what I call a *pseudo frame change*, which originates from the best of intentions, but can result in executives shooting themselves in the foot. What senior leadership often *says* it wants from its global "high potentials" is a "pipeline" of strategic thinking capable of generating winning strategies; but what senior leadership often *does* is lock these employees within existing corporate frames. In such circumstances, two conditions must be addressed: (1) senior leadership must understand the learning process required for strategic thinking; (2) senior leadership must support and model that learning process when developing high-potential candidates.

A typical scenario tends to play out in the following manner. High-potential candidates from various countries are selected to develop their strategic thinking. These people, who are the brightest and the best from around the world, are being groomed, through succession plans, to step up eventually to executive positions. Frequently, the candidates are shipped to headquarters for a stint in which they are doused in the corporate methodology or given a development assignment in a challenging market to build their leadership skills and accumulate knowledge. Both approaches can be beneficial. Once in these development assignments, the candidates are expected to attend strategy meetings, congregate with key strategists at the company, and be grilled on the methods of analysis used. The expectation is that these bright minds will generate the next winning strategy—or so the message goes. But often, this course of action undermines this intent.

If these high-potential candidates are to have any hope of advancing their strategic thinking and developing their roles as leaders, they need to acquire and become adept at critical reflective processing, not just analytical skills. Even the most polished analytical skills fall short when we are converting experiences into successful strategy.

Most often, these high-potential candidates are, essentially, placed firmly inside the corporate frame to learn its construction (i.e., the corporate way). Learning the corporate way is important for building a knowledge base and reinforcing the organizational culture. But frequently this learning is where the strategy-development process ends—and where the strategic thinking problem begins. These high-potential individuals learn the existing corporate frames and all of the subtle cues about changing those frames—or not.

Because of this socialization, these candidates may easily mistake strategic planning for strategic thinking. As a result, typically, they fail to adopt a habit of challenging the corporate frames and remain unclear about their strategic role: Is it to maintain existing frames, or is it to truly shatter and reframe? Furthermore, rarely do these high-potential candidates take the time to familiarize themselves with their greatest strategic asset—their own unique frames. Without critical reflective ability, they cannot challenge and test their own frames, nor can they test the existing corporate frames on which strategy is currently made.

Unless frame testing occurs, the personal beliefs and assumptions of the high-potential individuals and those of the company are never made apparent. Granted, this sometimes happens by chance, but luck is not the aim of a process. In order to create an innovative, adaptive, and sustainable strategy, these individuals must shatter (deconstruct the existing frame) and reframe (reconstruct it). Ultimately, those who succeed at strategic thinking understand, articulate, and test their own existing frames, as well as those of the company.

Typically, candidates learn a knowledge base of making strategy within existing corporate frames, but the critical step of shattering and reframing is often omitted from strategic development programs. This is an unfortunate omission, since critical reflection is, after all, the aim of a strategic thinking initiative.

Senior leadership needs to endorse explicitly and model the critical reflective processes as part of learning to think strategically. If critical reflection is not stated explicitly and demonstrated, the best strategic efforts amount to little more than making extensions to the existing frames—pseudo frame change.

Content Reflection, Process Reflection, and Premise Reflection

A useful way to start practicing critical reflection is to distinguish among three specific kinds of critical reflection: *content* reflection, *process* reflection, and *premise* reflection.[10] These distinctions are useful to both clarify the definition of reflection and further understand the deeper, dive domain of learning. Table 17.1 outlines content, process, and premise reflection.

TABLE 17.1   Content Reflection, Process Reflection, and Premise Reflection

	Type of Critical Reflection		
	Content Reflection	**Process Reflection**	**Premise Reflection**
Description	Focuses on *what*	Focuses on *how*	Focuses on *why*
Approaches	Restate problem Identify key issues Summarize major points State indicators of trends and patterns Identify factors and variables Confirm data Verify sources	Map steps, actions and reactions, and approaches used Explore how the problem emerged/grew/shifted Trace step-by-step actions, reactions, and responses Discuss progression and sequence Discuss scope, impact, and influence Discuss relevance and reliability of indicators	Challenge the relevance and nature of a strategic problem: "Why is this issue relevant to strategy?" "Is this my concern?" "How else could this be framed?" "Is the key concept a valid concept?" Validate data, inferences Challenge assumptions, beliefs, and values underlying the key problem Make explicit and challenge the rationale underlying strategy decisions
Relevance	Surf learning Cognitive instrumental	Surf and dive learning Cognitive instrumental Critical thinking	Dive learning Cognitive and affective Critical reflection Critical inquiry Critical dialogue

Content Reflection

The focus of content reflection is on the content or description of a strategic problem. Content questions aim to focus our thoughts on the "what." What aspect of the problem are we paying attention to? Content questions enable us to get more specific information and details about a topic, and tend to be transactional in nature. For example, if the strategic problem is one of diminishing global market share for a particular automobile, the strategist might look for indicators of trends and attempt to associate those behaviors with development initiatives. Where is the problem occurring? When did this start? How much will an advertising campaign turnaround cost? How much time will it take? What are the key factors to examine?

Process Reflection

Process reflection involves thinking about the procedures that led to the problem or the approaches used to implement the strategic solution—the "how." Process questions push us to examine how we make strategic decisions. How did the problem come about? How exactly did we get here? How did others do it? Process questions enable us to trace the steps and to challenge the quality of the rationale that underlies our strategic decision by describing the process we used to make the decision. The strategist interested in the diminishing global market share of a particular automobile might dig deeper and ask how the data and analysis were selected and analyzed. The strategist might investigate how she knew that the statistical indicators were relevant, reliable, and comprehensive. She might question the progression or sequence of events. She might ask whether or not the effort to find indicators of weakening oil supply was adequate. If the same problem came up in another country, business unit, or product, would the same procedure solve the problem? Is the timeline really appropriate for success? Process reflection is a rational and linear kind of reflection, which does not always include an affective or an intuitive component. Process questions often use surf-level thinking, but can draw on the deeper, dive-level of thinking.

Premise Reflection

Premise reflection leads us to question the relevance of the problem itself. Premise reflection serves to bring us closer to the "why" and "what if…" A strategist might ask: "Is market share my real concern? How else could this problem be framed? Is market share the only or the primary indicator of success? Can I control market share? Is market share dominance a valid concept?" In premise reflection, the strategist questions the assumptions, beliefs, or values underlying the problem. Premise reflection consists of a strong affective dimension—we feel an unmistakable "twitch" that bolts our attention and may prompt us to resist. Premise reflection leads us to the deeper, dive domain of learning and allows us to determine the degree of confidence we have in our conclusion, based on the soundness of our strategic thinking process and the clarity and authenticity of its underlying premise.

Content, process, and premise questions are essential for learning to think strategically. In my practice, I have found that the questions most commonly asked in strategic sessions are content questions. Process questions require a focused and guided attention and are not asked as often. And premise questions are extremely rare. If leaders aim to develop an innovative and sustainable strategy pipeline within their organizations, then they need to muster the courage and master the capability of asking deep, dive questions, which create premise-level reflection. The development of strategic thinking requires moving beyond the acquisition of new knowledge and into a process of challenging existing assumptions, values, and frames.

Notes

1. Hogarth, *Educating Intuition*.
2. Kahneman, *Thinking, Fast and Slow*, 202.
3. De Bono, *Lateral Thinking*, 42.
4. Mezirow, *Transformative Dimensions of Adult Learning*, 87.
5. Schon, *The Reflective Practitioner*, 241.
6. Schon, quoted in Mezirow, *Transformative Dimensions of Adult Learning*, 104.
7. Taleb, *The Black Swan*, 218.
8. Kahneman, *Thinking, Fast and Slow*, 202.
9. Schon, *The Reflective Practitioner*.
10. Mezirow, *Transformative Dimensions of Adult Learning*.

18

Reframing

As a result of shattering our strategy frames through a rigorous and iterative process of divergent thinking and critical reflective processes, we have an option to refine and reframe our strategy issue. The ability to reframe a strategy issue is an outcome of successful strategic thinking. Ordinarily, we frame situations very quickly, using our experience to make meaning of issues at hand.[1] The reframing of a problem reveals the mistakes we made precisely because of our familiarity or our expertise, or because we have cemented our perception of the world and cannot see it in any other way, and this view gives way to a different way of positioning a strategic issue.

Reframing becomes even more complicated when the context in which the information is learned and the context in which it may be used are different. When dealing with uncertainty, contradictions, and conflict in strategic thinking, we informally learn to conduct frame experiments. These frames impose a kind of coherence on messy situations, and we discover consequences and implications of our selected frames through testing.

Six Framing Traps that Impede the Ability to Reframe

While everyone can strengthen the critical reflective processes required to reframe to some degree, we want to be on the lookout for some personal traps which can impede our ability to reframe. While each of these six traps can serve a business in some situations, when it comes to strategic thinking, they are impediments—manifestations of our habits of mind.

Immediate Gratifiers

These are the people who want results—now! They are all about action, with no time, experience, or appreciation for the thinking that underlies and improves strategic action.

Once we begin to lose our ability to imagine or create, we cannot envision the future, and strategic thinking capacity vanishes.

Know-It-Alls

Know-it-alls tend to make instant judgments based on frozen, same-frame thinking. They believe their frame because it is the only way they "know." Challenge and testing feel wrong and threatening. Know-it-all thinking stops dialogue, freezes us in place, and leads us to ignore information and insights that support other positions.

Experts

An expert mindset can be a double-edged sword. Sometimes, highly expert people make up their minds so quickly that they overlook critical flaws in the process because of their deep knowledge, successful experience, and acquired and trusted intuition. Expert minds are like computers that can scan vast amounts of data with few interruptions. Because of their vast experience and familiarity, experts can fail to consider surprise elements which may be crucial factors in their strategic problem. Those who lack specific expertise and think more slowly can have an unexpected advantage. Such a person may follow a more deliberate and careful thinking process—noticing more signals, weighing all the factors involved, noticing where data are missing, identifying blind spots, or noting paths of questioning which have not been taken.

Satisfieds

These people are satisfied and content with the status quo and see no reason to change. This kind of resistance to change is based on a rationale that if we want to preserve our privileged place in a particular corporate or social niche—the one that lets me in regardless of whom it shut out—then critical thinking or critical reflection is a threat to our sense of self and our position. We sometimes need to be reminded that discomfort, imbalance, and discontent are powerful motivators for learning and for strategic thinking.

Conformists

Similar to the satisfieds, conformists appear in organizations that have a club sort of mentality. Once we decide that our group is superior, our mind focuses only on who is one of us and who is not—and what actions, objects, frames, or thoughts maintain that distinction. Symbolism overrides thinking. For example, rituals and conformity can be useful in times of economic stability because they allow an organization to create bonds and feelings of solidarity. But when challenge is required, the same-frame thinking of conformists makes the group's ability to detect the signals of change and to envision a new thinking impossible. This impossibility has disastrous implications for developing strategic thinkers and highlights the need for diversity of thought in strategy meetings.

Over-Simplifiers

As situations become more complex and contradictory, a common tendency when making sense is to over-simplify. Because we feel overwhelmed, we sometimes falsely believe that all complex and contradictory things can be reduced to more basic parts. We deny the real complexity because we do not know how to make meaning of competing and contradictory things. The temptation for over-simplification in a chaotic and fast-paced environment is tremendous, and we often become vulnerable to shortcuts and quick fixes.

If we want to strengthen our ability to think strategically, we need to identify any existing habits of mind that could become a trap to our strategic thinking. We can develop this awareness by continuously expanding our experience base, paying attention to habitual and familiar frames, and practicing with a skillful and artful coach, colleagues, or friends who support the use of critical inquiry, critical dialogue, and critical reflection.

Expertise and Experience: The Double-Edged Sword

Expertise, as we mentioned in the six traps, is both a charm and a curse in terms of reframing a strategic issue. Expertise lets us quickly categorize a situation as typical. Similarly, expertise shows us where to focus our attention and what to ignore. But sometimes we can become so complacent or over-confident about what we think we know that we are caught off guard when the unexpected happens. This is the flip side of expertise—it can blind us and give us a false sense of knowing. Expertise enables us to ignore cues and options that we do not think are worthwhile.[2]

When we are tasked with strategic thinking, this expert mindset can lead us to overlook relevant but novel cues, to ignore potentially useful ideas, and to fail to notice important opportunities. In his 20-year study of expert predictions, psychologist Philip Tetlock reported that those experts "with the most knowledge are often less reliable. The reason is that the person who acquires more knowledge develops an enhanced illusion of her skill and becomes unrealistically overconfident."[3]

Reframing is a very common strategic thinking challenge for senior strategists with whom I work, primarily due to their expertise and experience. An important part of learning to think strategically is that non-experts need to be able to challenge the experts in a group. (See Critical Dialogue in Part V.) The seasoned strategists whom I interviewed underscored a striking comment—that expertise in confronting a strategic problem is much more valuable than expertise in answering the problem.

When we look at or listen to data, an adept strategic thinker will question whether anything in the picture is unusual. We need to imagine new patterns even when the old patterns are very vivid. The reframing problem shows that our intuition is fallible. Even when intuition is based on expertise, we may still have overlooked something important. Too often, experienced strategists can fall into a routine that blinds them to new possibilities.[4] The habit of critical reflection is essential for breaking through this barrier of expertise.

Many novice strategists get locked into a view of themselves as technical experts, and they find nothing in the strategy process that warrants reflection. More often than not, these novices have become too skillful at techniques of selective inattention and situational control—techniques that they use to preserve their habit of mind. Uncertainty is perceived as a threat, and its admission is a sign of weakness. Others, more adept at reflection in action or on action, also may feel profoundly uneasy because they cannot verbalize their know-how and cannot justify its quality or rigor, but they regard the imbalance and tension as an opportunity for deeper critical inquiry and reflection.

> *Expertise in confronting a strategic problem is much more valuable than expertise in answering the problem.*

In order to facilitate the shattering and reframing process, strategists must have both an understanding of the informal learning process involved in strategic thinking and a basic vocabulary they can use. Both can facilitate and enhance enormously the strategic thinking process. Often, our expertise is what allows us to be trapped for entry into the elite chambers of strategy, at the tip of the triangle. Yet this membership too often becomes the trap that trips, because we do not fully understand how to develop our strategic thinking capability.

One simple exercise for helping to shatter and reframe both the expert and other traps is to explicitly identify, test, and track what you know that you know and what you know that you do not know. While this exercise may sound obvious, it can lead to surprises and an interesting dialogue. A simple table, something like Table 18.1, can get things started. Select a single strategy dimension as shown in Figure 14.1 for a given issue—for example, technology or finance—and just start filling in the table. After some time you will want to compare and begin to clarify your thinking through dialogue with colleagues. The expectation is that you will seek out those people who are certain to have different frames, knowledge, and experiences.

Reframing a strategic issue relies on our ability to identify our habits of mind, challenge what we "know," and to become aware of our intuitions. Just because intuition is fallible does not mean that we cannot make good use of it. Our eyes are not perfect—they blur and have blind spots, and they often require lenses to correct for distortions. Yet we don't reject the information we receive from our eyes. So, too, we need not refute what we learn through our intuition. We need to pay close attention to our intuition and cultivate

TABLE 18.1 Example of Knowledge Tracker for Strategic Thinking

Category: Technology

What I Must Know	What I Know	What I Don't Know	What I Think I Know	Somebody Else Knows	Keeps Changing	Can't Trust

it with the same degree of seriousness that we give to analysis. As common sense would suggest, intuition researcher Philip Tetlock reminds us, "Experts are just human in the end. Experts are led astray not by what they believe, but by how they think."[5]

Notes

1. Hogarth, *Educating Intuition*.
2. Tetlock, *Expert Political Judgment: How Good Is It? How Can We Know?*
3. Tetlock, *Expert Political Judgment: How Good Is It? How Can We Know?*, 233.
4. Kahneman, *Thinking, Fast and Slow*.
5. Tetlock, *Expert Political Judgment: How Good Is It? How Can We Know?*, 233.

VI

Summary and Questions

Counter to traditional strategy development approaches, intuition is a vital component of learning to think strategically. Intuition is developed through accumulated and compiled experience. Seasoned strategists use their tacit knowledge and intuitive knowledge to recognize familiar patterns and irregularities for certain situations to which they cannot give a reasonably accurate or complete description.

Patterns and frames strongly influence the way in which we approach a strategic issue. Recognizing personal and organizational patterns of thought and developing an awareness of "blind spots" are critical to strategic thinking. Additionally, good strategists balance the rational and a-rational thought processes for effective strategic thinking. By including diverse frames of reference into the strategic thinking process we can ensure a degree of variation in the interpretation of information.

Consciously escaping fixed patterns of thinking and developing a new, innovative arrangement of patterns can help to establish the foundation for frame shifting and shattering. As a process, reframing can change our view and position on a strategic issue. Strategic thinkers must also be cognizant of the personal traps that can impede their ability to reframe. Common strategic thinking traps include immediate gratification, know-it-all thinking, having an expert mindset, satisfaction with the status quo, conformity, and over-simplification of a complex issue.

The use of critical reflective processes is fundamental for shifting and shattering frames. By understanding and engaging in critical inquiry and critical dialogue, we can focus and navigate the content-, process-, and premise-level reflection of a strategic issue.

1. What are some ways that you could model the critical reflective processes within strategy sessions? Who do you know that engages in the critical reflective processes effectively?
2. How can you practice reframing issues related to your strategy concerns?

3. Are there any of the six framing traps that you frequently identify within your team? For yourself? How do those traps affect your ability to reframe issues? Does your organization foster or even reward any of the strategic thinking traps?

4. Think of a surprise or perhaps a catastrophe that has occurred within your organization or a familiar organization. How could it be reframed and leveraged as an opportunity?

5. Think of a time when you heard someone ask a great question that triggered premise-level reflection. What was your reaction? Why? What made that question great?

...BUT WHAT ABOUT THE NUMBERS?

Strange Bedfellows: Intuition and Analysis as Partners in the Strategic Learning Process

You cannot feed the hungry on statistics.

David Lloyd George (1863–1945), British statesman and prime minister

Reporting facts is the refuge of those who have no imagination.

Luc de Clapiers Marquis de Vauvenargues (1715–1747), French soldier

19

The Roles of Analysis and Intuition in Strategic Decision Making

"No more marketing research. No more focus groups. No more promotions and commercials—we've been sinking money in this black hole for a couple of years. No more. I should've trusted my gut feeling long ago!" That was the declaration made by Louisa Perez, the country manager of an American soft-drinks corporation operating in Venezuela, to her executive committee. For the first time in her life, she could not get answers to a problem from the research and analysis. For the longest time, she had had an uncomfortable feeling that something was not right, but she ignored the feeling in favor of more analysis. Louisa is known within the company as a meticulous analyst; her decisions are always based on well-researched data. She has been annoyed with the song that the locally hired managers sing every day: "My gut feeling tells me this, my gut feeling tells me that." Louisa has guts—she just never felt like basing her strategy on these gut feelings.

She continued:

> It's amazing—we're beaten to a pulp in the orange soda drinks segment of the
> Venezuelan market by a newcomer that doesn't invest any money in marketing its
> own product. It just dumps the drink concentrates at the feet of local bottlers and
> waits for more orders—which come like clockwork.

Later, at a dinner with the sales team of the local distributor, Louisa could not help but share her frustration with a young sales manager seated beside her. He smiled awkwardly and said:

> I'm sorry, Mrs. Perez, that nobody told you about it earlier. But I believe the reason
> your product's sales are going down has nothing to do with your marketing efforts.
> Some dishonest soda fountain operators have figured out a way to open sealed con-
> centrate containers and dilute the beverage with tap water. The competitor's con-
> tainers are much easier to tamper with than yours—that is why they keep buying

*them; it's not the quality of the soda. Your company's technological prowess and the
growing numbers of dishonest operators have driven you out of the market.*

Louisa's gut feeling turned out to be right. The problem was not about jingles and research.
Now, she faces another dilemma—to start researching the new phenomenon or to skip
the research and deal with it by relying on her newfound strategy tool: intuition.

Part VII consists of three chapters. Chapter 19 looks at the complementary roles of
analysis and intuition, and considers how intuition is a balance for analysis and how
analysis provides a check for intuition in strategic thinking. Chapter 20 discusses the
traditional strategic decision-making process and then offers an integrated strategic decision-making alternative. Chapter 21 discusses coordinating intuition and analysis to
strengthen strategic thinking.

*Rational analysis can never substitute for intuition
within the process of strategic thinking.*

Intuition within the context of strategic thinking has to be balanced with deliberate,
rational analysis. But rational analysis can never substitute for intuition within the process of strategic thinking. Cognitive knowledge must be integrated with having "a feel"
for the situation, which is otherwise known as *tacit* knowledge. While analysis has its
function and intuition is not perfect, trying to replace intuition with analysis is a huge
mistake, if the intention is to think strategically.

Analysis is a supportive tool for making intuitive decisions. The concept of rational,
logical thinking is one of selection based on the process of rejection. Information and
ideas are put in order and tested according to linear criteria; then, they are discredited
and discarded if they do not fit. When time and information are available, analysis can
help to uncover cues and patterns as well as provide new points of focus for the creation
of different patterns and reframing. Also, analysis can help to evaluate a decision. But
analysis cannot replace the intuition that is at the center of the strategic decision-making
process. Strategy does not always obey the logic of our framework.

Despite increasingly analytical approaches to making strategy, it remains principally
an iterative process of two distinctly different cognitive clusters—one that is reliant on
conceptual, divergent, and critical reflective processes and the other a cluster of rational,
convergent, logical, linear capabilities (see Chapter 4). We need to explore the connection between analysis and intuition in an effort to develop strategic thinking. Ultimately,
we need to learn how to conduct analyses which improve intuitive thinking—and to
distinguish what types of decisions are most appropriate for analytical thinking and for
intuitive thinking. Intuition expert Gary Klein notes:

*Our intuitions function like our peripheral vision to keep us oriented and aware of our
surroundings. Our analytical abilities, on the other hand, enable us to think precisely.*

We may believe that everything we think and decide comes from our analytical thinking, the conscious and deliberate arguments we construct in our heads, but that's because we're not aware of how our intuitions direct our conscious thought processes.[1]

In situations that require strategic thinking, sometimes we need to rely more on intuition and other times we need to draw more on analysis. According to intuition experts and research, when the situation keeps changing, when the time pressure is high, or when the goals are vague, analysis is not enough. We have to go with what we "know."[2] These situations require risk taking, yet they can also yield strategic rewards if we invest in building a repertoire of successful intuitive experiences. By contrast, when our strategic decision involves a lot of computational complexity, such as determining whether there is a cost advantage, we are doomed or duped if we do not do the analysis.

*Numbers are not always any more
trustworthy than intuition.*

Because our intuition can mislead us, we often opt to track events using objective measures—which are quick and easy things to share. Relevant or not, this objectivity feels safe. To use objective measures, we develop metrics that will record what we need to know—a rate of change, a degree of progress, or some other feature that will help us make decisions. Market-share metrics, for instance, tell us the extent to which a company dominates its industry.

On the other hand, intuition comes to us through subconscious and sensory reactions and perceptions, not through numbers, so hunches just pop into our minds without leaving any trail about how they were formed. In contrast, metrics provide firm documentation for our decisions. If someone questions us, we can point to the numbers to explain our decisions. Intuition cannot really help us to figure out overhead rates or make budget projections.

Unfortunately, numbers are not always any more trustworthy than intuition. Accurate, reliable numbers are often difficult to obtain, subject to multiple interpretations, and even harder to apply. Quantifying the elements of a situation does not guarantee that we will make a good decision. Metrics can even interfere with intuition. For example, the hard numbers of a particular niche market don't necessarily add up to a story that explains why we feel a strategic decision is just plain wrong. There is considerably more to a strategic decision than a chain of numbers.

Nevertheless, we cannot dispense with numbers. They force us to align our intuition with reality. For example, numbers keep us from continuing a strategy whose image masks the reality of reduced capacity, changed circumstances, overextended budgets, or disappointing rates of return. Therefore, numbers cannot be discounted or discredited entirely.

Intuition as a Check on Analysis

How does intuition keep analysis in check? Intuition helps us to monitor our attention by signaling to us to be more alert in high-stakes situations. For example, we "smell a rat" or get that gut feeling that something is not quite right. Intuition can help us spot problems earlier and warn us that our decisions, and actions based on those decisions, are insufficient to reach our goal. It is our intuition that enables us to pick up on subtle inconsistencies in patterns, which triggers a feeling, which then leads to a certain decision or action. Because of this, we draw confident and incredible conclusions from very little information. Intuition is what we use when we try to see patterns when we look at data and facts. The patterns are not linear, so they are not always obvious. This is when intuition becomes our best friend—we look over a set of data or variables and suddenly a pattern becomes visible. The ability to recognize patterns is intuitive. Our experience is what arranges things into patterns.

One strength of metrics is that they give us a snapshot without the cumbersome details of the process by which that snapshot was acquired. This absence of history and context accelerates communication in strategic meetings, because details of the method for obtaining data are not usually shared. This means that we have to judge the numbers on face value—the risk is in not knowing if we can trust the numbers.

I am not suggesting that we reject or be shielded from data; rather, we need to use critical dialogue and inquiry to scrutinize and test the data. We need to ask, "Whose data?" "Where did they come from?" "Why were they collected?" "Whose interests were they intended to serve?" "Whose interest do they actually serve?" "Why were they compiled in a particular way?" and "Who paid for the data collection and analysis?" in order to get the story and the context behind the numbers. Seeing numbers out of context can cause us to misinterpret information and lead to regrettable strategic decisions and conclusions. In this strategic environment of ambiguity and paradox, analysis will take us only so far.

Analysis as a Check on Intuition

While it is important to emphasize the role of intuition in strategic decision making, of equal note is that intuition alone does not generate or constitute strategic thinking. What are some of the limitations to intuition? Why does intuition sometimes prove unreliable? Several important limitations to the use of intuition come from the types of decisions we face, the opportunities we have had to develop our intuition, and the inherent nature of expertise. Intuition researcher Gary Klein suggests three reasons why our intuition may not serve us well.[3]

First, while complex and uncertain decisions make intuition difficult to apply, these are the very kinds of situations in which we need to use highly skilled intuition more than ever. Since much of strategic thinking includes dealing with very complex, incomplete, and uncertain information which is constantly changing, we must develop our intuition to a degree that we can trust it as a reliable tool. Analysis alone does not suffice.

Intuition must be tested against analysis, and analysis must be tested against our intuition in these highly complex and constantly changing circumstances.

Developing intuition based on pattern matching is hard when the strategic situation we are trying to resolve is complicated. Even if we think that we recognize a pattern, we may be fooling ourselves, which is why we must be adept at using critical reflective processes (i.e., dialogue, reflection, challenge, testing) to challenge our perceptions, frames, and assumptions. There are no substitutes for testing and reflecting.

Second, the strategist may not have had a chance to acquire expertise. We may not have a chance to build a strong experience base because we cannot get feedback about our judgments. The absence of a strong experience base can lower our confidence when using our intuition.

Third, the experience base of our intuition may be distorted. Even if we know how to acquire and evaluate our intuition, we still have to worry about the validity of the feedback we receive. Therefore, we must habitually test validity through dialogue and critical inquiry.

Rational and intuitive thinking are not mutually exclusive. When both are well developed, our composite knowledge is extremely advantageous when learning to think strategically.

Notes

1. Klein, *The Power of Intuition*, 66.
2. Kahneman, *Thinking, Fast and Slow*; Ariely, *The Upside of Irrationality*; Klein, *The Power of Intuition*; Duggan, *Strategic Intuition*; Hogarth, *Educating Intuition*; Tetlock, *Expert Political Judgment: How Good Is It? How Can We Know?* While all of these authors have their own vocabulary, definitions, and a somewhat different interpretation of intuition based on their own respective studies, all contribute to the body of literature and to a better understanding of the role of intuition and analysis with regard to strategic thinking. While the conclusions they draw are different, this serves to expand the base of knowledge on intuition.
3. Klein, *The Power of Intuition*, 67–70.

20

Decision-Making Approaches to Strategic Thinking

Decision making is central to strategy making and therefore it must be practiced, challenged, and refined as we learn to think strategically. First, we will look at the familiar and traditional Western approach to strategic decision making, and follow with an approach that integrates intuition and rationality.

Traditional Strategic Decision Making

Traditional strategic planning approaches, steeped in the customs of the technical rational scientific school of thought, emphasize some variation of the familiar, classic six-step model of decision making:

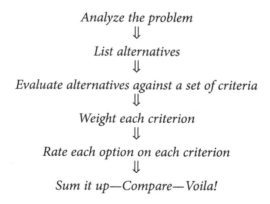

Analyze the problem
⇓
List alternatives
⇓
Evaluate alternatives against a set of criteria
⇓
Weight each criterion
⇓
Rate each option on each criterion
⇓
Sum it up—Compare—Voila!

This linear model of decision making strikes many of us as very comforting and appealing. The model is straightforward, and is based on solid analysis and logic. It is systematic, rational, and methodical. Leaving nothing to chance, a good decision is guaranteed if we just follow the process. This model allows us to justify our decision intelligibly to others—there is something reassuringly "scientific" about it.

The catch is that this linear model provides a false sense of assurance. It is a sanitized sequence that omits the untidy parts of the complex problem-solving process. The messy, nonlinear parts of problem solving are imperative to distinguish strategic thinking from strategic planning and are necessary for strategic innovation, adaptability, and sustainability.

As we have discussed in great detail, critical reflective processes are essential for challenging the underlying assumptions of a current strategic issue in order to ensure that it is examined and explored. Complex strategy decisions call for a combination of cognitions that include critically reflective processes. Reflection in action may be slow and arduous, or quick and decisive. When a strategist reflects in and on his action, the possible targets of reflection are as varied as the kinds of factors, variables, and patterns before him, and as wide ranging as the multitude of underlying frames, assumptions, and belief systems that he brings to his reflections.

Reflection may be about the tacit norms and reasons that underlie a particular judgment, or on the theories implicit in a pattern of events, decisions, or reactions. Also, reflection could be on the feeling about a situation that has guided a particular course of action or decision. Possibly, reflection could be about the way in which the strategist has framed the problem encountered, or on the role he has constructed for himself within a larger organizational or business context.

Although reflection in action is an extraordinarily complex process, it is commonplace among successful strategists. For many strategists it is the defining trait of their success because of its impact on complex decision making.

We must be willing to enter into new kinds of confusion and uncertainties when we engage in critical reflection on action.

Our attitude toward inquiry influences greatly our attitude toward the reality, and, therefore, our attitude affects the strategic decisions we make. We probe the information and stories of the directors of the key business units and systematically pursue the implications of our familiar and chosen frames. At the same time that we try to shape the situation to our frame, we must hold ourselves open to any "playback" from or of the situation.

While judgments must be grounded in relevant data, conclusions should remain open to reevaluation, which can be stressful. We must be willing to enter into new kinds of confusion and uncertainties when we engage in critical reflection on action and decision making.

To apply reflection in and on action to strategic thinking, the following tenets of learning are recommended:[1]

1. Give and get valid information. Valid information is essential for informed decisions.
2. Seek out and provide others with directly observable data and correct reports so that valid attributions can be made.

3. Create the conditions for free and informed choice.
4. Try to create, for ourselves and for others, awareness of the values we embrace in making the decision, awareness of the limits of our capacities, and awareness of those factors that are beyond our control.
5. Increase our internal commitment to decisions made. Try to create conditions, for ourselves and for others, in which we are committed to an action because it is intrinsically satisfying—not because we anticipate external rewards or punishments.

Integrated Strategic Decision Making

As we strengthen our capacity for strategic thinking, we must remain mindful of and adept at integrating the roles of intuition and rationality. Critical reflection is an approach that can help to integrate intuition and rationality effectively in strategic decision making. Figure 20.1 illustrates the complementary roles of intuition and rationality in the overall strategic decision-making process. Although, in reality, intuition and rationality coexist, they tend to alternate in performing a predominant function within the strategic decision-making process.

Upon encountering a strategic circumstance or dilemma, intuition is what waves the red flag or nudges us under the table. By leveraging our experience and knowledge in a non-analytical and discreet manner, intuition gets our attention and helps us to recognize

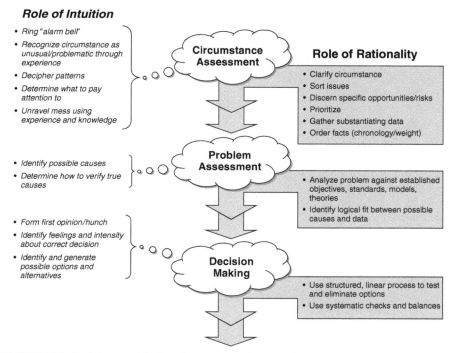

FIGURE 20.1   Integrated Roles of Intuition and Rationality in Strategic Decision Making

something as problematic. Intuition helps us to determine where to focus our attention and helps us to sort issues.

Then, the role of rationality kicks in by clarifying and systematically discerning issues and opportunities which warrant further consideration. Rationality is essential for ordering facts in a linear and logical way. Meticulous prioritization, data collection, and analysis are crucial in order to move forward the assessment of circumstance.

As our problem assessment progresses, our intuition works to identify possible causes and to verify true causes. Without a well-honed intuitive sense, problem analysis can remain clinical, sanitized, and ineffectual, in that problems are exposed only superficially and analyzed without much, if any, examination of the "truthfulness" of their cause. Rationality then plays the critical role of identifying relevant information and analyzing facts. Rationality serves to evaluate a logical fit between possible causes and data, by analyzing the problem against established objectives, standards, formulas, and models.

The final decision-making step is where the tension between intuition and rationality is most apparent. The consequences of making a strategic decision today can be daunting—huge stakes within an unpredictable future make the risk factor enormous. Executives whom I interviewed noted consistently that intuition usually leads their strategic decision making; and if their intuition is not countered by rationality, runaway intuition can be as detrimental as it can be beneficial. Intuition provides our first judgment or gut reaction in decision making. The role of rationality is essential and imperative, then, as a "testing" method, to verify the hunches and preferences we have intuitively made. We need to work through the rigors of a disciplined rational process while noting and suspending our initial claims.

The focused and skillful use of both intuition and rationality offers a structured process of checks and balances in strategic decision making. Developing and reinforcing critical reflection as part of learning to think strategically can ensure that intuition and rationality are aligned, for each is an insurance on the other.

Note

1. Argyris and Schon, *Organizational Learning II: Theory, Method, and Practice.*

21

Coordinating Intuition and Analysis to Facilitate Strategic Thinking

As we have examined thus far, neither analysis nor intuition alone is sufficient for strategic decision making. The challenge is to find a way to balance intuition and analysis. We do not want to abandon metrics, but we do not want to be fooled by numbers either. We need to find ways to use data effectively to support and correct our intuition, so that we can benefit from both analysis and intuition as ways of interpreting strategic events.

The synthesis of intuition and analysis that seems most effective for strategic thinking is when we permit intuition to direct our analysis of the circumstances and guide the strategic thinking process. This way, intuition helps us to recognize situations and decide how to react, and analysis verifies our intuitions to make sure they are not misleading us. Table 21.1 highlights the optimal use of intuition and numbers in strategic decision making.

There are several other things that we can do that combine intuition and analysis, including (1) mapping the strengths and weaknesses of strategic options without attaching metrics, and (2) not replacing intuition with procedures as a means of taking control of gray areas—a very common mistake. Another integrated approach is to fuse numbers and intuition by using stories in the form of metaphors, analogies, parables, and fables—a narrative can describe how the metrics came to be. These stories can explain how a few primary influences caused the circumstance we are trying to grasp and navigate. Stories add nuance and context as we make meaning of metrics—and those same metrics help us to structure our stories.

Further, strange as it may sound to those who have not experienced it, I often coax the strategists with whom I work to "draw" their strategic problem, along with details of any risks and conclusions. Drawing the strategic problem is a great way to integrate intuition and analysis and it develops thought flexibility by shifting cognitive clusters.

TABLE 21.1   Constructive Uses of Intuition and Numbers for Strategic Decision Making

Use Intuition to Support Strategic Decisions by	Use Numbers to Support Strategic Decisions by
Initiating strategic concept and framework ("gut sense")	Testing intuitive framework
Formulating frameworks	Establishing strategic targets and goals
Identifying patterns ("hunches") that are negative and positive	Making comparisons
Making sense of incomplete, partial, inaccurate information	Ensuring compliance
Making sense of rapidly changing data	Spotting trends and patterns
Mentally simulating scenarios ("dress rehearsing")	Evaluating strategic performance
Exploring new possibilities and alternatives with stories Expanding and enriching context of data	Testing stories and creating and re-creating new stories
Constructing new frameworks	Constructing new frameworks

SCENARIO

Arjun was tagged as a nascent frontrunner within the fiercely competitive world of technology start-up companies. He was admired as a brilliant analytical thinker. As the CEO of a renowned Silicon Valley firm, he was hounded by ever-aggressive investors to create a new, innovative strategy. He needed a groundbreaking strategy. It needed to be ingenious; and he needed it soon.

Arjun was spinning like a hamster on a wheel trying to generate an innovative strategy. Tormented by his inability to generate such a strategy, he grew increasingly anxious as the calendar weeks became months. He stayed glued to his computer screen, hopeful that a strategy would soon emerge from the reams of data. He was scared and paralyzed.

Regardless of the many caffeinated brainstorming sessions his team had, and an exorbitant invoice from hiring a strategy consultant, the end result was merely a variation or a slight pivot of their current strategy template. The clock was ticking and competitors were nabbing business and products.

After meeting with Arjun and with his executive team, I suggested that he might want to take out a pencil and draw the problem so that he could see it. He winced at the suggestion and grew skeptical the longer he thought about it. He grumbled something about not having sketched anything beyond two stick figures in kindergarten. His initial protest was fortunately, short lived. The minute Arjun put pen to paper and focused on drawing the problem, he became immersed and energized. The process of drawing suspended his rational thinking and momentarily allowed him to tap into an a-rational mindset.

As we spoke later that month, Arjun enthusiastically mentioned that when he was actually drawing, he felt liberated. He could see a whole new dimension to the problem. Details and circumstances that had been largely invisible to him were now part of his overall picture. Drawing his problem had highlighted variables that were hidden in the data. He claimed he had re-positioned their business at least nine times as he drew and re-drew persistent threats contained in various imaginary scenarios. Another epiphany he reported was the eagerness of his global team to become involved in his newfound approach to formulating a strategy.

Not only did he recite the old cliché of a picture being worth a thousand words, but he also noted that the exercise was expansive. He commented on the "fascinating conversation between my hand and my mind." Once the risks and factors were sketched, he could see the limitations and constraints of his current thinking.

Much to his amazement, the more he drew the more he wanted to draw, irrespective of the chortles and jovial threats to post his masterpieces. His sketches brought peals of laughter, but they nevertheless became a magnet to attract those who would typically have been excluded from his strategy conversations.

Arjun shifted his mindset from an over-reliance on using rational thinking and analytical data to generate a strategy, to engaging in an a-rational process of drawing his strategic problem. This shift offered a means to diverge his thinking and critically examine his strategy problem in a way that is not possible when locked into a rational mindset. "Reinvigorating, energizing, and enlightening. That pretty well sums up what it was like!" revealed Arjun to a crowded room at their annual shareholders meeting. While he may not be entered in the annals of art history with the likes of Dégas or Picasso, he ultimately was able to sketch the elements of a complex strategic problem and satisfy the concerned investors, as well as keep his job.

Just because someone has run the numbers does not mean that we have to believe his conclusion. Numbers are as vulnerable to interpretation as is our intuition based on experience. Once we know what a metric is, we can usually find a way to play with or around it—to show that we are doing well according to the official measuring stick, even though we are not making progress toward the larger objectives.

Regrettably, traditional strategy development approaches tend to focus almost exclusively on the cognitive cluster comprised of linear, logical, rational, and convergent thinking—useful for analytical thinking—at the expense of application, awareness, and appreciation of the cognitive domain consisting of divergent thinking, critical reflective processes, intuition, tacit knowledge, a-rational thinking, and affect. Aside from the attention given to emotional and social intelligence,[1] the relevance of the affective, a-rational domain to strategic thinking remains largely ignored, diminished, or discredited.

Do we wonder, then, that we are struggling to develop strategic thinkers? The cognitive cluster required for strategic thinking (see Chapter 4) takes a considerable amount of time, tolerance for ambiguity, heightened sensitivity, and a strong desire and discipline to develop. Furthermore, in practice, the traits of this cognitive cluster are largely invisible and occur informally. As we attempt to combine intuition and analysis, we must also accept a degree of ambivalence, which is part of the complex reality of strategy.

Regardless of its limitations, honing our intuition is critical as we learn to think strategically; therefore, we need to develop our intuition into a reliable instrument. There is no magic formula or shortcut which improves such judgment. We can only develop our intuition for making decisions by prioritizing its development. This means continually challenging ourselves to make tough judgments, honestly appraising those decisions in order to learn from the consequences, actively building up an experience base, and learning to balance and blend intuition with analysis.

Successful strategists and those responsible for developing a cadre of strategic thinkers include intuition in their learning approach because it is precisely the reason why others trust their opinions and decisions. These strategists are known to be right on the mark—the ones who spot the early signs of problems and recognize opportunities without having to gather all the relevant data and perform all the required analysis—they just "know." Through years of experience, they have developed and translated that experience into a level of confidence necessary to make important judgments. If key strategists understand where their intuition originates, if they can discern when their intuition may be misleading, and if they can convince others to take their intuition seriously, then they are able to justify their authority.

Note

1. Goleman, *Working With Emotional Intelligence*.

VII

Summary and Questions

Executives often rely too heavily upon either data analysis or intuition to the detriment of their strategic thinking. While data analysis is an important tool to understand the strategic environment, an over-reliance can lead to same-frame thinking in the strategic thinking process. It is important to balance rational analysis with intuition when making strategic decisions. One cannot replace the other, as they are complementary.

Intuition is necessary to ensure that our data analysis makes sense. However, it is equally important to use analysis to ensure that our intuition is correct. Effective and consistently accurate strategic thinking is accomplished through deliberate application of rational analysis and intuition, in tandem.

Furthermore, critical reflection can also assist us to incorporate intuition and data analysis into the strategy decision. It can also support us in applying prior knowledge to new contexts when determining the validity of our intuition. Successful strategists use intuition to help identify patterns, trends, and problems early. They understand the origins of their intuitive thoughts and know when their intuition might be flawed, and they compensate by alternating their intuition with analysis.

1. Think of an instance when you were involved in a strategic decision where the data and intuition were not in agreement. How did you make the decision? What role did the data play in the decision? What role did intuition play in the decision? How could rebalancing the use of data and intuition have changed the decision and the outcome?
2. How does having a flawed framework affect intuition? How can you identify a flawed frame and change the frame in order to effectively use intuition in decision making?
3. Are you aware of any of your own flawed frameworks? How could you know? What could be the origins of your flawed intuitive thoughts?
4. Why is it important to identify the risks you could incur by ignoring or discrediting intuition in your strategic decision making?

WHAT ROLE DOES CULTURE PLAY?

You'd Be Surprised: Culture as a Factor for Learning to Think Strategically

"What kind of bird are you, if you can't fly?" chirped the bird.
"What kind of bird are you, if you can't swim?" retorted the duck.

From Peter and the Wolf *by Sergey Prokofiev (1891–1953), Russian composer*

22

The Role of Culture in
Strategic Thinking

Why address strategic thinking in relation to socio-national culture? The role of culture in strategic thinking is a topic that is often either at the forefront of the minds of those responsible for the strategic success of companies and other organizations, or buried deep in oblivion. Globalization has forced us to examine the role of culture with regard to strategic thinking. As Part VIII will point out, we need to understand the learning process involved in strategic thinking in order to position constructively the role that culture plays in strategic thinking.

This part consists of two chapters. Chapter 22 looks at the role of culture in relation to strategic thinking, typical problems encountered, and the cultural dimension of hierarchy as it impacts upon frame formulation. Chapter 23 discusses the challenge of introducing strategic thinking across cultures. Chapter 23 also includes a section on shattering and reframing across cultures and common factors to consider when dealing with other cultures in developing strategic thinking.

Executives, managers, professionals, entrepreneurs, customers, suppliers, shareholders, governments, and competitors of various cultural backgrounds in vastly different locales are all connected in an intricate global web. Individually and collectively, these players are influential in some aspect of strategy: policy reform, business development, leadership development, talent management, relocation assignments, executive searches, change management, and so on. Expatriates, repatriates, and nationals are all involved in developing the internal capacity to create and re-create innovative, sustainable, and adaptable strategy.

As conveyed in previous chapters, successful strategic thinking does not occur in a vacuum. Such thinking can occur only when those involved are able to identify and challenge underlying assumptions, to make frames explicitly, and to shatter and reframe their own basic beliefs and those of the organization. Supporting the frame-changing process means endorsing the use of critical reflective processes (critical inquiry, critical reflection, and critical dialogue) to constructively challenge anyone involved in the strategy process. Also, successful strategic thinking means that everyone is invited to question the business, political, social, and economic environments and to test the company's capabilities on a continuous basis and without retribution.

In my work with corporate strategists, government policy reformers, and innovative entrepreneurs around the world, I am constantly bombarded with one question: "Why can't I find any good strategic thinkers here?" In fact, this question is often the springboard to many of my client relationships. In working with strategic thinking issues all across the globe, I have found leaders in every country, every industry sector, and within private and public organizations who drive at the second, more compelling part of the question: "What can I do to make 'these people' think strategically?" What many clients want to hear, of course, is a simple diagnosis indicating that their strategic thinking problem is due to "cultural differences," followed by some neatly packaged three-step solution, and accompanied by a timeline. They are eager to receive standard course proposals and correlated metrics tables. (These dreamers are in for quite a surprise!)

Unfortunately, the remedy is not quite that simple or clear. Typically, I find that senior executives and corporate boards use a strategic planning framework as a basis for complaints about the absence of strategic thinkers, but this is like saying that you want to go fishing so you head to the desert. This strategic planning framework is symptomatic of the executives' lack of, or misunderstanding of, the cognitive processes underlying strategic thinking and strategic planning. These executives fail to differentiate between strategic thinking and strategic planning, and are unaware of the role that culture plays.

Most often, I find that clients tend to lack a process or criteria by which to identify and develop strategic thinkers, because they lack knowledge about the informal, iterative learning process or have no awareness of the attributes needed to proceed. Furthermore, rarely do these executives have foundational information about the cultures with which they are working. Once these missing pieces are made clear, culture becomes just another variable to identify and to acknowledge in facilitating learning to think strategically.

Culture's Impact on Pattern Recognition

What role does socio-national culture play in learning to think strategically? Culture plays a big role, as it shapes our frames and, in turn, teaches us what to pay attention to. Culture informs the patterns we come to recognize, and rewards us for learning them. Specific patterns are inherently cultural, since they teach us what to fear, where to attach values, and which values to assign to our frames.

Culture per se is not a differentiating factor in the learning process of strategic thinking. Culture is but one factor that influences our experience. The strategic thinking process is identical, regardless of culture, because strategic thinking is driven by the informal human learning process. The informal learning process required for strategic thinking exists at a level that supersedes culture—socio-national culture, organizational culture, or functional culture. But if one is unaware of the informal learning process that underlies strategic thinking, one might mistakenly and easily blame culture as the culprit for a shortage of strategic thinkers across the globe.

Culture per se is not a differentiating factor in the learning process of strategic thinking. Culture is but one factor that influences our experience. The strategic thinking process is identical, regardless of culture, because strategic thinking is driven by the informal human learning process.

Management and public policy researcher Khalid Alyahya's studies on Middle Eastern senior managers support the notion that, at some point, national culture becomes irrelevant to thinking and learning. His extensive research on management cultures in the Middle East concurs with other findings which claim that, to a certain extent,

> *people act and ... organizations operate the same way regardless of where they are located, ... regardless of the culture or historic experience of a society. Democratic practices such as empowerment, decentralization, and participation that prove to be successful and effective in one setting are transferable to other national settings.*[1]

What is most important for global organizations is for their managers and executives to model and establish an expectation for critical reflection and to reframe experience. This reflective capacity enables us to learn from our experiences, and fosters learning for strategic thinking.

Too often, I find that culture is a convenient veil with which to cover our frustrations and unanswered questions about the strategic thinking process—particularly when we are working with leaders from outside our primary culture. Things are further complicated by the fact that strategic thinking is an over-used and under-defined term, as previously mentioned. Furthermore, the informal learning process of strategic thinking is generally not well understood, so we attribute the whole messiness to culture and may attempt to absolve ourselves of responsibility for development.

All cultures have customs and deeply embedded values that help us to determine what we know, how we know it, and the degree to which it is safe for us to use challenge, dialogue, and critical reflection in our organizational contexts.

Although culture per se is not a primary factor in learning to think strategically (the learning process is), culture has a visible impact on the patterns that we learn to recognize and the frames we use to outline and assess strategic data, information, and decisions. For example, culture determines the way we assess creditworthiness for mergers, it influences why we predict political stability for investment, it affects how we judge a provincial governor's or deputy minister's trustworthiness for a joint venture, and it determines how we plan our market-entry strategy.

All cultures have customs and deeply embedded values that help us to determine what we know, how we know it, and the degree to which it is safe for us to use challenge, critical dialogue, and critical reflection in our organizational contexts.

Typical *Faux Pas*

What kinds of cultural things typically go wrong in global strategy-making meetings? Very often, I find that we think we know more than we actually do about foreign markets, about the capabilities of our local businesses with regard to implementation, and about local agendas and priorities. Furthermore, we have inconsistent degrees of comprehension about the way that global operations are positioned relative to the organization's core strengths. One strategic learning imperative is to take the time to critically reflect and critically dialogue with others to determine the limits of what we know and what others know at the start of the strategy-making process (see Table 18.1).

Regardless of geographic location, rarely do we find a company which has a consistent understanding or expectation of a strategic thinking process. Mind you, having this consistent understanding is distinctly different from having an official, formal, strategy-making routine in place. The kind of instrumental, mechanical, strategic planning process that is well known basically consists of people showing up at a certain time and place with requested information and analysis and conducting a surf-level discussion within existing corporate frames of reference. This discussion tends to be logistically rich and learning poor.

Very often, when we are making strategy outside our primary culture, critical information is missed or misinterpreted because it is not available through the usual market-research processes. Essential frames may be omitted from strategy discussions because the relevance of the perspectives is not visible in the same way as it is back home. Furthermore, key contributors are frequently overlooked, due to language or geography, time zones, and technology issues; we tend to convince ourselves that getting their partial insight or fragmented information is good enough.

Cross-Cultural Dimensions that Impact upon Frame Formulation

We carry our existing frames with us across continents and time zones without realizing that they may be juxtaposed on a pile of other existing frames that are very different from our own. While this lack of realization can be destructive to strategic thinking if left uncovered and unchallenged, it can become a constructive and competitive source of innovation if the frames are identified, tested, shattered, and reframed. In order for this shattering and reframing to happen, we must engage in the deeper, dive domain of learning to examine the role that culture may play in our attitudes and beliefs, particularly with regard to the notion of challenging others and being challenged ourselves.

Cross-cultural theorist Geert Hofstede, in his 1980 seminal work *Culture's Consequences*,[2] identified five dimensions that exist in every culture, to varying degrees. These dimensions influence the frames of reference that we develop over time. While Hofstede's studies have been criticized in a number of ways, his cultural dimensions provide us with a convenient way of classifying the differences among cultures and have continued to be a subject of revision and debate for subsequent cross-cultural theorists.

Alfons Trompenaars and Charles Hampden-Turner modified these dimensions in their 1993 book, *The Seven Cultures of Capitalism*, to include seven dimensions: universalism vs. particularism, analyzing vs. integrating, individualism vs. communitarianism, inner-directed vs. outer-directed orientation, time as sequence vs. time as synchronization, achieved status vs. ascribed status, and equality vs. hierarchy.[3] Many excellent sources are available on cross-cultural dimensions, and an understanding of the dimensions can serve as a basis for inquiry, to challenge the assumptions underlying strategic decisions.

Regardless of the specific terminology, all of these cultural dimensions play a role in shaping our frames of reference. When working with clients around the world, I am frequently asked to pare down the cultural dimensions to the single, most influential aspect related to learning to think strategically. Doing this is, of course, impossible. The complex combination of cultural dimensions and individual personal traits which impact upon our capacity must be accepted *en masse* when learning to think strategically.

Nevertheless, for the purpose of demonstrating the impact of the combination of cultural dimensions on strategic thinking, I reluctantly and cautiously will stick my neck out and mention *hierarchy* as but one manifestation of the combined dimensions—and only to exemplify the impact that culture has on learning to think strategically. Hierarchy leaves its sticky fingerprints on every aspect of strategy making, and I find, because of its pervasive influence, that hierarchy is important to address early on when working with executives. Hierarchy is evident in a multitude of ways, which makes it a convenient starting point for challenging beliefs and igniting critical dialogue about content, process, and premise assumptions.

Hierarchy as a Factor to Be Reckoned With

How a culture perceives hierarchy within a business or government environment can determine the experience that leaders typically have with challenging information and expressing divergent opinions. From our respective cultures, we learn specific things about hierarchy. For example: Who can we question? Under what circumstances? What is a "question" as opposed to a "threat" or an "insult?" How do we structure a question? What is the right way to respond to questions? Why? When do we attempt to save face or to display status through questions and responses?

In some cultures, for example, challenging a colleague, a superior, or a visitor is considered disrespectful because this challenge is interpreted as an attack, an interrogation, or humiliation; such a challenger is labeled as disloyal or untrustworthy. This label can make it difficult to incorporate a rigorous routine of critical inquiry necessary for learning to think strategically. Developing the trust required for making and implementing critical strategic decisions may be difficult as well.

Perhaps most importantly, the quality of strategy can be substantially weakened if the deeper, dive domain of learning is not embraced and practiced by everyone involved with strategic issues in every geographic location.

In some cultures, to remain within the surf domain of learning is considered to be polite business and good interpersonal interaction because nobody dares to be challenged, except in accordance with hierarchical rules—this protects against a loss of face. In these cultures, using critical dialogue and inquiry openly for testing may be more difficult. At the same time, a particular individual within that culture may have strong critical reflective capacity, but public and open challenge and testing may be culturally difficult to do. The dilemma can become one of relative consequence.

SCENARIO

Recently, Junichiro had been promoted to be the Asia president of a German international investment bank. A big part of the position was obviously strategy, and the stakes were high. He had a stellar strategic planning and execution track record. In fact, this record is why he was promoted into the position. But his rope began to fray when his strategic thinking ability was put to the test. His role within the bank had changed overnight from being a brilliant strategic planner to becoming a successful strategic thinker. Without the capacity to create and re-create strategy, there would be no strategy to implement.

He was caught between a rock and a hard place. He knew that within Japanese business society he would quickly lose the respect of the very people who promoted him, especially if he questioned them overtly or publicly. At the same time, his own neck and the bottom line of the bank depended on him to routinely scrutinize every particle of data and analysis. He realized that he needed to think differently in order to do this. Panicked, he sought help.

During our initial meetings, Junichiro mentioned that he had never learned to "think"; what he had learned was to be very adept at rapid pattern recognition and correcting imprecisions. In fact, his adeptness is how he had made a name for himself, because in minutes he could automatically sift through mounds of data and accurately solve complex problems. He quickly discovered that this was not enough for strategic thinking.

In order for Junichiro to commit to taking the risk of learning the critical reflective processes that he understood were essential for learning to think strategically, he had to resolve the polite, on-the-surface Japanese cultural requirement that clashed with the particular practices required in critical reflection. This first step was a confidence builder. He identified several key strategic thinking strengths he already possessed (honed intuition, experience of using reflection in non-work contexts, access to positive role models, and a fierce desire to win). Also, he distinguished strategic thinking from strategic planning in his executive and management vocabulary. And, as the new company president, he set an expectation within the corporate culture of practicing critical inquiry—challenging, testing, and refining strategic ideas.

Furthermore, Junichiro retained his personal and cultural preference for dealing with people one-on-one, and he subtly modified his indirect style so that he did not feel as though he was "attacking" his Asian colleagues. This modification was important for him to remain authentic. Junichiro took great care to preface his critical inquiry with an explanation of the mutual and collective benefits of such a process. He invited his Asian colleagues to reciprocate, and he demonstrated appropriate language of questions—making a game of the process. Also, he took care to thank each person before and after each critical-dialogue encounter, expressing gratitude for their support of the bank's long-term strategic capacity. Once Junichiro had drawn up this list of conditions that he felt were necessary culturally, he was satisfied that he could commit himself to the learning process. The very process of drawing up the list engaged him in identifying and testing his own assumptions and beliefs about the learning process involved in strategic thinking.

Most importantly, remember that just because we "don't," doesn't mean that we "can't" learn to recognize different patterns and develop different frames of reference. I have worked with exceedingly capable strategic thinkers in Saudi Arabia, Egypt, and Russia—all strong hierarchical cultures with clearly established cultural norms for questioning. Pattern recognition and shattering is learnable. Culture is not an excuse to hide behind. Certainly, culture has a strong influence on the patterns that we learn to recognize and the frames we learn to use, but our human capacity to critically reflect is limitless. Therefore, we can learn to shatter and reframe through critical reflective processes, if we seek to and commit.

Regarding the influence of hierarchy: some cultures consider disregarding hierarchy to be disrespectful and disloyal, particularly when junior executives or those from a certain group (e.g., women, newcomers, outsiders, functional groups, nationalities) express alternatives or imagine beyond their prescribed status in society or outside the hierarchical bounds of a specific team or job description.

Quite commonly, I find that executives from these cultures (organizational cultures as well as socio-national cultures) lack an ability to notice pattern variations because they are short of the experience base. Their culture taught them to follow a tightly defined, prescriptive approach to pattern identification—and this approach was so limited that imagining new ways of seeing things does not even register, since they have no experience doing so. Their forte is in paying attention to and quickly noticing a set of "correct" or "incorrect" patterns in a given circumstance. While this focus has advantages, it is a habit of mind that needs to be tested in order to learn to think strategically.

After several months of working on strategic thinking with a newly promoted and ambitious Chinese global head of manufacturing for a multinational paper company, this executive described the difference that he noticed in his own decision making after concentrating on critical reflective processes:

It used to be impossible for me to make decisions that were not given to me because I didn't even know what "think more strategically" meant. But there is a lot of pressure on me in my new job. I couldn't "see" anything except [for] what had been pointed out to me. I didn't know how to notice things. I was afraid to look for other things. The only things I "saw" were the things I was permitted to look at; everything else was blacked out in my mind.

In my case, it was always important to notice what other people expect you to see—the aim in my culture is to avoid seeing anything that you are not supposed to see. It was like everything else was in the dark, and, naturally, I was afraid of the dark. I was supposed to be afraid of the dark. [Anything that is] new or different hides in the dark [for protection]—and now, that is what you are telling me and helping me to practice! I feel a little bit afraid, but I am amazed already at what I can see now that I am looking. I think I only needed permission and a guide. It is only now that I realize all the other things that are happening at the same time. I am already making better and bigger decisions and it's surprising to me, but I have a wonderful feeling of freedom and control in this way of thinking.

Notes

1. Alyahya and Vengroff, "Human Capital Utilization, Empowerment, and Organizational Effectiveness in the Middle East: A Comparative Perspective," 6.
2. Hofstede, *Culture's Consequences.*
3. Trompenaars and Hampden-Turner, *The Seven Cultures of Capitalism.*

23

The Challenge of Introducing Strategic Thinking Across Cultures

Having lived and worked abroad for more than two decades myself, I feel very strongly about the strategic need to transcend culture and to refocus as quickly as possible on the informal, iterative learning process of strategic thinking. I do not mean ignoring culture, but that we must acknowledge and appreciate culture within the larger learning context. The intent of strategic development is to increase the capacity for learning to think strategically, and culture is just one, albeit significant, piece.

Yet the influence of culture on shaping collective and individual frames can have an impact on nearly every aspect of strategic decision making. Therefore, we must understand some common frames which need to be shattered and re-created across cultures. One of the more common strategic challenges is information gathering. Credible, valid, verifiable, relevant, and timely information is often hard to come by, and yet it is integral to strategic decision making. Cross-cultural expert Ernest Gundling notes that, while there may be numerous reasons why information is not shared readily,

> *In general, concerns about sharing information directly are more pronounced in hierarchical, group-oriented cultures where enduring personal relationships are a key personal asset. To place in jeopardy your relationship with a senior member of the hierarchy or a key network member could have dire long-term consequences.*[1]

> *In many countries, who gives information is given greater significance than what the information is.*

Business information that is standard in some countries, such as annual reports, auditing and accounting reports and data, marketing data, and economic reports, may not be available or even exist in others—for a variety of reasons. Furthermore, the quality and the objectivity of available information can be problematic. In many countries, who gives information is given greater significance than what the information is. No one dares to question either the data or the individual who provided it because to do so would threaten the hierarchy that sustains the culture. In these cases, there is no line that distinguishes fact from fiction.

The political environment can also influence information gathering and complicate strategic decision making. When working in a country or with people from countries with a history of politically oppressive regimes, the legacy of fear and suspicion lives on long after the political landscape has changed. The ghosts of experience continue to haunt even the most bold and progressive people. Providing relevant and truthful information to anyone outside a tight circle of family and a few friends is considered foolish and risky. Furthermore, the shadow of a thriving Mafia or remnants of a former regime can guide the information flow of local and international businesses, and leaders are likely to be guarded and hesitant about sharing information about anything—revenues, plans, or client relations—for fear of how it might be used against them.

As a means of introducing a strategic thinking imperative into a non-Western or culturally diverse environment, it is helpful to position strategic thinking as a directive, by having an authority figure from headquarters or from a well-respected government ministry officially sanction the critical reflective processes as being an integral part of making strategy or policy reform competitive. Presented as a corporate culture expectation, the pronouncement can and should be followed by crucial modeling among senior leaders and guided coaching that is respectful of individual practice. This approach bows to the dimension of hierarchy and legitimizes the unfamiliar new practice. It also gives permission to executives and managers to commit to practicing such things as critical inquiry and testing.

In other words, with this kind of positioning, the expectation of using a critical reflective process and a divergent process for the development of strategic thinking is explicitly stated as an imperative or directive from the top. This establishes parameters that place the corporate culture above any socio-national culture for eight hours of each day within a specific context. This way, the emphasis is not on behavioral change but, rather, on a fundamental process of embedding change that includes behavioral practices which undoubtedly counter existing belief systems on many levels. This practice will be disruptive, but dealing with disruption is part of adaptive and innovative thinking, which is essential to competitive strategic capacity.

Shattering and Reframing Across Cultures

As we have discussed, culture can be influential on our ability to shatter and reframe. Cultural values tend to direct our focus; culture highlights the patterns we are "supposed to see." And culture creates a context in which we practice and experience the right and wrong ways of identifying, interpreting, and evaluating these patterns. Culture is how we learn our first frames of good and bad. We learn to look at a situation in a particular way and make decisions according to prescribed frames. Through culture, we also learn the degree of value given to both analysis and intuition.

Shattering frames requires that we are able to challenge and test ourselves, others, and the habits of mind, beliefs, and underlying assumptions that support the traditions of the organization. Therefore, we must be willing to risk comfort and familiarity in favor of the uncomfortable and uncertain. We need to be able to live with all the what-ifs that will haunt us as a result of shattering: What if my questions are laughed at? What if my data/information/hunch contradicts the commonly accepted way? What if I don't know the answer to my own question? What if I posit a question or topic that is a "forbidden frame"?

Time and again, clients from around the world confide and comment that it is actually very liberating and freeing to use the deeper, dive domain of learning, rigorous and risky as it may be, because they do not have to give up their authentic selves. Instead, they are able to choose, discard, borrow, and adapt at will. In my experience, this tedious and emotionally strenuous process of shattering cannot be taught in a traditional manner, but it can be modeled and coached. I have found that when clients engage in shattering, the strategic thinking process is identical, regardless of culture, because the strategic thinking process is driven by an informal and iterative learning process.

Sometimes, clients are anxious about the strategic thinking learning process, fearful that they might find themselves reclining on a couch, hanging from tree limbs, or positioned on a yoga mat. This learning is an intensive, exhaustive, and formidable process, but one that is generally lacking in melodrama. Knowledge about the three-stage process of informal learning (preparation, experience, and reevaluation) discussed in Part III and the five attributes (imagination, broad perspective, juggle, no control over, and desire to win) presented in Part IX is essential for executives in any culture to understand if they are to think strategically.

> *Personal and organizational determination and*
> *commitment levels are much more important for*
> *learning to think strategically than any one*
> *particular cultural frame.*

Once the informal learning process and the five attributes are understood and attended to, culture sort of evaporates from the strategic thinking process. The validity of data is greatly enhanced, integrity issues are made apparent, and better strategy making and implementation are a result. Learning to think strategically is well worth the investment if a company or government truly wants to grow a global pipeline of strategic thinkers. The road can be quite long and full of bumps, but making this journey is certainly worth it. Personal and organizational determination and commitment levels are much more important for learning to think strategically than any one particular cultural frame.

Anyone Can Learn to Think Strategically

Although it is a surprisingly pervasive belief in corporate corner offices, and in executive development circles, believing that someone may be unable to think strategically just because she or he comes from a certain culture is a myth. Once again, I emphasize that culture is simply one factor that influences our experience. There is a beauty to experience—it can be broadened, deepened, acquired, and transferred over the course of our entire life.

SCENARIO

Abo was a fiercely determined, strategically successful African tribal leader who was also illiterate, due to sustained and dire economic, political, and social circumstances. His country had the good fortune of his being appointed to a government ministerial post as part of a nation-building process that was being instituted. I had the great pleasure of being invited to work on strategy development with the various government ministers and was told it would probably be easier for me if I just politely ignored Abo, because it would be impossible for him to fathom strategic thinking, but I found his contributions to be original, his questions to be insightful, and his wit to be irresistible—he was an experienced (and perhaps a natural) strategist.

In spite of my modest expectations, this man tested my beliefs about learning strategic thinking—heretofore, illiteracy had not been part of my strategic development experience. Abo, it turned out, was very adept at using the informal learning process in the same way as literate corporate executives. He methodically gathered and analyzed massive amounts of information from diverse sources, humbly acknowledging that much of it was incomplete and inaccurate. He was not at all hesitant to ask focused questions that exposed underlying complexity and contradictions.

It quickly became apparent that he had a thinking habit that was admirable and inspiring to other government ministers. He asked critical questions to test the motives and beliefs of himself and anybody else in attendance. His probes were insightful and provocative, and they tested for implications and consequences that were broadly based. He dutifully tested and retested his own and others' viewpoints, and he claimed that his feisty nature was a result of being doubtful, curious, and eternally hopeful—not dissimilar to those descriptors put forth by the ancient Greeks that included dealing with seeming polarities. This combination compelled him "to fight for what I know in my heart is right." He was an incredible problem solver with an ability to make connections between seemingly unrelated matters in the hope of sowing the seeds of new possibilities.

Abo was a highly experienced strategic thinker who simply didn't read or write. He was thinking at very deep levels and had extraordinary critical reflection capability. When he spoke, his words were artful and profound, and he had developed a talent for transferring learning across various contexts. With ease and pleasure he used his learning experiences in the wartime and peacetime villages and mountains to draw analogies and metaphors for the new government challenges—his storytelling was riveting. It was as if he had years of experience in dealing with members of the new parliament and international agencies, because his intuition was honed in his prior experiences. He was very wise in the ways of politics, such that none of these strategic policy problems was new to him; only the context had changed.

In addition to further developing his strategic thinking strengths, he chose to focus development on the flip side of the strategy-making coin—building his linear, logical cognitive abilities such as sequencing information and understanding the logic of cause and effect—necessary skills for strategic planning. He also jumped at the chance to enroll in a literacy program to make up for lost time.

Admittedly, this is an extreme example, but only because I point it out as exceptional. Cases similar to this (e.g., illiteracy, dyslexia, and speech, hearing, and physical disabilities) abound in organizations and in communities around the globe. My point is twofold. The first point is that we can all learn to further develop the critical reflective processes that are essential to strategic thinking. The second point is that we need to be aware that our own cultural frames can limit our ability to see strategic thinking talent, because talent may not fit the pattern of what we believe it should look like. Based on her study of entrepreneurs and strategic thinking, Croatian professor Lara Jelenc concludes that "There are many myths and interpretations of its meaning ... largely due to the problem of articulating the cognitive character of strategic thinking."[2]

Understanding the five attributes (see Part IX) and the informal learning process (see Parts II and III) inherent to strategic thinking is critical if we aspire to develop others and ourselves. Simply bringing together a group of highly intelligent or well-educated people is insufficient for strategic thinking to occur. Strategic thinking requires a mutual understanding among people about the strategic intent and an awareness of the process involved to achieve that intent. This learning process is dependent on a high capacity for critical reflection, trusted intuition, and meaningful critical dialogue, all balanced with meticulous analytical skills among the people involved. Strategic capacity building requires that this multifaceted process become embedded in the organization's culture.

The following seven suggestions are useful for introducing strategic thinking across socio-national culture.

1. *Clarify intent.* Is the aim to develop strategic thinking or strategic planning? We need both, and the cognitive clusters need to be complementary functions in order to achieve a winning strategy. Learning is easier if a clear focus is articulated.
2. *Pick and choose broadly and encourage self-selection.* Not everybody in an organization needs to be a strategic thinker. While reflective processes can be developed to varying degrees, we also need strategic planners—especially if an excellent strategy has a prayer of being successfully implemented. Offer information about developing strategic thinking to everyone with strategic responsibility, but allow people to self-select initially, in order to create role models and momentum.
3. *Give permission to use a deeper, dive level of learning,* which includes the critical reflective processes of inquiry, challenge, reflection, and testing.
4. *Provide an abundance of information about the strategic thinking learning process* up front. This creates a foundation for trusting the process and encourages self-directed learning.

5. *Use an informal development process*, such as coaching or mentoring, and be patient with the timeframe that may be needed. Don't pressure people to see results—remember, this is an informal learning process. Focus instead on including and practicing critical inquiry in daily business tasks and increasing the critical dialogue on day-to-day issues. Much of the learning process may be invisible, and much of the early learning may be incidental (i.e., trusting senior leadership, trusting the critical reflective process, trusting changed relationships, and so on).

6. *Don't assume.* Clarify what you know and what others know and what you do not know and what others do not know.

7. *Avoid using "culture" as an excuse* for not developing strategic thinkers in every area of the world. The informal learning process and attributes required are of a human, not cultural, nature.

In summary, we need to understand what influences the way we frame our experiences as well as the assumptions and beliefs that we hold about strategy issues. We must understand the culture into which the learning framework fits. Learning to shatter and reframe beliefs that are culturally influenced must occur in order to learn to think strategically. Admittedly, this shattering and reframing can be more or less challenging from one culture to the next, but it is part of human adaptation and thought innovation. It can be learned, and it is inclusive of all cultures.

Notes

1. Gundling, *Working GlobeSmart.*
2. Jelenc, "The Impact of Strategic Management Schools and Strategic Thinking on the Performance of Croatian Entrepreneurial Practice," 28.

Summary and Questions

Although socio-national culture structures do indeed influence our habits, mindsets, pattern recognition, and frames of reference, they are not the primary factors in learning to think strategically. The capacity to think strategically is driven by the informal human learning process and it is identical across countries and cultures. If, however, we are unaware of the informal processes that exist at a level that supersedes culture and underlies strategic thinking, culture can easily become the culprit for a perceived absence of strategic thinkers.

Critical reflection, critical inquiry, and critical dialogue are imperative to determine the limits of what we know at the start of the strategic thinking process when developing a global strategy. Too often, in cross-cultural strategy settings, information is missed, frames are omitted and ignored, attributions are made, and key mindsets are overlooked.

The pronounced hierarchy that is inherent in some cultures can stifle strategic thinking and must be acknowledged to effectively implement strategic thinking practices. In many cases it is helpful for an organization's senior leaders to promote the idea of strategic thinking and critical reflective processes in order to generate acceptance of strategic thinking practices within their organization.

To introduce strategic thinking across different cultures, it is helpful to clarify intent, choose contributors to the strategic thinking process who represent broad backgrounds, encourage people to self-select into strategic thinking sessions, and to give permission and support to employees at all levels and within all functions to ask critical questions. It can also be beneficial to widely disseminate information about strategic thinking and to utilize an informal development process.

Any organization that is committed to developing a strategic thinking process can do so, regardless of the socio-national culture. Strategic thinking requires more than a roomful of the most intelligent people; it requires people who understand the intent and the process of strategic thinking within the broader strategic framework. Strategic thinkers exist around the world.

1. Why is an understanding of the socio-national culture important to developing strategic thinking?
2. How might the process of asking deep, dive-level questions that expose and challenge fundamental assumptions disrupt an organizational or socio-national culture? What are the implications of a disruption?
3. What suggestions could you offer to constructively introduce the critical reflective processes required of strategic thinking within a socio-national culture that values hierarchy? That values a collective orientation?
4. What are some of the cross-cultural challenges you might anticipate when introducing strategic thinking within your organization? What are some of the risks involved? What could be some of the benefits to the business? What can you do to leverage the impact on learning strategic thinking?

IS ANYBODY BORN WITH
THIS KNOW-HOW?

The Myth of the Chosen Few:
Five Critical Attributes for
Learning to Think Strategically

A man, though wise, should never be ashamed of learning more,
and must unbend his mind.

From Antigone by Sophocles (442–42 B.C.), Greek philosopher

24

The Five Critical Attributes

Luckily, and in spite of all the implied messages that are dispersed about strategic think-ing as a reserve of the chosen few, strategic thinking is indeed learnable. Is it teachable? Perhaps not directly—but it is learnable.

The temptation to accept a myth about who can learn to think strategically is under-standable in a strategy environment that is overloaded with complexities, contradictions, and confusion. A myth, after all, controls the possibility of conflicting evidence—myths help us to make meaning of conflict and ambivalence.

With regard to strategic thinking, there are four reasons that propagate the myth of the *chosen few*—those who do think strategically. First, over-use of the term *strategy*. Without a clear definition of strategic thinking or a distinction between strategic plan-ning and strategic thinking, we easily create, and get caught in, confusion.

Second, strategy is generally talked about as something we get to make when we become (more) important. Not being a strategic thinker is a well-known, sacrosanct excuse used to prevent people from promotion. So surely, those who make strategy must be among the chosen few.

Third, we recall the capstone strategy courses in most business school curricula and the tip of the triangle in corporate strategy structure. Both imply elitism and perpetuate illusions of grandeur. Criteria and definitions remain implicit and mostly vague, so we are left with the impression that whatever is required of strategists, we lack; which serves to reinforce the myth of the chosen few. In truth, most of what occurs in the strategy meetings of these elite pockets of organizational power is not about strategic thinking—it is about strategic planning. So it's a bottle that hasn't been uncorked, a party that hasn't happened!

The fourth myth is that successful strategy is deceptively simple. It either works or it doesn't. This myth deludes us into believing that making strategy is about the luck or magic of those clever chosen few. However, the underlying thinking process is mostly invisible, informal, and not well understood.

To dispel these deeply held and widely believed myths is not easy. If, however, we understand the attributes that support the learning process involved in strategic thinking, we can begin to imagine ways to develop our capacity to learn to think strategically.

Part IX comprises three chapters. Chapter 24 discusses five attributes identified by seasoned and successful strategists as being critical to learning to think strategically:

- Having a vivid *imagination.*
- Keeping a broad perspective.
- Being able to *juggle*, or attend to competing, incomplete, and inaccurate information all at once.
- Dealing with things that you have *no control over.*
- Possessing an adamant and relentless *desire to win.*

Chapter 25 describes the interplay among the five attributes. And Chapter 26 discusses the notion of adaptation as a strategic expectation.

Irrespective of culture, industry, and age, leaders who are conceptual, divergent, nonlinear, and intuitive thinkers tend to have a natural inclination toward strategic thinking. By the same token, concrete, linear, analytical thinkers tend to have a natural edge in strategic planning. As with any highly complex and high-stakes endeavor, there are those who have a natural propensity for strategic thinking and those who may find it challenging. However, a challenge can be overcome, and a natural inclination is only a "booster shot."

Personal cognitive capabilities need to be respected, and differences should be perceived as complementary to and compatible with the strategic thinking process. In other words, concrete, linear, analytical thinkers can most certainly learn to become more conceptual, critically reflective, intuitive, and a-rational—though they may squeal from time to time. Conceptual, intuitive thinkers can, likewise, learn to become more linear, logical, and rational—though they, too, may squawk at times.

Everyone is capable of improving and informally developing the five essential attributes, to varying degrees. Because of this potential, organizational leaders must ensure that everyone within an organization has access to resources that support the learning process used for strategic thinking through:

- Information about the strategic thinking process.
- Opportunities to observe critical dialogue among senior leaders.
- Practice through participation in critical dialogue regarding strategic issues.
- Encouragement to engage in creative endeavors.
- Engagement in the critical reflective processes.

With such exposure and learning expectations, some natural strategic thinkers will emerge from the shadows, creating a first link to the pipeline. Skillful planners who wish to strengthen their strategic thinking capacity will also come forth, creating another link to the pipeline. From there, interest is generated and others tend to be attracted and drawn into the pipeline.

Having worked with both accomplished and aspiring strategists, I contend that genuine strategic thinking growth is largely about making sure that people understand what is required for learning to think strategically and allowing them to take the lead in their own learning. This learning process differs dramatically from one person to another.

Once strategists understand the learning process that underlies strategic thinking, they can and do come up with their own best ideas and approaches to support the development of the five attributes and critical reflective processes. When aspiring strategists lead the learning process, their commitment to wrestling with entrenched habits of mind, identifying patterns, and taking the risk to trust some informal learning increases considerably.

> *The aim is not to create a strategic thinking campaign but, rather, to create a pipeline of strategic thinkers across functions and at all levels within an organization, for competitive purposes.*

Importantly, not every person in an organization needs to be a strategic thinker. The aim is not to create a strategic thinking campaign but, rather, to create a pipeline of strategic thinkers across functions and at all levels within an organization, for competitive purposes. Rest assured that each of the following attributes can be developed to some level of mastery through discipline, determination, and practice.

The executives whom I interviewed for the research underlying this book were asked to describe what they paid attention to when making good strategy and what was the most essential requirement for thinking strategically. I expected that the executives' different backgrounds might generate different attributes that they considered essential to learning to think strategically. But I was surprised to find that the five attributes presented here were consistently and emphatically articulated: a vivid imagination, broad perspective, juggle, ability to deal with things that you have no control over, and an adamant desire to win.[1] These five attributes are not arranged in order of importance, since they are all equally essential to learning to think strategically.

Imagination

> *The real voyage of discovery consists not in making new landscapes, but in having new eyes.*
>
> *Marcel Proust (1871–1922), French novelist*

Activating our imagination is a critical factor for learning to think strategically. Dealing only with information or linear matter is insufficient. One of the Japanese financial executives in the study stated:

To start, I have an idea or a problem. As I become aware, I usually start to ask questions, and, of course, then my imagination begins to act. (leans forward, talks very quickly and gradually louder) And depending on what I do about it, I can get into trouble (laughter) or have some fun! You know, imagination is, I will say to you, a very, very important part of good strategy making. This is probably the best part, and it is necessary to enjoy it—to spend time with your imagination! (smiles, sits back) I think it's a big mistake not to include imagination [in making strategy]. It is something that happens inside—and can happen anywhere. You know, other people tend to ruin this part, so I do it privately and don't tell anybody it's happening! (laughter)

A Polish senior manufacturing executive also explained the importance of imagination in making strategy:

You must always try to imagine what else or how else things could be. Imagination! This is something nobody talks about in strategy sessions; maybe they think it's not so serious or sophisticated. Or maybe it is that you cannot buy it. (laughter) But it's the jewel nobody expects in the pauper's attic.

One American executive stated: "A really important part of making good strategy is being able to imagine things. You can't just work with facts and data. Your mind and imagination have to kick in if you're going to be any good."

The CFO of the technology company concurred with other successful strategists in the study: "Your imagination kicks into high gear, you read everything and talk with everybody—no stone goes unturned; you keep rolling them around."

Strategic thinking requires the cognitive duo of divergent and deep, dive thinking. Divergent thinking helps us break mental habits, see new patterns, and imagine possible connections. Deep, dive thinking involves having continuous and meaningful internal conversations that are critically reflective, and having external conversations that are insightful and challenging—conversations with others that focus on data, experience, and insight that stretch our frames and expose us to other possibilities of knowing.

Occasionally, some of my business clients lump creativity and intuition together. These aspiring strategists assume, mistakenly, that if they focus on developing creativity they will automatically improve their intuitive judgment. Unfortunately, the two do not always function well together. Creativity comes from combining different, seemingly unrelated, dimensions of experience. Creativity, by definition, is not tied to our past experiences, whereas intuition is a byproduct of patterns we have previously experienced. Therefore, an intuitive approach to creativity may rely on previous experience, but it also transcends that experience.[2]

Creativity comes from combining different, seemingly unrelated, dimensions of experience.

We know that successful strategists delight in using their imaginations when thinking strategically and that we all have the capability of transferring learning from one context to another.[3] This transfer of learning is an essential part of the imagination that is so vital to strategic thinking; we need to know it and trust it in order to leverage it for strategic advantage.

> *Ironically, at a time when innovative strategic*
> *thinking is among the most pressing concerns,*
> *business schools are upping the ante on analysis,*
> *with the serious intent of churning out people who*
> *will make innovative strategy.*

One of the most perplexing problems regarding strategic thinking is that we treat business and creativity as if they do not belong together. The reality is that they do. They only seem like odd partners because we assume their opposition and position them as such. Within this framework, we feel compelled to pick one or the other; but for businesses to thrive in a competitive global economy, by way of sustainable strategic capability, it is imperative to see them as complementary.

Ironically, at a time when innovative strategic thinking is among the most pressing concerns, business schools are upping the ante on analysis, with the serious intent of churning out people who will make innovative strategy. To return to an earlier metaphor, using only analysis to create innovative strategy is like hoping to fish while heading to the desert. If strategic innovation is what business schools wish to cultivate, then students would be much better off engaging in photography, painting, design, or, perhaps, guitar or piano lessons in order to "know" creativity. These outlets will contribute substantially to their long-term ability to create innovative strategy, simply because they will have first-hand creative experience on which to draw. Creation itself is a generative process. Creativity is about combining the original and the new. Unfortunately, the resultant tension that launches divergent thinking drives many aspiring strategic thinkers to halt the creative process and return to their prior habits of mind and same-frame thinking. This serves only to perpetuate and preserve the existing organizational frames and habits of mind. Our formal and conventional education, paradoxically, teaches us that when we feel this sort of tension the appropriate solution is to frame the situation as a "problem." We are often guided to select one approach or another. Unfortunately, by remaining in this traditional frame of problem solving and eliminating tension, we stop short of ever progressing in the creative thinking process. The tension that is provoked by the contradiction and opposing mindset is merely a signal inviting us to move through the situation by using the divergent "and" thinking process, rather than "either/or" thinking (see Chapter 28).

It is fascinating to me that although the core business of any successful company depends on its ability to re-create innovative strategy, the creative people are often left out of strategy meetings. They tend to be excluded from a process that is dependent on their greatest asset, creativity. Often, we assume that truly creative people do not know the "business" side. What, then, would happen if we excluded financial experts from the strategy meeting because we assumed they did not know the "creative" side of the business? Truly creative people often report that they feel sidelined or disconnected from the business. Furthermore, in many businesses there is an aversion to the very word "creative," and yet innovative thinking is not possible without it.

The strategic thinking process requires the inclusion of those individuals who hold very different perspectives and experiences to help challenge, test, and refine the underlying frames and assumptions that support current business strategy. Also, innovative strategic thinking requires an understanding that shattering and reframing are part of the divergent and creative process needed for strategic success.

In order to develop innovative strategy, the role of imagination must be acknowledged, celebrated, and integrated into the strategic thinking process. At a time when companies say they are desperate to have a more innovative strategy, their daily decisions often undermine them and prevent them from moving in that direction.

Broad Perspective

> *If the doors of perception were cleansed, everything would appear as it truly is, infinite.*
>
> *William Blake (1757–1827), English poet and artist*

The second attribute is the ability to see a situation from a broad perspective. This attribute has two parts: to literally "see" the strategic problem from a bird's-eye perspective and in panoramic view; and to draw on a vast and diverse range of frames and points of view. The executives who were interviewed maintained that the ability to see things from a broad perspective is crucial because this view allows them to see many things at the same time and to begin to imagine seeing things differently—both as they are and as they might be. When asked how he broadens his perspective, an American technology executive explained:

> *I just talk to people, trying to hear about their experiences … all kinds of people. That's what you realize about strategy and why I like making strategy. If you want to develop a big picture or see a big picture, you need to talk to people. I mean everywhere you go, in the market line, at the beach, at the movies—even at my parents' house, flying, you name it. Wherever there are people, somebody's willing to talk. If you listen to all of them and pull back, way back, you start to see things more broadly. You have to look at the picture differently though; when you look at the whole picture, you can figure out how strange things actually fit in—and your options explode.*

Interestingly, the executives often referred to developing a broad perspective and expanding critical dialogue in the same thought. They claimed that talking to a vast and diverse range of people on a regular basis helped them to develop their capacity for broad perspective. They also implied that critical dialogue led them to a broader perspective.

One of the Japanese executives exclaimed:

You must find a way to be in the highest balloon, because it gives you the very best view. You must talk to everybody all the time, not just a few people during one time of the year. You have to be a big or good listener in order to see the wide perspective.

A Chinese executive said: "I like to look broadly at things and imagine what they might look like in different arrangements—and this is really important, I believe, for making strategy." After reflecting on the question of the most essential requirement for thinking strategically, an American financial executive responded:

You know, another thing I guess I'd say is perspective. That's why you've got to get out and talk to people—it broadens your perspective. And that's what strategy, or good strategy, is all about. (pause) The best vantage point is from the highest point—that bird's-eye view.

The technology CFO from Hong Kong explained:

I like to see the big picture—that's why I like making strategy. Even though it is difficult to do, you must make it a habit to talk to many people, about every issue. This is how you get the broad perspective that you need to make successful strategy.

The CEO of a financial company commented that one of the most important reasons to broaden perspective is "to improve your way of thinking. So get to the highest point, to get the best broad view. That's the best way to improve thinking because you see things differently, and then you have more possibilities for thinking."

The most successful way these strategists broadened their perspective was by diversifying and expanding their interactions and contacts, because expanding them forced the executives to challenge their frameworks and to see and imagine other patterns. Interestingly, nearly all of the executives interviewed attributed their experience of living and working outside their home country to broadening their perspective in ways that nothing else could. While not everyone tasked with making strategy can or will choose to live and work in another country, going outside our comfort zone is enormously beneficial, and breaking with the familiar is a means to broadening our perspective.

Social scientists Susan Weil and Ian McGill maintain that "a person or organization which knows only their own village will not understand it. It is through dialogue across villages that we are enabled to consider what we intend and what we do from new perspectives."[4] This perspective suggests an experiential link to an expanded perspective.

These executives had an extensive capacity to shift between rational thinking and a-rational thinking, and an uncanny ability to see connections and create synergies among seemingly unrelated things. Making these connections is the essence of creativity and is necessary for taking a broad perspective.

Juggle

It isn't what we don't know that gives us trouble, it's what we know that ain't so.

Will Rogers (1879–1935), American actor and humorist

The third essential attribute is the ability to comprehend many things at once, specifically being able to deal with incomplete and inconsistent information, inaccurate data, and information in flux. This attribute is among the biggest challenges for global strategists.

> *The ability to see and to work with opposing relations and paradoxes is indeed an attribute identified by effective strategists as a requirement for strategic thinking—as opposed to planning, where the ability to eliminate paradoxes and ambivalence is required.*

A technology executive in the study responded to the question about what he pays attention to and what is essential for learning to think strategically by exclaiming:

> *Learn to juggle! [You're] bombarded with tons of information and data, especially about economics and political processes … and it changes all the time. [You] need to start thinking about how everything affects everything else. You juggle in your mind— that's how you're able to deal with so many unknowns and unpredictable things.*

Juggling is about far more than multi-tasking. In his seminal work that challenged the rational model of decision making, Nobel Prize winner Daniel Kahneman noted,

> *Like a juggler with several balls in the air, you cannot afford to slow down; the rate at which material decays in memory forces the pace, driving you to refresh and rehearse information before it is lost. Any task that requires you to keep several ideas in mind at the same time has the same hurried character. Unless you have the good fortune of a capacious working memory, you may be forced to work uncomfortably hard. The most effortful forms of slow thinking are those that require you to think fast.*[5]

This juggling attribute is in stark contrast to the prioritization and reductionist thinking required of strategic planning. Strategic thinking demands that we see and work with opposing relations and paradoxes—whereas strategic planning requires us to eliminate paradoxes and areas of ambiguity. Sometimes, juggling can feel awkward, or downright overwhelming. The Polish manufacturing CEO quipped: "It is very easy to gather information. Most of it is of no use—or it is not true—it is incomplete always! *(pause)* You must know this and treat it like you carry hot potatoes!"

A technology company executive emphatically stated:

The importance of filtering and figuring out ways to use tons and tons of information, most of it incomplete and inconsistent, is a must. If you can't work with a lot of incomplete or contradictory information, you'll never be a good strategist. If you can and you enjoy it, and you're driven, then you have a chance.

In describing what he pays particular attention to when making strategy, one of the Japanese financial executives said:

I pay attention to everything all at once. (laughter) It's not good to separate or categorize things when you make strategy—everything must be included and you must figure out a way to think like this if you want to win. If you practice, at first it will look [like] a blur. Then you must keep step[ping] back until you either see something you recognize, or maybe you will see the whole as a new idea. (pause, followed by a big breath) That is how to make sense of too much information! And you must never trust it [information].

The country manager of a pharmaceutical division covering a remote area of Southeast Asia smiled and shook his head as he read his job description aloud: "responsible for corporate compliance and making strategy." Laughing, he described it as "inhaling and exhaling at the same time!" And he's right. On the one hand, he is responsible for enforcing compliance with myriad corporate, industry, and country regulations, rules, and meticulous procedures—tasks requiring extreme convergent thinking. On the other hand, he is expected to come up with a successful, sustainable, adaptable, and innovative strategy in an unbelievably competitive market—a charge requiring divergent and intuitive thinking. An ability to juggle the competing strategic demands and to fully use the complex cognitive cluster is a reality of thinking in a global business strategy environment.

The pharmaceutical executive juggles an everyday strategic challenge of being responsible for compliance (where the role is to ensure that others remain within the existing framework) and also being responsible for strategic thinking (where the role is to move beyond the current framework). This example demonstrates one of the great juggling challenges for global executives, because monitoring compliance and thinking strategically require drawing on very different cognitive clusters.

No Control Over

Anyone can hold the helm when the sea is calm.

Maxim 358, by Publicius Syrus (first century B.C.)

The fourth attribute is the ability to deal with things over which we have no control. A Japanese financial executive explained:

> I'd say always prepare for the unexpected—you never know. But you'd better plan for a lot of them—things you never expected—they'll be there! (moves forward, talks faster) And I'd say to pay attention to what you can't control. (sits back in chair, talks louder, and gestures with hands) This is backwards from what they teach you in all these courses and books, but it's what I think from my own experience.

The American financial company executive reminded us of the following:

> The world is full of the unpredictable, and these are the things that make or break business strategy. You need to be on top of these unpredictable things, get comfortable thinking about them. (moves forward, puts both hands on tabletop) When you're talking about developing a good strategy in this kind of a merger-and-acquisition environment, you can't waste your time on things you can control—you'd better spend it thinking about what you can't control.

One of the Polish executives put it another way:

> We must think about what we don't know and expect the worst always. And it's no use having a party about what you now control, because you don't know tomorrow. Control is only in our imagination. If you think in this way, you will ask good questions.

This attitude was shared by a German manufacturing company executive, who explained: "We need to think about everything, especially the things we don't have any power or control over. These are the things we must include in good strategic thinking."

A Japanese executive commented: "Thinking about strategy is not so predictable—and it is pain[ful]. I must work mostly with unknown information, many missing pieces … but always think about the big picture."

To underscore the importance of being able to deal with things you cannot control when making strategy, an American executive declared: "You're driven to find ways to overcome the unpredictable and changing obstacles and disasters, things you're totally dependent on yet have absolutely no control over."

Contrary to what is taught in many formal strategic planning courses, the executives in this study indicated overwhelmingly that, for strategic thinking, it is critical to pay attention to what they could *not* control, rather than to focus on what they could control. This appears to have been a result of their personal experience. For example, a Danish executive who was also a ceramicist mentioned his metaphor of clay—that he cannot control the physical properties of clay; they are what they are. Yet, when working with clay he pays close attention to these things over which he has no control, in order to work *with* these events.

Interestingly, the executives viewed their lack of control as a kind of tool for leveraging risk. The elements of risk and fear were referenced throughout the interviews by all of the executives as an emotional motivator for learning to make strategy. Also, risk and fear contributed to the executives' incidental learning, particularly about not trusting sources of data, which conversely led them to trust themselves. They learned to *reframe* situations to enable themselves to see new opportunities and to think and trust a-rational and intuitive thinking in situations over which they had no control.

Perhaps this attribute of dealing with things over which we have no control helps to explain why these successful strategists thrive on a high level of challenge and why they identified the ability to deal with things over which they have no control as being one of the five essential attributes for making strategy. This ability—to deal with things over which they had no control—appealed to and tested the executives' competitive drive and strengthened their desire to win. Things over which they had no control offered challenge, which in turn offered meaningful learning, which eventually led to successful strategic thinking. The factor of fear was a motivator, and they learned incidentally to value negative experiences as being important to the learning process. This learning experience allowed them to take risks with decisions over which they had no control. Through their experience, they learned that negative factors were really just challenges for them to overcome in order to win.

Recent research shows that tension is created when we deal with decisions that include constantly changing and unknown variables. As a result of his studies, Daniel Kahneman pointed out that, "Inconsistencies reduce the ease of our thoughts and the clarity of our feelings."[6] In tough situations, successful strategists act as if they have already won, because they do not believe they can lose—akin to what poet Rainer Maria Rilke penned: "Follow your fear."

The strategists whom I interviewed experienced the great power that came with releasing the very thing that shamed them, and they converted their source of fear into a source of pride. Their conversion was possible because of their uncompromising desire to win. For these executives, the element of risk enticed them and played to their competitive nature. Learning to deal with things over which they have no control seemed to give them a competitive advantage. If everyone has access to the same data, paying attention to what they do not know or cannot control requires imagination in order to devise a winning outcome.

Desire to Win

What counts is not necessarily the size of the dog in the fight—it's the size of the fight in the dog.

Dwight D. Eisenhower (1890–1969), American general and thirty-fourth president of the United States

The fifth and final critical attribute is a strong, relentless desire to win. This is the passion and conviction behind all strategic change. For the executives with whom I spoke, the element of competition influenced strongly their ability to learn to think strategically.

In response to the question "What has allowed you to be successful in making strategy when others have not been?" the CFO of a financial company instantaneously replied: "I like to be ahead of everybody else. If you don't have that drive, you're not the one to make strategy—it won't be strong or good enough."

The Polish manufacturing CEO emphasized that in order to be successful in making strategy, "You must be determined to win, have a fighting spirit." He explained: "Making good strategy—it's about figuring out how to win—this compelling need to get things right, perfect, or win. It's mandatory to good strategy making. Without it, you're simply making plans."

New strategies can emerge from competition, confusion, and confrontation, as these create a necessary tension. Without it, innovative strategy can never proceed. Dialogue, discussion, and debate are all required communication techniques that the successful strategists tended to use for leveraging competitive, confused, and confrontational situations.

In response to a question about what has allowed him to be successful in making strategy when others have not been, the American CEO of the technology company exclaimed:

The stakes are too high to not win. You've got to win. You'd better be able to take risks, be extremely well informed, and always build in backups. (pause) And you'd better win. (grin) Sometimes it doesn't seem like work—it's more like a game (laughter)—and we want to win. We must win!

The German manufacturing executive stated succinctly: "I like to win. I like the challenge of the game. And when you run one of the world's best textile companies, you must win, or you lose. It's simple."

A Japanese financial executive confessed sheepishly: "I am very stubborn, *(laughter)* or at least everyone says this about me—so maybe it's true. It must be this way if I want to make good strategy. I don't lose!"

The desire to win was a strong undercurrent in the thinking of all the successful strategists whom I interviewed. This will to win was one area where they seemed to make a definitive case for black or white—they either win or they lose. A strong argument could be made that having an intense desire to win had attracted these executives to a highly competitive business environment in the first place. But their relentless perpetuation of competition is what is remarkable. This drive to win is precisely what enabled them to excel and thrive in a competitive environment and earn their reputations as successful strategists.

A passion and determination to survive and thrive connects all five of the attributes, in that it is the primary motivator for learning to make a winning strategy. A compelling desire to win can reframe reality. This after all, made Lady Macbeth the most powerful woman of Scotland. She created the future because she alone demonstrated the greatest desire; and everyone in Shakespeare's *Macbeth* followed her agenda before their own.

Notes

1. Sloan, "A Case Study of How Nine Executives Learn Informally to Develop Strategy in a Global Context."
2. Hogarth, *Educating Intuition*.
3. Sloan, "A Case Study of How Nine Executives Learn Informally to Develop Strategy in a Global Context."
4. Quoted in Boud and Garrick, *Understanding Learning at Work*, 221.
5. Kahneman, *Thinking, Fast and Slow*, 37.
6. Kahneman, *Thinking, Fast and Slow*, 200.

Interplay of the Five Attributes

The combination of this particular set of five attributes supports the critical reflective processes and the divergent and deep-dive dimensions that are required of the informal strategic learning model presented in Part III. Different combinations of the five attributes, in a simultaneous interplay, are used during each of the three stages: preparation, experience, and reevaluation.

I would argue that the set of five attributes establishes a mental precondition conducive to engaging in the reflective processes and that the routine use of the critical reflective process model fosters the set of five attributes—in a cyclical and generative way. As a result, paying close attention to and developing the five attributes is an important aspect of developing the cognitive cluster used in learning to think strategically (see Chapter 4).

Although the specific interplay of these attributes is different for each individual, collectively they are essential to learning to think strategically. A compelling and fierce desire to win can propel the critical reflective process. A vivid and active imagination generates curiosity and creativity in the reflective process. The quest for broad perspective is enhanced by both a desire to win and imagination, offering the individual a perpetual array of new possibilities that requires continuous testing. The ability to juggle, to constructively deal with many conflicting things at once, invites challenge and tension to the reflective process, especially when it is combined with the ability to constructively deal with things over which we have no control.

Interestingly, while there is a strong interplay among the five attributes, the nature of the five attributes is paradoxical. Just as their interplay is essential to strategic thinking, they can also lead strategists to frustration, obsession, and anxiety. And yet, according to the executives I interviewed, the five attributes are also the very means by which they overcome this tension. In other words, the five attributes are both the affliction and the antidote.

For example, the Japanese financial CEO explained that in his quest to achieve a broader perspective, he felt overwhelmed and desperate by having to attend to so many things over which he had no control. He expressed tremendous feelings of angst when attempting to balance competing feelings of trying, on the one hand, to unleash his creativity and at the same time to rein in his imagination. He expressed distress at having to monitor his nearly compulsive desire to win. Yet he did not ascribe a negative connotation to the descriptors he used (i.e., "frustration," "overwhelmed," "distressed"), but, instead, gave these descriptors a positive connotation—he became animated and energized as he recalled numerous such experiences. Instead of succumbing to this unease, the tension created as a result of the interplay among these attributes motivated and challenged him. They propelled him in his pursuit of making strategy.

The executives regarded situations that could easily have been considered detrimental to making strategy as an opportunity to exercise imagination. Frequently, they used reflection in action to reframe the circumstance as an opportunity for a win. In this sense, being able to engage the attribute of imagination functioned as a motivator because the executives could create options and alternatives to gain a competitive advantage. According to their descriptions, the executives regarded having their imagination challenged as a kind of sport or game that was fueled by their desire to win.

Communication Techniques for Attributes Integration

The deeper, dive learning domain is used extensively to connect the attributes to one another. Storytelling, dialogue, and debate are communicative learning techniques favored by many successful strategists, not only to inspire creativity and to stimulate their imagination, but also to build, sustain, and connect the five attributes. Storytelling created a means by which they could deal with things over which they had no control, and provided a reference point for testing subsequent experiences and a means of sharing information. Interestingly, stories in the form of metaphors, parables, and analogies were commonly described as a way of transferring strategic learning across contexts.

Because storytelling is reflective in nature, many of the strategists with whom I spoke indicated that they received more knowledge by putting the information into a story context than by exchanging facts. They tended to use this technique to challenge their assumptions and reflect both in and on action. This perspective is congruent with informal learning, suggesting that "only after a chance encounter, random events and circumstances do people construct a logical story to explain their learning to themselves and others."[1]

A story can serve as an impetus for gathering data. For example, a small factual detail is brought to light in the telling of a story, making the listener realize that this detail could be crucial. This realization prompts an inquiry for more information from a variety of sources. Or, a story may serve to broaden and deepen the data by providing context. A German manufacturing executive noted:

We just like to come together and talk about what we read—it seems we all read different things—and of course we also read the same publications. And we tell stories, a lot of stories about different scenarios. It's better than just talking all the time. I think storytelling elevates my thinking.

Curiously, storytelling can also be used as a kind of testing tool. Several of the strategists highlighted how stories can change in the telling, even while the facts of the circumstances of the story remain constant. Have you ever noticed how the story of a major business success changes depending on when the story is told? For example, within minutes of an announcement, six months later, or 12 years later? Who the audience is (e.g., a news commentator, your kids, a recruiter, a new hire, your rival). How often it has been told, and who tells it. The more it is told, the more it is tested. The first telling of any story is likely to be quite different in its description of details, the sequence, the pace, and so on than subsequent versions of the same story.

The ability to continually add layers of context and color is an inherent strength of storytelling, and, because stories change all the time, they allow strategists to continually use their imagination to combine information and try out various scenarios with their colleagues. The hypothetical scenarios served to engage the executives in reflection in action. As they presented a story, they received a flurry of reactions, questions, and new data which challenged the original story. Reflection occurred, followed by revisions to the story; subsequently, either part of the story was retold or a brand new story was shared. More questioning followed, which led to more information and eventually more reflection … and so the cycle continued.

In my research, storytelling repeatedly surfaced as a method for refining thinking about strategy. By drawing on each other's thinking and hearing others' stories, the executives were able to frame and reframe situations by putting things into a broader perspective and, therefore, to view situations, variables, and options differently. In this sense, the executives appeared to use what is sometimes called a symbolic frame,[2] which is effective in ambiguous or uncertain circumstances where roles, relationships, and goals are unclear.

The executives in the study were acutely aware that they were tasked with making global strategy within a chaotic environment, and storytelling allowed them to create symbols, which diminished unpredictability. "The symbolic frame considers the roles of myths, symbols, stories, … actors, rituals, ceremonies, humor, play, and metaphors in organizational life."[3] The strategists in this study perceived a disorderly and confused environment as a challenge to advance their strategic agenda, and storytelling served as an effective communication technique for clarification and unification to this end.

In conclusion, developing and exercising the combination of five attributes is important to developing the cognitive cluster that we use when learning to think strategically. A compelling and fierce desire to win propels the reflective processes. A vivid and active imagination generates curiosity and creativity in the reflective process. The quest for broad perspective is enhanced by both a desire to win and imagination, offering the individual a perpetual array of new possibilities that require continuous testing. And the ability to juggle, to constructively deal with many things at once, invites challenge and tension to the reflective process when it is combined with the ability to constructively deal with things over which one has no control. The specific combination of attributes involved is not the same every time, but the interplay of these attributes is consistently used when we engage in strategic thinking.

Notes

1. Marsick and Volpe, *Informal Learning on the Job. Advances in Developing Human Resources*, 7.
2. Bolman and Deal, *Reframing Organizations: Artistry, Choice, and Leadership*.
3. Marsick and Volpe, *Informal Learning on the Job. Advances in Developing Human Resources*, 85.

26

Adaptation as a Strategic Expectation

If the aim of good strategic thinking is to create a strategy that is sustainable, innovative, and winning, then, by definition, good strategic thinking needs also to be adaptive. In order to become more adaptive, any development initiative must be focused on strengthening and expanding our repertoire of intuition as a means to developing this particular cognitive cluster that underlies strategic thinking (see Chapter 4). Developing this cognitive cluster strengthens adaptive capacity, which can become generative in nature.

> *Strategic adaptation is most often about recovery or trying to survive a crisis which has appeared suddenly and which threatens the strategy.*

The notion of adaptability is not new, and it is generally not included within a strategic thinking context. As noted in Chapter 2, if we look at strategic thinking from the perspective of complexity theory, it is, first and foremost, about adaptation. And if we recall the ancient Greek notion of strategy, we recognize the implicit reference to the need for adaptive and flexible capability in order to deal with the polarities, uncertainties, complexities, and contradictions inherent in strategy. Drawing on Darwinism, we know that the largest, the strongest, or even the most intelligent of species are not those that survive—but those species that survive are the most adaptable to change.

Strategic adaptation consists of building on what has already been established, while exploring new possibilities in the present to benefit the future. Strategic adaptation, unfortunately, is not all about improvisation and fun. Research shows that strategic adaptation is most often about recovery or trying to survive a crisis which has appeared suddenly and which threatens the strategy.[1] This research is consistent with transformative learning in the deepest level of the dive domain (see Part IV).

In his well-researched book, *The Upside of Irrationality*, Dan Ariely notes that

adaptation is a very important novelty filter that helps us focus our limited atten-
tion on things that are changing and might therefore pose either opportunities or
danger. Adaptation allows us to attend to the important changes among the mil-
lions that occur around us all the time and ignore the unimportant ones.[2]

In reference to the starting point of strategic thinking, a Japanese executive explained:

To start, you must have a purpose. Sometimes I start because I'm afraid of some-
thing, many times I suppose it's this. (laughter) And you understand that being
afraid is a problem. So in some sense perhaps I start with a problem, and then I
just move to different places to look at the problem.

And the Hong Kong technology company COO explicitly stated:

I think I learn as much from things that hurt me as from things that help me—probably
more if I take the time to think. It's like you have a net you drag through life. You bring
along all your "collectibles," your experiences, with you. And there are times when they'll
help you and times when they'll get in your way. Those are the times you can learn the
most from. They're your experiences, and it's up to you what you do with them.

Adaptation is closely linked to reflecting in and on action as a learning process. Reflection in action and reflection on action have become conscious habits over the years for many of the executives I interviewed—both kinds of reflection are habits they learned and valued from their experience. They seemed to be aware of, expect, and trust the chaos, tension, and unexpected elements, and they did not feel compelled to control the disorder. Instead, they accepted anxiety as part of the challenge and expressed both satisfaction and enthusiasm about using reflection in action. Through their experience they had unknowingly made it part of their strategic thinking processes.

The executives in the study, as so many in my practice, described their ability and confidence to turn an obstacle into a game, and a game into a win. They appear to have learned to facilitate their own learning by reflecting on and reframing a challenge until it became a strategic opportunity for them. I continue to be fascinated by accounts of this adaptive process—a continuous and dynamic interplay of the five attributes and the three-stage informal learning process at work.

For example, all three of the executives from a Polish manufacturing company mentioned government interference as a contextual hindrance. They referred with disdain to the degree of involvement of the government, the bureaucracy, the perception that the government's intention was to provide interference rather than support for businesses, the slow pace at which the government moved, and their past experience with punitive governmental powers. Also, the three executives indicated that the government was an "unknown" element, a "factor beyond their control," and an impassioned "source of fire" that appeared to fuel their sense of determination. Incidentally, they had learned to transform the negative factor of government into an element of challenge and a motivator for learning.

The Hong Kong technology executive explained factors that contribute to his being a successful strategy maker:

I think it's a combination of who I am and my luck, honestly. I'm basically a very driven and hardworking guy. I need to really like or be fascinated by what I'm doing—even as a kid I never just did what somebody told me. (laughter) And I like to pretend different things inside my mind. I don't give up easily. (laughter) That's probably a good trait, at least most of the time.

An adaptive strategist is able to respond rapidly and effectively to unexpected events, and can quickly shift from a planned sequence of actions to an alternative that is more appropriate.[3] Something I have noticed in my own practice, which was supported by the findings of the study underlying this book, is that successful strategists did not explicitly mention "mistakes" as part of their learning, nor did they respond to probes about the role of "mistakes."

A closer look at this avoidance or omission revealed that the strategists in the study did in fact acknowledge their mistakes, but they did not call them mistakes per se. They tended not to distinguish missteps from experimentation or trial and error. Their descriptions implied, however, that they incorporated learning from these experiences into their continuous cycle of critical reflection and revision during the experience and reevaluation stages of the informal learning process. Also, they used dialogue and storytelling as techniques to test and to preempt errors and to adapt in order to move forward.

One of the financial executives brushed aside the word *mistake* and went on to explain:

I don't really think about mistakes, or I'd just get stuck ... gotta move forward. It's more like I'm adjusting to things all the time. When things don't work out, that moment becomes part of the new future. It's strange. When this happens we look again at the data and then we pull apart the analysis. This is the part I really like because I think in a different way. It's the tough part, but I always learn from it. We imagine all these possibilities and make up a lot of stories. Telling stories is good, you know, because they help you understand what went wrong. And we talk about all kinds of things we have to try. This kind of thing happens all the time; it's just part of learning to make adjustments and it's hard to explain. There are lots of these adjustments that need to be made to strategy, lots of things go wrong. But they're not really mistakes—they're just part of the process.

Successful strategists with whom I have worked invariably exhibit a strong degree of self-reliance. They do not dwell on negatives or obstacles—they expect them and perceive them as challenges and as learning initiatives. Mistakes simply allow them to refocus their attention and force them to see things differently.

An over-reliance on detailed plans and regimented procedures crowds out adaptive potential.

Adaptation is similar in some respects to improvisation. We cannot plan an improvisation—we assess the situation and act or react. Intuition is essential for improvisation. In strategy making, we rely on intuition to decide when to adapt, to determine the degree to which a situation is deteriorating, and to decide which routine or action script we should use to adjust. Furthermore, we rely on our intuition to decide whether or not to trust our adaptation, because the changes we want to make may result in subsequent or even worse problems.

Chaos theory warns that the closer we get to thinking we understand a pattern and believing we can control it, the more likely we are to be surprised and frustrated when it turns out to be quite different from what we imagined. Therefore, strategists must practice thinking that supports dealing with contradictions. Daily life regularly reminds us that our minds and our businesses are not always systems in balance. If we regularly allow our minds to play with highly unlikely possibilities in relation to some pattern or trend, then the future will not come as such a surprise. We will have a large repertoire of experience with such possibilities, which strengthens our intuition and increases the likelihood of adapting.

Details Can Doom Adaptation

Frequently in my practice, I find that although country and regional business heads are tasked with strategic responsibilities and are highly committed to developing local strategic thinkers, they nonetheless, tend to cancel opportunities for strategic adaptation by creating an over-reliance on excruciatingly detailed plans and procedures among their senior managers. Research has shown that an over-reliance on detailed plans and regimented procedures can diminish adaptive potential.[4] An overdependence on plans and procedures actually becomes an impediment and runs counter to developing strategic thinking capability. Just as an over-reliance on a memorized script can impede improvisation, so too can a meticulously detailed plan derail the ability to think strategically.

In contrast to strategic thinkers, strategic planners often aim to specify every individual detail, leaving nothing to chance. Unfortunately, the more details there are, the harder it is to adapt, the more fragile the plans become, and the more susceptible a strategic plan becomes to missing its anticipated outcome.

In their book, *Managing the Unexpected*, Karl Weick and Kathleen Sutcliffe discuss three ways that detailed plans can stifle adaptability.[5] First, plans make us insensitive to the anomalies that tell us it is time to adapt, because plans describe what is relevant and what is not. Anything that is irrelevant to the plan does not get much attention. Second, plans may include contingency actions for coping with difficulties, but these contingencies were drawn up in advance and are usually void of context, the constraints, and any new opportunities that tend to crop up the moment the plan is being implemented. And third, plans are designed to have us repeat "optimized" patterns of activity. But high-reliability organizations cope with unexpected events by adapting to circumstances rather than by depending on plans. Adaptation is not simply building a new strategic plan to replace an old one. Rather, adaptation means modifying a plan that is in progress via a strategic thinking process—like jumping on a moving train or trying to catch a bird in flight. Most often, the plans we develop need to be improved and modified as we learn in action, because businesses compete in a grossly complex, constantly changing, uncertain global context which is saturated with incomplete and inaccurate information. Adapting strategy is much more difficult than planning strategy, because there are innumerable variables, both known and unknown.

Often, executives stumble over the paradox that the greater the uncertainty we face when making strategy, the more advantage there is to managing that uncertainty by planning to adapt. In other words, paying attention to our hunches or our common sense is what is needed. We tend to know intuitively that the more uncertain and unpredictable our strategic environment, the more useless our detailed plans become. Strategic thinking is not about the creation of a static plan but, rather, about setting a dynamic thinking process in motion. An important part of facilitating strategic thinking capacity is to create the expectation of adaptation. We need to be strategically adaptive to deal with such a chaotic and unpredictable environment.

Adaptation is a broad and complex process which "operates at deep physiological, psychological, and environmental levels, and it affects us in many aspects of our lives. Because of its generality and pervasiveness, there is also a lot that we don't yet understand about it."[6]

> *Strategic planning is not the antithesis of strategic thinking; rather, it is complementary to it and needs to be balanced within the overall strategy-making process.*

The concept of *bounded rationality* was first introduced by Herbert Simon, who won a Nobel Prize in 1978 for his work on decision making and problem solving. His idea was that there are too many facts and too many combinations of facts for us to make any important decision by simply gathering and analyzing all the facts.[7] He found that the more complex the decision, the faster the complications added up, and the more "knowing" how to make a decision in ways other than cognitive sequential analysis became necessary.

We need a method which allows us to make effective decisions in these all-too-familiar strategic situations. Technical analysis and computer models can help, but only by providing a sophisticated synopsis or consolidated information. Given that most global strategy is created under these highly complex circumstances, the decisions we make are connected to many conditions that lack metrics, yet weigh heavily on the overall strategic-risk quotient. Therefore, when we consider learning to think strategically, we must pay attention to honing our adaptive capabilities in order to balance our analytical skills.

Strategic adaptation, however, is not always a good idea, and improvisation is not inherently beneficial to strategic thinking. A well-developed intuition allows us to "know" when to change a plan and when to leave it alone. Intuition raises our internal red flags and alerts us to the benefits of taking action and the unintended consequences that arise from adaptations. Our ability to adapt is only as good as our intuition, which is based on our experience.

Strategic planning is not the antithesis of strategic thinking; rather, it is complementary to it and needs to be balanced within the overall strategy-making process. Meticulous attention to detail is imperative to the planning and the implementation phases of strategy. If we expect to adapt our strategy, we must tacitly accept the unpredictability of strategy and openly try to work with this unpredictability, instead of trying to out-plan it.

Notes

1. Ariely, *The Upside of Irrationality*.
2. Ariely, *The Upside of Irrationality*, 159.
3. Ariely, *The Upside of Irrationality*.
4. Klein, *The Power of Intuition*, 151.
5. Weick and Sutcliffe, *Managing the Unexpected: Assuring High Performance in an Age of Complexity*.
6. Klein, *The Power of Intuition*, 151.
7. Simon, *Models of Man*.

Summary and Questions

Nearly anyone can learn to think more strategically. To learn to think strategically, we need to develop a set of five attributes: a vivid *imagination*, a *broad perspective*, be able to *juggle* incomplete and competing pieces of information, deal with things over which you have *no control*, and have a fierce *desire to win*. The best strategic thinkers use these five attributes in concert to enhance their strategic thinking. Genuine strategic thinking growth is largely about making sure that people understand what is required for learning to think strategically and allowing them to take the lead in their own learning.

We can use metaphor, drawing, storytelling, dialogue, discussion, and debate to integrate the five attributes into our development processes. Since metaphor, drawing, and storytelling have critical reflective qualities, they are helpful when communicating during the strategic thinking process. These are often underutilized, yet highly impactful types of informal learning that can assist in developing strategic thinkers. Drawing and metaphor in particular, activate and assist in visualizing, diverging, and challenging the strategic problem.

Strategic thinking must be adaptive. If the intent is to engage in strategic thinking, we should refrain from becoming too involved with details, as details can inhibit and deter adaptability. Strategic thinking and strategic planning should be complementary. We want to leverage the strengths of each in order to propel an organization toward its strategic aim.

1. Why is the creation of a "pipeline" of strategic thinkers throughout an organization beneficial to the sustainability of an organization's future? How could you support this?
2. Which of the five attributes are your strengths? Why? How does this impact your ability to contribute to strategy conversations? How could you further develop these strengths?

3. Which of the five attributes are your weakest areas? Why? How does this impact your ability to contribute to your strategy conversations? What changes could you make?

4. Can you think of a time within an organization when over-attention to details was responsible for derailing a strategic aim? What factors contributed to this? How could it have been averted?

HOW CAN WE BECOME BETTER STRATEGIC THINKERS?

Engaging in Informal Learning Approaches: Strengthening the Five Attributes and the Critical Reflective Processes

I have never let my schooling interfere with my education.

Mark Twain (1835–1910), American author

Developing the Five Essential Attributes

You may be relieved to know that this part does not include a list of how-to exercises and activities. Rather, I am recommending things that work for clients in my consulting practice to support the long-term sustainable development of strategic thinking; these things are heavily reliant on informal learning, yet easily adaptable to formal workshops and lectures, which are more structured. I invite you to use this book as a source for creating your own developmental ideas, to experiment, and to modify current approaches.

The overall recommendations that I put forth in this part focus on strengthening the five essential attributes discussed in Part IX (imagination, broad perspective, juggle, no control over, and desire to win) and on developing critical reflective processes as introduced in Part VI, allowing strategists to link learning in their expanded life experience to a global business strategy context.

Chapter 27 discusses the role the arts can play in developing strategic thinking. Chapter 28 describes three practical ways to address the development of critical reflective processes: "and" thinking, action learning, and lateral thinking. Chapter 29 presents a list of suggestions for individuals, learning facilitators, business schools, and organizations.

If we assume, as many organizations do, that human capital is the only true competitive global strategic advantage, and if we also assume that the global reality, in which we make strategy, promises only to become more complex and challenging, then common sense tells us that we need to make a long-term business investment in strengthening and expanding the strategic thinking capacity of our organizations.

> *If businesses are to remain largely technical operations, most organizations are fairly well equipped with excellent resources for strategic planning. But if organizations are expected to be competitive within the realm of growing complexities, contradictions, and change, and if business schools are to be*

*perceived as something more than just expensive
technical schools, most are far from being prepared
with excellent resources for strategic thinking.*

With regard to strategy, organizations are beginning to recognize the gap between what they need (strategic thinkers) and what many are continuing to develop by default (strategic planners). The days are long past when analysis, science, and mathematics could be compartmentalized from "the other stuff" required of complex global business strategy—because significant and sustainable security, health, economic, and social interests are at stake. If our future business and government leaders are going to develop and defend our values through strategy and policy initiatives, they have to understand what they are. The humanities and arts teach just that.

If businesses are to remain largely technical operations, most organizations are fairly well equipped with excellent resources for strategic planning. But if organizations are expected to be competitive within the realm of growing complexities, contradictions, and change, and if business schools are to be perceived as something more than just expensive technical schools, most are far from being prepared with excellent resources for strategic thinking. If this situation is to change for the better, businesses, executive development programs, and business schools need to engage in some significant frame shattering and reframing regarding their approach toward strategy development.

While there are many things that can be done to strengthen strategic thinking, I recommend a somewhat unconventional approach of emphasizing engagement in the arts and humanities. The humanities, the arts, and critical reflective processes are accessible and affordable around the globe—most often, we simply don't think about their expansive breadth and depth with regard to developing the capability of strategic thinking.

The Arts to the Rescue

So what does participation and experience in artistic endeavors bring to the development of strategic thinking? You can breathe easy, as it has nothing to do with artistic talent per se. The aim is not to achieve fame and fortune as an artistic master but, rather, to "open the doors of perception," as poet William Blake wrote in *The Marriage of Heaven and Hell.*

This first subsection explores the basic theme of participation in artistic endeavors as a recommendation for learning to think strategically. Odd as it may sound, such participation can support learning to think strategically and the critical reflective processes because the arts and humanities offer infinite scope and depth, and are inclusive of all five of the critical attributes. The arts also require adeptness of the critical reflective processes, and are reliant on the cognitive cluster that underlies strategic thinking (see Chapter 4).

While an expansive life experience may include a multitude of activities which broaden our horizon and open new vistas, one of the most comprehensive and powerful strategic thinking influences I have experienced in my own business life, and those of the strategists whom I interviewed, is exposure to the arts. Learning to think strategically is strengthened not merely from participating in an artistic process, but when paired with critical reflective processes.

We can acquire first-hand learning through the experience of "doing" photography, painting, writing, singing, dancing, playing an instrument, and so on. Also, we can learn through second-hand experience—what the early twentieth-century philosopher William James called "knowledge about" the arts and humanities, for example, by listening to an orchestra, watching a dance, reading a novel, or seeing a play. Naturally, what we read, hear, see, and feel about the play, novel, painting, or dance performance contributes to our "knowledge about," which often triggers our deeply held beliefs. We find ourselves taking sides with a particular character and passionately defending or vilifying the actions of another. Experiencing the arts is a great way to broaden our repertoire of experience, surface assumptions, transfer learning, identify patterns, and become aware of the convictions on which we take strategic action and make decisions.

When either first- or second-hand artistic experience is coupled with critical reflective processes such as critical inquiry, critical reflection, and critical dialogue, personal interpretations and premise beliefs can be tested and new alternatives brought to light. Our reflection about our artistic experiences is what happens as we create alternative endings, when we disagree or are disappointed with an unsatisfactory conclusion.

While both cognitive clusters (see Chapter 4) are used to create meaning from an engagement with the humanities or arts, it is the cognitive cluster underlying strategic thinking that moves the experience to a deeper, dive level. Nonlinear, a-rational thinking, divergent and convergent thinking, critical inquiry, critical dialogue, and critical reflection all come into play when we become engaged in an arts experience. With drama, a novel, or a film, there is often a visceral feeling that compels us to take a particular position. Engaging in critical reflection and critical dialogue about the assumptions we hold regarding these incidents is a great way to build analogies and to facilitate the transfer of the learning of such an experience to strategy problems. The content of the drama or novel need not be business related, because it is the process reflection, the premise reflection, and metaphoric conversion that are essential to transferring the artistic experience across contexts.

An arts encounter can become a metaphor for a business strategy experience (and vice versa) if critical reflection and critical dialogue follow.

Participation in an art form not only exposes us to new patterns through heightened sensory stimulation and imagination but, also, this participation engages experientially both the affective and cognitive learning dimensions that are needed for strategic thinking. Experiencing the arts (either in doing or in knowledge about) requires us to use both the surf and the deeper, dive learning domains. These artistic experiences allow us to practice essential aspects of strategic thinking without really "thinking" about it.

Believe it or not, I find that my clients who regularly engage in an artistic endeavor generally "get it" very quickly.

An arts encounter can become a metaphor for a business-strategy experience (and vice versa) if critical reflection and critical dialogue follow. Cognitive agility and imagination are strengthened as we look for parallels and patterns within a business context.

The practice of transfer of learning from one context to another presents us with one of the most impelling strategic thinking learning experiences.

Benefits of Engaging in the Arts

As we have just mentioned, participation in the arts supports the development of the five attributes (imagination, broad perspective, juggle, no control over, desire to win) by providing opportunities to practice the following:

- Expand perspective.
  We see, hear, and feel different interpretations of the same data; balance individual and group roles; experience the impact of elemental changes in structure, form, texture, dynamics, distortion, diminution, and exaggeration; and experience historical and cultural contexts on the interpretation of data. For example, although the musical notes printed on a page are fixed, they can be interpreted in many different ways. We recognize a tune, yet it is different each time because of the instrumentation, the tempo, the acoustics, the performer, our mood, and so forth. The smile of Mona Lisa remains the same, beautiful, and fixed over the centuries; yet it changes with each viewing.
- Deal with many competing things at once.
  We pay attention to the mastery of technique and focus simultaneously on the overall form, the structure of a piece, changing emotions, and creativity. We learn to juggle many things at once, focusing and shifting our attention with ease.
- Engage imagination.
  The arts foster creativity and infinite possibilities. We see new relationships and connections between things and as a result of our decisions, actions, and responses.
- Experience tension.
  An affective dimension is inherent in the arts. We have a feeling that generates an intense reaction, which creates options of exploration and divergence, or a release. Pride and humility accompany an awareness of our habits, performance, or creations.
- Pay attention to things we cannot control.
  We understand that we cannot control every specific aspect of the final movement of an orchestral performance—only our part. The properties of oil paint are what they are—heightening our attention and elevating our appreciation, and perhaps sensitizing our curiosity.
- Develop emotional awareness.

We experience a wide range of emotions when viewing a photograph or listening to a brass quintet—from disgust, revulsion, pain, aggression, and sadness to happiness, pleasure, eroticism, and ecstasy.

- Deal with paradox.
  We deal with the finished *and* the incomplete; repetition *and* free form; continuity *and* deviation; prescription *and* creation; structure *and* experimentation; sameness *and* surprise.
- Accept incomplete information.
  A creation is never truly a completed work. Just as successful strategy is always past tense, a successful performance is only a moment in time passed, and is never finished.
- Take a risk.
  Learning something new requires commitment and risk. We place ourselves in the vulnerable position of being a non-expert, a novice, and possibly being judged incompetent.
- Learn discipline.
  Regular practice is required for improvement. Practice requires discipline, sacrifice, precision, sequence, repetition, drill, and consistency. Discipline is required to balance technique versus feelings, which is required for artistic mastery.
- Appreciate practice.
  Practice requires feedback and determination. We learn to appreciate a distinct sense of time (no shortcuts), movement toward something we strongly desire, nonlinear progress, and a combination of thinking and feeling.
- Learn the creative process through technique.
  Creation does not just happen; learning the technical rudiments is necessary in order to create.

Although I am a big proponent of fostering informal learning as a means to strengthening the five attributes, I also adamantly support the intermittent use of highly structured formal "learning about" the arts. For example, formal learning from workshops, presentations, and provocative lectures can help us "learn about" artistic information (e.g., topics such as form exaggeration and figure distortion in abstract painting). Strategists can eventually develop the cognitive capability to transfer this learning across contexts and identify parallels and metaphors in their respective strategic environment.

Again, as noted in the beginning of this chapter, the emphasis is not on artistic perfection or technical expertise, but on engaging in some type of creative endeavor for the purpose of strengthening strategic thinking.

28

Developing Critical Reflective Processes

Masterful use of critical reflective processing (critical reflection, critical dialogue, critical thinking, and critical inquiry) is another way to address the development of the five attributes that are necessary for learning to think strategically: imagination, broad perspective, juggle, no control over, and desire to win. I want to underscore that critical reflective processes do not necessarily result in strategic thinking, but they are an essential component.

This chapter is comprised of three sections. The first discusses how reflective processes strengthen the five attributes. The second section explores "and" thinking. The third section presents a brief overview of two learning-process approaches—action learning and lateral thinking—as ways to support the development of critical reflective processes and, in turn, the five attributes.

Critical Reflective Processes Strengthen the Five Attributes

As we have seen throughout this book, the five attributes both overlap and are interdependent. Rather than addressing each of the five attributes separately, looking at how critical reflective processes can strengthen the combination of the five attributes is more practical and realistic. How do we strengthen the combination of the five attributes? As discussed in Chapter 27, active participation in any creative or artistic pursuit requires the use of critical reflective processes.

Incorporating the critical reflective processes into an arts experience can be a powerful (and efficient) way of strengthening the five attributes. Let's look at the following ways this can occur:

- Macro–micro connection
  We constantly oscillate between macro and micro perceptions, experiencing the relationship between the part and the whole. Also, we experience the consequences of having a single perspective and the benefits of taking a broad perspective.

- Focus
  We practice concentration when the focal point continually changes. Also, we learn to pay attention to different cues and signals, such as the use of amplification and minimization, accents, or silence to gain or refocus attention. Additionally, we learn to focus on the appropriate domain of learning required at a given moment. The instrumental surf domain requires a skills response, while the deeper, dive domain requires a more intuitive level of feeling—eventually, practicing focus enables us to make focus a tacit ability.
- Reflection in action
  Through practice and repetition, we refine reflection and reaction. There is no endpoint in an artistic endeavor because reflection and experience are continually at work. We constantly ask: How else? What else? When else? Who else? Why not?
- Surprise
  We experience surprise as a means of shifting our focus. Our pattern recognition is altered, and we shift or divert our attention. Our affective-learning dimension is heightened—we laugh, gasp, gulp, or cringe in response to a dance movement, a costume, or a line in a play.
- Intuition
  We learn to trust our intuition through using it and reflecting on it. Trusting intuition happens naturally in the arts—as we acquire experience through practice, feedback, and repetition, we develop our intuition and become confident with using it.
- Affective awareness
  We experience the subtleties and variances of emotions and the impact that emotions have on an arts experience or performance. Also, we become aware of feelings attached to the reactions that an artistic experience invokes.
- Integration
  We synthesize and integrate the affective domain with the cognitive domain, the analytic with the intuitive, and the instrumental with the deeper, dive-learning domain.
- Systems thinking
  We figure out the influence and impact of the relationships between performer, audience, technician, media, business operations, teacher, composer, and so on.
- Learning transfer
  We transfer this artistic learning to strategic thinking—one experience becomes a metaphor for the other, which facilitates pattern recognition, framing, shattering, and reframing.

As we see from this list, the use of critical reflective processes (critical reflection, critical inquiry, critical thinking, and critical dialogue) supports the development of the five attributes necessary for learning to think strategically.

Another way to support the development of these attributes is through the creation of scenarios and alternatives to problems. Surprisingly, we often resist examining strategic alternatives in depth because doing so can lead to confusion, ambivalence, and "messiness." Asking questions about alternatives and assumptions seems like common sense, but we rarely do this in a rigorous, disciplined, and open manner during traditional strategy meetings because expediency, political ramifications, and same-frame thinking tend to prevail.

Critical reflection, critical inquiry, critical thinking, and critical dialogue develop the five attributes required of strategic thinking in that they sharpen reflection in action and reflection on action. When reflection in and on action is repeated sufficiently and the results are successful, this critical reflection becomes second nature and, ultimately, we learn to trust the intuitive judgment that comes from our frequent experience—a huge and immeasurable advantage for learning to think strategically.

"And" Thinking

Critical reflection, critical inquiry, and critical dialogue are also necessary to improve our ability to make sense of opposites, contradictions, polarities, and paradoxes in a way that generates new ideas, new thoughts, and new possibilities. I call this cognitive capability "and" thinking—a highly complex kind of thinking that works with the inherent tension created by a polarity.

Much of the global context of strategy making requires an ability to deal with complex, competing, contradictory information and paradoxes. Our business and policy world requires adeptness with a cognitive cluster that moves us far beyond dualistic thinking. Making strategy that is adaptive does not afford us the time and does not always benefit from using elimination and reductionist thinking.

> *"And" thinking is based on the inherent tension*
> *created by a polarity—resulting in new meaning,*
> *thoughts, and new ideas.*

"And" thinking is a major variance to the technical rational approach to problem solving and decision making. It can be an especially complex and difficult way of thinking, because it runs counter to the notion of reductionist thinking that relies on a process of eliminating any contradictory and opposing thoughts. As a further note, "and" thinking is different from "both" thinking. While "both" thinking is also comprised of two elements, these elements may not necessarily be polarities.

"And" thinking requires that we temporarily suspend judgment and experience the tension, as a means to or as a source of creative tension, and search for new possibilities that may seem exaggerated, pointless, and ridiculous. Working *with* this tension leads to divergent thinking and deep, dive questions, and requires an integration of all five attributes discussed in Chapter 24.

Curiously, I find American strategists would often
rather take a risk of being wrong all the way than
live with the tension of ambivalence that is inherent
in "and" thinking.

Curiously, in my work with corporate and government strategists in many countries, I have noticed that (we) Americans often tend to prefer extremes when it comes to thinking about strategy. Frequently, my American clients insist on a this-*or*-that decision very early in the strategy-making process, as soon as the tension from opposing or competing issues becomes apparent. Some of the common underlying assumptions that begin to surface through critical inquiry and critical dialogue include a premise notion that fence-riding is wrong or weak, good strategists should be able to control everything, tension is a source for elimination, and there is only one best way.

Interestingly, Americans seem to like the expedience that comes with being definitive in the moment: pick *or* choose, this *or* that, and either/or. With few exceptions, I find American strategists would rather take a risk of being wrong all the way than live with the tension in "and" thinking. However, what is required for dealing with the complexity of global strategic thinking is precisely this—being comfortable with the tension of dealing with complex and unpredictable circumstances which include opposites, contradictions, and paradoxes.

"And" thinking forces us to uncover the competing and opposing parts of a strategy in an effort to examine faulty assumptions and explore innovative alternatives. Often, polarities within strategy issues can remain invisible unless we seek them out and challenge them as part of strategic thinking. Our business world is a paradoxical network of global *and* local, general *and* specific, modern *and* postmodern environments. Also, it consists of fragmentation *and* globalization, heterogeneity *and* uniformity, passive consumption *and* active customization, individualism *and* tribalism, and the old *and* the new. Furthermore, we need to pay attention to developing both affective *and* cognitive, rationality *and* intuition, dialogue *and* debate, and convergence *and* divergence.

To think strategically, we want to expect "ands" and the unmistakable tension. We need to experience this tension, recognize it, invite it, and work *with* it.

"And" thinking forces two opposing or contradictory
ideas or opinions into a single new thought or novel
concept and can create tremendous tension and
imbalance—to the point of outbursts and innova-
tive breakthroughs.

"And" thinking forces two opposing or contradictory ideas or opinions into a single new thought or novel concept and can create tremendous tension and imbalance—to the point of outbursts and innovative breakthroughs.

Two Learning Processes: Action Learning and Lateral Thinking

Two learning processes, which I encourage anyone interested in strategic thinking to use in order to develop critical reflective processes, are action learning and lateral thinking. I recommend these two in particular because they develop critical reflective processes, they are flexible and integrative, and they can be either highly structured and formal or very informal.

Action Learning

Essentially, action learning (AL) is an approach consisting of learning and action. While AL programs vary considerably, according to AL expert Michael Marquardt of George Washington University, all AL programs comprise six components: problem, group, questions, action, learning, and coach.[1]

Reg Revans introduced the concept of AL in the United Kingdom in the 1940s.[2] Since then, there have been many interpretations and variations of AL applications. In a nutshell, AL is a systematic and structured approach to developing cognitive and affective discipline, skills, and thinking habits—essentials for learning to think strategically, because AL assists with learning transfer across contexts.

With regard to strategic thinking, AL integrates informal and formal learning and is an excellent way to establish individual and organizational use of the deeper, dive-learning domain for strategic problem solving and decision making. Once initial problems are formulated, there is ample room to uncover patterns of thinking, inferences, and so on. Though the strategic thinking process is complex and dynamic, its components can be structured to a certain extent. AL encourages participants to experiment and make discoveries about their own learning as they embark on solving strategic problems. Furthermore, AL develops a cadre of people who have the capacity to use critically reflective processes in strategic thinking.

Linear and logical critical thinking can be included as a structured part of an AL process as a means of balancing the nonlinear and creative nature of the five essential attributes. Critical thinking establishes a logical chain of reasoning that is useful to unravel assumptions and to test new frames and ways of thinking. In critical thinking, a pattern of reasoning, starting with the basic construct of a reason, leads to a conclusion, and the conclusion is established and elaborated. The process moves toward complexities like the deconstruction and construction of an argument, where one develops and tests hypotheses, analyzes assumptions, and evaluates inferences or causal explanations. Fluency and confidence in using critical thinking are necessary for shifting back and forth between dialogue, discussion, and debate, as well as for testing the rational validity of ideas generated using a-rational thinking.

The implementation of AL can vary significantly, depending on a company's specific goals, timeframes, and the individuals involved. What is most important, however, is that strategic imperatives are translated into business initiatives that can drive AL.

Lateral Thinking

Lateral thinking (LT) is an approach for strengthening the strategic thinking attributes of imagination, broad perspective, and juggling. According to the originator of lateral thinking, Edward De Bono, "Lateral thinking is both an attitude and a method of using information."[3] LT is a kind of nonlinear, a-rational thinking that is concerned with changing patterns. Instead of taking a pattern and then developing it, as happens with vertical thinking, LT aims to restructure the pattern by putting things together in a different way. By its very nature, LT is compatible with and supportive of developing adaptive, innovative, and sustainable strategy.

De Bono further notes that, in using lateral thinking,

> *one acknowledges the usefulness of a pattern, but instead of regarding it as inevitable, one regards it as only one way of putting things together. This attitude challenges the assumption that what is a convenient pattern at the moment is the only possible pattern.*[4]

Since successful strategy is always past tense (i.e., it never happens the same way again), LT is enormously relevant and important for learning to think strategically because it emphasizes movement and future.

De Bono contrasts two terms: vertical thinking and lateral thinking. While acknowledging that lateral and vertical thinking are complementary, he differentiates the two by noting that vertical thinking is selective, meaning that it excludes other ways of thinking about accomplishing tasks. This vertical method is derived from technical rationality, such that we strive to identify the most promising approach to a problem. By contrast, LT is generative and openly seeks to include other ways of approaching a problem. The intent of LT is to generate as many alternative approaches as possible, and this divergent effort supports the mental process required for strategic thinking.

> *Lateral thinking enhances the effectiveness of vertical thinking by offering it more to select from.*

In his well-known book, *Lateral Thinking*, De Bono explains that the necessity of withholding judgment when using LT is useful in three ways:

> *to arrange information in a way which would never have come about in the normal course of events; to hold an arrangement of information without judging it; and to protect from dismissal an arrangement of information which has already been judged as impossible.*[5]

The ability to suspend judgment is one of the most basic principles of LT, and this ability is one of the fundamental points of difference from vertical thinking.

With regard to strategic thinking, LT is useful for generating ideas, while vertical thinking is useful for developing and implementing ideas. LT enhances the effectiveness of vertical thinking by offering it more. The implications for using LT to strengthen the five attributes are obvious, but strategists and facilitators of learning must also be willing to clarify whether the situation calls for strategic planning or strategic thinking—that is, vertical or lateral thinking, respectively.

Learning to think strategically is not something learned overnight. It requires emotional (affective) and intellectual (cognitive) learning, the inclusion of life experiences, the sum of the five attributes, and adeptness at using critical reflective processes.

Notes

1. Marquardt, *Action Learning Solving Problems and Building Leaders in Real Time*.
2. Revans, *The Origin and Growth of Action Learning*.
3. De Bono, *Lateral Thinking*, 52.
4. De Bono, *Lateral Thinking*, 52.
5. De Bono, *Lateral Thinking*, 229.

29

Where We've Come From and Where We Can Go: Some Suggestions

Throughout this book, we have been encouraged to seek a balance and integrate opposing and contradictory perspectives, or *metos*. We have followed the swinging pendulum from the ancient Greek concept of strategy, which assumed an unresolvable tension and mutuality between chaos and ordered *cosmos*, all the way over to technical rationality of the modern era, with its obsession on the linear, rational, scientific approach to strategy making. Still, in search of the Holy Grail for learning to think strategically, we find ourselves at a crossroads, eager to move forward and apply what we have learned.

Learning to think strategically is complex and enormously challenging—yet paramount among leadership responsibilities. It requires abilities that are not generally taught in formal, traditional strategy courses, but instead are learned informally. Strategic thinking requires experience, and time for critical reflection, inquiry, dialogue, and commitment to developing the five attributes. This final chapter consists of four subsections, each focusing on suggestions for a particular group: individuals, learning facilitators, business schools, and organizations.

Suggestions for Individuals

There are many things individuals can do to support the development of strategic thinking. First and foremost, as mentioned in Chapter 27, participate in a creative art form— any art form—even if you are not "that type." Whether you choose piano lessons, painting, carpentry, photography, or cooking, make sure you enjoy it and feel engaged when "doing" it. There is no wrong way to play or improvise.

When exploring new mediums and exercising new skills, sometimes you need a partner, such as a good friend, a coach, or mentor, who can guide you through critical reflective processes (critical dialogue, critical inquiry, critical reflection) until they become habits. This kind of supported engagement can help with later transfer of learning to a business- or government-strategy context.

Alternatively, or additionally, you could keep a journal about your experience, tracking your progress, reactions, and observations: what you are doing, thinking, and feeling; what is easy; what is a struggle; what you are noticing about your thinking and your progress. Recall the five attributes and use them as a guide for your journal reflections and questions. By drawing parallels (literally and figuratively) about what you are noticing and experiencing in your artistic pursuit, you are laying the foundation for strategic thinking.

In case I lost you back at "piano lessons" and "painting," rest assured that the learning from these types of efforts can be used in a competitive business setting. For instance, as I mentioned earlier, when working with executives to develop a strategy, one of the most valuable exercises I ask of them is to "draw" their strategic problem. Initially, some look at me with comic disbelief in their eyes and deflect the invitation with a passing reference to stick figures, but visualizing a problem or a strategy can produce some terrific "a-ha's," amazing clarification, and innovative thoughts.

Similarly, when critical reflective processes are introduced, I find that aspiring strategists often respond apprehensively. They have a sense that critical reflective processes are probably good for someone they know—but not appropriate for them! Often, executives are ambivalent and nervous about challenging and testing current thinking because this is not a practice accepted within their organizational culture. They are concerned about being ridiculed and afraid that their colleagues will disapprove of their reframing. Again, they tend to like the concept, but would prefer to forego the experience.

To ease into these difficult learning processes, I find that offering strategists some knowledge of the surf and dive learning domains provides them with a purposeful means of approaching the level of thinking to which they aspire in meetings ... and practice nearly always alleviates some of the anxiety associated with the strategic learning process.

Suggestions for Facilitators of Learning

So what can be done to support the development of ambitious and aspiring leaders who wish (or need) to learn to think strategically? First and foremost, those responsible for facilitating learning can create a climate that is conducive to strategic thinking by providing the following:

- *Offer information* about the learning process used for strategic thinking, the role of informal learning, cognitive clusters, intuition, learning domains, transfer, and the role of critical reflective processes. Clearly and explicitly differentiate between learning strategic thinking and learning strategic planning.
- *Encourage sufficient space and time* to reflect.
- *Practice inquiry and dialogue* so that learners have a baseline, feel confident, and gain experience in using questions, active listening, and dialogue.

- *Ensure that learners are involved in strategy making,* for this involvement is the best way to practice reflection in and on action.
- *Trust* that executives and managers can and do have meaningful learning experiences that transfer and contribute to strategic thinking, and invite them to identify these experiences.

Roles for Learning Facilitators

The ability to do many things at once has become a way of life for leaders of all organizations. For better and for worse, technology can do an incredible number of remarkable things—sometimes to the point of confusion. As human beings, we often feel pressure to match the performance standards of technology. As we attempt to facilitate learning to think strategically, three points are useful to keep in mind.

First, remember that from a strategic thinking perspective, successful strategy is always past tense; therefore, take an adaptive stance and assume that things will continue to change. Keep moving mentally. Don't rely on past approaches or mindsets for future success.

Second, successful strategic thinking requires agility in using both cognitive clusters: the linear, logical, analytic, convergent cluster, and the nonlinear, a-rational, divergent, intuitive, imaginative cluster. Because the linear, logical side is deeply entrenched already in traditional learning and organizational development practice, sharpen the focus on the nonlinear, a-rational, divergent, intuitive, and imaginative one.

And third, successful strategy is adaptable, sustainable, innovative, and winning. Such strategy requires developing the five attributes (imagination, broad perspective, juggle, no control over, desire to win) and using the informal learning process to ensure the development of these attributes.

So, what does this mean for organizational learning facilitators? This knowledge opens opportunities for organizational learning facilitators to assume any or a combination of the following three roles.

Key Strategist

A partner at all levels of organizational strategy meetings, a key strategist contributes content data and offers a specific perspective. A chief learning officer, for example, has an organizational responsibility to speak directly to the contribution of individual development and to social and strategy dimensions, and to embed challenge into the culture in an effort to create a pipeline of strategic thinkers within the organization.

Concept Creator

The concept creator advocates for a process which changes radically the way in which strategy is made. Instead of discussing whether to use an inside-out/outside-in approach or a top-down/bottom-up strategy or structure/infrastructure, concept creators encourage an inclusive, adaptive, nonlinear, divergent, a-rational strategic thinking approach as a genuine concept re-creation.

Process Facilitator

Process facilitators often partner with the chief learning officer and organizational learning specialists who support executives and line managers. Process facilitators play a supporting role to those who challenge, revise, and test the data as well as their thinking throughout the strategy-making process.

Innovative Techniques for Promoting Strategic Thinking

The following suggestions provide facilitators of learning with new techniques for promoting and strengthening the cognitive and affective skills required for strategic thinking. Learning facilitators can strengthen the learning process of strategic thinking by being willing to:

- Give permission to people to act as the contrarian during strategy meetings. Rotate this role until everyone feels comfortable playing this role with everyone else during meetings. Establish pride and respect in playing the contrarian role. Rotate people in and out of various groups—allow plenty of opportunities for people to inquire and dialogue.
- Formally teach techniques to ask deep, dive questions.
- Formally teach and practice debate, discussion, and dialogue.
- Invite provocative or antagonistic speakers, and urge them to shake up your thinking with fresh perspectives and challenges. Bring in outside speakers who have good thinking habits but who come from worlds which are unfamiliar and very different from your own. Listen, reflect, and dialogue about corporate, competitive, public, political, educational, social, ethnic, and religious issues and perspectives.
- Use metaphors, analogies, fables, and parables as documentation and divergence mechanisms, which enable complex concepts and results to be transferred readily.
- Respect non-work experiences. Learning occurs throughout all activities, not just in the classroom or within working hours or the confines of the workplace. Doing and action are frequently rewarded, to the exclusion of deeper thinking, which requires time, critical reflection, and inquiry. Observe, listen, and record the learning that comes from informal opportunities.
- Explicitly recognize and appreciate executives who endorse and practice informal development efforts that focus on critical reflective processes, in order to heighten awareness and identify role models. Such learning creates an everyday environment conducive to informal learning.
- Think of ways to repeat the things that worked. Pay attention, record, and reflect.
- "Draw" or construct a visual picture of your strategy. Use pens, markers, and objects prior to working on your spreadsheet.

By enabling everyone within the organization to learn a disciplined approach for strengthening the five essential attributes and critical reflective capacity, you can ensure that what emerges will be an informed, innovative, and sustainable strategic pipeline of sorts.

Suggestions for Business School Curricula

The appeal of business school curricula is that they are essentially a model of pragmatism and technical rationality. This model is also a weakness. The reality of the global business environment in which strategy is made has long ago outgrown this model. If business schools wish to move strategic thinking beyond a hope and a prayer, then the definition of strategy within curricula needs to be expanded to include learning to think strategically, rather than being limited to learning to plan strategically.

Reading and analyzing novels, dramas, painting, photography, films, and music are great ways to learn about basic human nature—and human nature as it intersects with products and services is, after all, what strategy making is all about. Becoming engrossed in a novel or play, or being moved by a particular piece of music, is a powerful experience. When we recognize that the strategic situations we encounter have been previously experienced, recorded in various forms, and reflected on by countless generations in various countries, our perspective begins to broaden, our pattern recognition sharpens, and our curiosity grows.

We begin to connect our current situation to that in the play, poem, music, dance, or picture through metaphorical thinking. Also, we gain insight through drawing, stories, paintings, and dramas from which to reflect and diverge. Through critical dialogue, continually, we transfer learning and come to understand how others have dealt with uncertainties, conflict, injustice, paradoxes, contradictions, and risk. This learning process belongs in business school conversations.

> *Learning is one of the very few business situations in which the process is more important than the result.*

Learning is about striving for balance and finding our bearings. The same goes for learning to think strategically. Learning is one of the very few business situations in which the process is more important than the result. Learning is the competitive factor that differentiates strategic thinking from strategic planning, namely because of its generative and sustainable nature. Therefore, we want continually to place ourselves in a state of imbalance in order to test and challenge our ability to learn.

While I am not advocating for the inclusion of art or music appreciation courses in business curricula, nor is there any reason to eliminate the analytic content from existing courses, I do recommend that attention be given to the flip side of the strategy coin. The five essential attributes and critical reflective processes need to be developed through informal means and also through an instructional approach.

There are two popular schools of thought about how to strengthen critical reflective processes. One is that critical reflective processes happen naturally; the second is that they need to be structured. I believe it is important to support the former with the latter if we are to accelerate learning strategic thinking. Business schools can set an expectation for the use of critical reflective processes and also include the processes in segments that can be practiced (e.g., listening, intuition, inquiry, lateral thinking, reflection, and dialogue) in a structured format using either an integrated or an isolated instructional approach.

An integrated approach might include incorporating such things as exercises in design, drawing, metaphoric writing, and intuition into the content of existing strategy courses. On the other hand, an isolated instructional approach might require a seminar allotted to critical inquiry or a workshop on design or storytelling. While some business schools are gradually including these, far more could benefit future leaders by doing so.

Although newly minted MBA graduates often are extremely adept at thinking within an analytical frame, I find that often they are not nearly as skillful when required to shift cognitive clusters. Frequently, across the globe, I notice that graduates of MBA programs lack the critical reflective processes needed to transfer, shatter, and reframe—precisely what is needed for innovative and adaptive strategic thinking. They are in a quagmire when trying to think strategically, unable to identify what their habits of mind and patterns are and unable to draw from and transfer experience across contexts. Without these skills, they cannot imagine and generate truly innovative strategy. Although many young MBA graduates have impressive life histories, their inability to critically reflect and to transfer learning across contexts diminishes their contribution to the strategy game.

When MBA graduates enter businesses and organizations, typically, they have a fixed-frame mentality regarding problem solving and decision making. They have learned (quite thoroughly) one way to examine a problem and often assume, falsely, that there is a best solution for each problem. While this assumption is useful for operational matters and simple problems, it is often counter-productive as support for the learning process needed in complex strategic thinking. Therefore, business schools could acknowledge and persistently work with both the surf and the dive learning domains across the curriculum, rather than permit the convenient and efficient surf domain of instrumental, transactional learning required in analytical courses.

In referencing the history of strategy, we can see the tremendous and long-lasting impact that the technical rational way of thinking has had on business school curricula. With regard to strategic thinking, the current perception is that many business school curricula are locked into a singular, outdated, analytical mode of thinking that emphasizes the frameworks in vogue during the Industrial Revolution. The focus continues, with the top-of-the-triangle, logical, rational thinking and objective representation taking absolute precedence over anything else. No wonder executives are often disappointed with the inability of experienced and emerging leaders to think strategically—they have simply not been taught. These highly linear, logical, rational skills need to be balanced and blended with learning that requires divergent, nonlinear, creative, and conceptual thinking abilities, which are less finite and less concrete and which include an emphasis on the affective as well as cognitive learning domains.

Suggestions for Organizations

Much of what has been outlined previously can also be applied to companies, governments, and other organizations. Strategic thinking is not merely behavioral or skill development; rather, it involves a high degree of complex cognitive and affective abilities. Also, organizations can create and encourage practice time to dialogue during strategy meetings. The aim of such dialogue should be on developing the five attributes of strategic thinkers—imagination, broad perspective, juggle, no control over, and desire to win—and the critical reflective processes. Dialogue about problems requiring rational decisions should be differentiated from problems needing an a-rational approach. Organizations can also focus on encouraging leaders at all levels to engage in creative endeavors to strengthen strategic thinking and embed a vocabulary, and on transferring learning across contexts. Shared vocabulary and concepts can be highly conducive to facilitating meaningful dialogue, which enhances the transfer process.

X

Summary and Questions

Engaging in any of the arts is highly beneficial to the development of the five attributes in both direct and indirect ways. Combined with the critical reflective processes, such engagement can strengthen our ability to think strategically in many ways. It hones the transfer of learning from one context to another, expands perspectives, stretches our imagination, offers experience with tension, develops emotional awareness, supports risk taking, and deals first-hand with paradox and polarities—specifically "and" thinking.

"And" thinking is a type of polarity thinking that is conducive to innovative and divergent thinking. The paradoxical and complex nature of many strategic problems requires an ability to identify the "and" polarity within the problem and to work *with* the inherent tension, rather than revert to convergent thinking to eliminate the tension. The tension that accompanies "and" polarities is beneficial in pushing the limits of what we can conceive as possible. A new concept or breakthrough moment may be the result of grappling with the tension of an "and" polarity.

Action learning and lateral thinking methods also strengthen the critical reflective processes as well as the five attributes that are required in strategic thinking. Action learning revolves around individuals learning through experimentation and using the critical reflective processes. Lateral thinking is about restructuring the problem and viewing it from multiple perspectives.

There are many ways to develop a "pipeline" of strategic thinkers, but there is no prescriptive method that works for every situation. It is up to individuals and organizations to determine which methods are appropriate and may work best for their situation.

1. Is there a creative endeavor or a preferred art form that you could access and engage in as a means to strengthening your own five attributes to become a more effective strategic thinker?
2. How could engagement in the arts develop your own critical reflective processes?
3. What role does informal learning play in developing the five attributes that are necessary for strategic thinking?

4. Think of a time when you *observed* a performance, museum exhibit, or another artistic event. Think of a time when you *engaged* in a creative endeavor. What was the difference? How does this apply to developing strategic thinking?
5. What challenges could you encounter in suggesting engagement in the arts as a means to strengthening strategic thinking within an organization? What opportunities might exist? What are some of the potential benefits to such a suggestion?

A "Cheat Sheet" for Individuals and Organizations

TIPS FOR INDIVIDUALS

- Instead of saying "no," ask a question. Ask questions that move from the surf to the dive level of thinking. To gain a new perspective, invite listeners and questioners who do not know the background, content, or the politics of a strategic issue.
- Take time to write down the feelings attached to your thinking in a journal or log. Over time, journal entries offer data to back up your intuitive sense of a pattern or trend. This journaling helps you to uncover assumptions, highlights traps in your thinking, and gives you confidence in your judgment.
- Critically reflect on things that provoke questions or strong feelings.
- Draw or design your strategy ideas instead of writing them. Write or tell parables, fables, allegories, and metaphors which illustrate your assumptions and beliefs about strategy issues.
- Upgrade and diversify the kinds of strategy conversations you have.
- Alternate among dialogue, discussion, and debate. Include dive-level questions.
- Scrutinize the content, the process, and the premise of a strategy matter separately; then, look at connections between and among them.
- Avoid solutions and a quick-fix approach to strategy problems. Instead, hold back and suspend judgment. Deliberately poke around until you find a surprise. Then inquire and reflect on that surprise.
- Show and tell the perspectives and the patterns you see in data. Explain what they mean, might mean, why, and why not. Pointing out patterns can accelerate the discovery process in strategic thinking, because imagining patterns you have not seen is sometimes difficult. Finding patterns will sharpen your focus and attention. Actually, using show-and-tell heightens the creative process and expands the breadth of visibility in strategic thinking.
- Slow down, in order to speed up later. Relax. Play. Reflect.
- Identify and focus on what you cannot control, rather than on what you can control.

- Identify role models who practice strategic thinking. Ask them to articulate their thinking, feelings, and experiences of the learning process.
- Change the people and places with whom and where you conduct strategy sessions. More of both is better.

TIPS FOR ORGANIZATIONS

- Shatter the tip-of-the-triangle model of strategy making. Instead, draw and develop from all levels, all functions, and all locales of the organization.
- Clarify the organizational intent by differentiating strategic planning from strategic thinking.
- Encourage and support activities such as participation in the arts and creative life experiences, in order to develop the five attributes and critical reflective processes. Alternate experiences in the arts with structured dialogue and critical reflective development sessions.
- Support and encourage learning processes, such as action learning and lateral thinking, as a means of strengthening the five attributes and transferring experience to a business-strategy context.
- Institutionalize time for reflection. Senior executives should articulate explicitly the value and relation between time, reflection, experience, and learning. Reflection can, and usually does, happen outside of work. What is important is that reflection be acknowledged and established as an expectation, supported with ideas of what reflection looks like, and that it then be processed and incorporated into strategic thinking.
- Support an awareness of intuition in order to develop experience and trust among executives as they use intuition as part of the strategic thinking process.
- Talk about discoveries and situations where critical reflective thinking contributes to strategic decisions as a great way of helping people learn to pay attention to critical reflection.
- Do not overestimate the impact of formal learning, just because this type of learning is an organizational habit or because it is convenient to quantify.
- Explicitly recognize informal learning as being valuable to the corporate culture.
- Avoid an obsession with measuring everything. Trust that powerful and significant learning can occur outside the four walls of organizational control.
- Organize "think tanks" across the organization and around the globe (live or virtual). The purpose of "think tanks" is to develop a pipeline of strategic thinkers by strengthening the five attributes and critical reflective processes, not to solve problems. "Think tanks" can become forums to practice and experiment with processes and an opportunity for senior executives to model and further develop strategic thinking.
- Include junior and mid-level managers in conversations about the strategic-learning process. This inclusion serves as a role-modeling opportunity to learn informally through experience. Junior managers should have access to the

experienced senior executives as a learning resource, and they should be supported with adequate time for reflection. This can be a great strategic pipeline builder.

- Establish critical dialogue and inquiry as a management expectation.
- Move lessons learned from the surf domain to the deeper, dive domain.
- Share more than transactional, instrumental, surface thinking about what went wrong, what changed, and the results. Include process and premise reflection to encourage the affective learning dimension.
- Expand the in-company group with whom executives regularly conduct informal dialogue and storytelling. Use storytelling and critical dialogue as an everyday alternative to bullet points and sound bites. The listening required of storytelling and critical dialogue can create enormous tension, which can encourage and enrich reflection.

Summary

After centuries of traveling the long and winding roads, practitioners of strategy and scholars alike have acknowledged the uncanny similarities between the current challenges of our global strategy making and those of the ancient Greeks. Although our present-day global strategy context is, in many ways, qualitatively and quantitatively different from that of our ancient predecessors, our context remains as unpredictable, ever changing, and rife with paradoxes as was the dawn of Western civilization. And while our learning repertoire is more expansive than that of our predecessors, common sense suggests that we can benefit from the knowledge of many previous centuries. As is often the case, this novel teaching turns out to be just a well-forgotten lesson of the past—the old is ever new again.

In order to promote strategic thinking as a valuable leadership capability, strategy must not be viewed as a product. Innovative, adaptive, and sustainable strategy requires that we exercise, habitually and interminably, a strategic thinking process. Leaders of today must learn to appreciate and embrace the complex tension inherent in learning to think strategically in order to competitively leverage a landscape that is turbulent, unpredictable, and rapidly changing, for the sake of tomorrow.

As noted at the Introduction, these chapters have been structured around three key questions: (1) How do successful executives learn to think strategically? (2) What learning approaches are used by successful executive strategists? (3) What factors and conditions are essential for learning to think strategically? My hope is that this book has generated questions in the minds of readers that will inspire practical, original, and informal ways of learning to think strategically—ways that acknowledge and build on the strengths of the learning legacies from the past and that drive us bravely into the future.

Bibliography

Abualjadail, M. "Problems Affecting Productivity of Public and Private Sector Employees in Saudi Arabia." Doctoral dissertation, La Verne, CA, University of La Verne, 1990.

Agor, W. H. "The Logic of Intuitive Decisionmaking: An Agenda for Future Research." In W. H. Agor (Ed.), *Intuition in Organizations*. Newbury Park, CA: Sage Publications, 1990, pp. 263–4.

Ahiauzu, A. I. "The African Thought System and the Work Behavior of the African Industrial Man." *International Studies of Management & Organization* 16 (1986): 37–58.

Alexander, D. L. "The Effect Level the Hierarchy and Functional Areas Have on the Extent Mintzberg's Roles As Required by Managerial Jobs." *Academy of Management* 26 (1979): 186–9.

Ali, A. and Swiercz, P. "The Relationship Between Managerial Decision Making and Work Satisfaction in Saudi Arabia." In E. Kaynack (Ed.), *International Business in the Middle East*. New York: Walter de Gruyter, 1986, pp. 137–49.

Alkahtani, A. "Involvement of Employees and Their Personal Characteristics in Saudi Construction Companies." *International Journal of Commerce & Management* 10 (2000): 67–78.

Al-Tweam, N. I. "Attitudes of Saudi Public Bureaucrats: A Study in Administrative Responsibility and Control of the Bureaucracy." Doctoral dissertation, Washington, DC, The Library of the Saudi Arabian Cultural Mission, 1995.

Alyahya, K. and Vengroff, R. "Human Capital Utilization, Empowerment, and Organizational Effectiveness in the Middle East: A Comparative Perspective." University of Connecticut and Harvard University: Global Development Studies paper, 2004.

Amidon, D. *The Innovation Superhighway: Harnessing Intellectual Capital for Sustainable Collaborative Advantage*. Woburn, MA: Butterworth-Heinemann, 2003.

Andrews, K. R. *The Concept of Corporate Strategy*, rev. ed. Homewood, IL: Richard D. Irwin, 1971.

Ansoff, H. E. *Corporate Strategy*. New York: McGraw-Hill, 1965.

Arbelaez, H. and Milman, G. "The Business Environment of Latin America and the Caribbean." *International Journal of Public Administration* 23 (2000): 1253–68.

Argyris, C. *Reasoning, Learning, and Actions: Individual and Organizational*. San Francisco: Jossey-Bass, 1982.

Argyris, C. *Knowledge for Action*. San Francisco: Jossey-Bass, 1993.

Argyris, C. and Schon, D. *Theory in Practice: Increasing Professional Effectiveness*. San Francisco: Jossey-Bass, 1974.

Argyris, C. and Schon, D. *Organizational Learning: A Theory of Action Perspective*. Reading, MA: Addison-Wesley, 1978.

Argyris, C. and Schon, D. *Organizational Learning II: Theory, Method, and Practice*. Reading, MA: Addison-Wesley, 1996.

Argyris, C., Putnam, R., and McLain Smith, D. *Action Science*. San Francisco: Jossey-Bass, 1985.

Ariely, D. *The Upside of Irrationality*. New York: Harper Collins Publishers, 2010.

Baddeley, A., Eysenck, M. W., and Anderson, M. C. *Memory*. Hove and New York: Psychology Press, 2009.

Bandura, A. *Social Foundations of Thought and Action: A Cognitive Social Theory*. Englewood, NJ: Prentice-Hall, 1986.

Barney, J. B. "Firm Resources and Sustained Competitive Advantage." *Journal of Management* 17 (1991): 99–120.

Bartholomees, J. B. "A Survey of the Theory of Strategy." In *USAWAC Guide to National Security Issues*, Vol. 1 5th ed. Carlisle, PA: Strategic Studies Institute of the US Army War College (SSI).

Bender, M. *Operation Excellence: Succeeding in Business and Life—The U.S. Military Way*, 1st ed. New York: AMACOM, 2004.

Bjur, W. E. and Zomorrodian, A. "Towards Indigenous Theories of Administration." *International Review of Administrative Sciences* 52 (1986): 393–420.

Bleeke, J. and Ernst, D. *Collaborating to Compete Using Strategic Alliances and Acquisitions in the Global Marketplace*. San Francisco: Jossey-Bass, 1993.

Bolman, L. G. and Deal, T. *Reframing Organizations: Artistry, Choice, and Leadership*, 2nd ed. San Francisco: Jossey-Bass, 1997.

Bottger, P., Hallein, I., and Yetton, P. "A Cross-National Study of Leadership: Participation as a Function of Problem Structure and Leader Power." *Journal of Management Studies* 22:4 (July 1985): 359–68.

Botticelli, P. "Competition and Business Strategy in Historical Perspective." Draft paper prepared for President and Fellows of Harvard College. Harvard Business School Publishing, December 1997.

Boucouvalas, M. "Consciousness and Learning: New and Renewed Approaches." *New Directions for Adult and Continuing Education* 57 (Spring 1993): 57–69.

Boud, D. and Garrick, J. *Understanding Learning at Work*. New York: Routledge, 1999.

Boud, D. and Walker, D. "Barriers to Reflection on Experience." In Boud, D., Cohen, R., and Walker, D. (Eds), *Using Experience for Learning*. Bristol, PA: The Society for Research into Higher Education and Open University Press, 1993, 73–86.

Boud, D., Keogh, R., and Walker, D. *Reflection: Turning Experience into Learning*. New York: Nichols, 1985.

Brockett, R. G. and Hiemstra, R. *Self-Direction in Adult Learning: Perspectives on Theory, Research, and Practice*. New York: Routledge, 1991.

Brodbeck, F., et al. "Cultural Variation of Leadership Prototypes Across 22 European Countries." *Journal of Occupational and Organizational Psychology* 73 (2000, March): 1–29.

Brookfield, S. *Understanding and Facilitating Adult Learning*. San Francisco: Jossey-Bass, 1986.

Brookfield, S. *Learning Democracy: E. Lindeman on Adult Education and Social Change*. London: Croom Helm, 1987.

Brookfield, S. "Tales from the Dark Side: A Phenomenography of Adult Critical Reflection." *Proceedings of the Adult Education Research Conference*, no. 35. Knoxville: The University of Tennessee, May 1994.

Brookings Institute, Center for Leadership Capacity Services. Office of Personnel Management. "Strategic Thinking." Internal document, 2011.1.

Brown, T. *Change by Design: How Design Thinking Transforms Organizations and Inspires Innovation*. New York: Harper Business, 2009.

Burgelman, R. A. "A Process Model of Strategic Business Exit: Implications for an Evolutionary Perspective on Strategy." *Strategic Management Journal* 17 (1996): 193–214.

Cell, E. *Learning to Learn from Experience*. Albany: State University of New York Press, 1984.

Cell, E. *Organizational Life: Learning to be Self-Directed*. Lanham, MI: University Press of America, 1998.

Chandler, A. D. *Strategy and Structure: Chapters in the History of the Industrial Enterprise*. Cambridge, MA: MIT Press, 1962.

Chandler, A. D. *Scale and Scope: The Dynamics of Industrial Capitalism*. Cambridge, MA: Harvard University Press, 1990.

Charles, A. and Gerras, S. "Developing Creative and Critical Thinkers." *Military Review* 89 (November–December 2009): 77–83.

Chase, R. and Aquilano, N. *Production and Operations Management*, 6th ed. Homewood, IL: Richard D. Irwin, 1992.

Chene, A. "The Concept of Autonomy in Adult Education: A Philosophical Discussion." *Adult Education Quarterly* 34 (1983): 38–47.

Collins, J. M. *Military Strategy: Principles, Practices, and Historical Perspectives*. Dulles, VA: Potomac Books, 2001.

Conley, P. *Experience Curves as a Planning Tool*. Boston Consulting Group pamphlet, 1970.

Courtney, H., Kirkland, J., and Viguerie, P. "Strategy Under Uncertainty." *Harvard Business Review* 6 (November–December 1997): 66–79.

Cranton, P. *Understanding and Promoting Transformative Learning*. San Francisco: Jossey-Bass, 1994.

Cross, R. and Israelit, S. *Strategic Learning in a Knowledge Economy: Individual, Collective, and Organizational Learning Process*. Woburn, MA: Butterworth-Heinemann, 2000.

Cseh, M. "Contextual Learning of Owner-Managers of Small, Successful Romanian Companies." *Contextual Learning Issues*. Academy of Human Resource Development (HRD) Conference Proceedings, 1999.

Cummings, S. and Wilson, D. *Images of Strategy*. Malden, MA: Blackwell, 2003.

Daniels, K. and Bailey, A. "Strategy Development Process and Participation in Decision Making: Predictors of Role Stressors and Job Satisfaction." *Journal of Applied Management Studies* 8 (1999): 27–45.

Davenport, T. *Human Capital: What It Is and Why People Invest In It*. San Francisco: Jossey-Bass, 1999.

De Bono, E. *Lateral Thinking*. New York: Harper & Row, 1970.

DeKluyver, C. A. *Strategic Thinking: An Executive Perspective*. Upper Saddle River, NJ: Prentice-Hall, 2000.

Dewey, J. *Art as Experience*. New York: Pondview Books, 1934.

Dewey, J. *Experience and Education*. New York: Collier Books, 1938.

Dewitt, B. and Meyer, R. *Strategy Synthesis: Resolving Strategy Paradoxes to Create Competitive Advantage*. London: Thompson, 1999.

Dixon, N. M. *Perspectives on Dialogue*. Greensboro, NC: Center for Creative Leadership, in-house publication, 1996.

Dodd, D. and Favaro, K. *The Three Tensions: Winning the Struggle to Perform Without Compromise*. San Francisco: Jossey-Bass, 2007.

Dotlich, D. and Noel, J. *Action Learning: How the World's Top Companies are Re-Creating Their Leaders and Themselves*. San Francisco: Jossey-Bass, 1998.

Doz, Y. and Prahalad, C. K. "Headquarters Influence and Strategic Control in MNC's." *Sloan Management Review* 23 (Fall 1981): 15–29.

Dreyfus, H. L. and Dreyfus, S. E. *Mind Over Machine: The Power of Human Intuitive Expertise in the Era of the Computer*. New York: Free Press, 1986.

Duggan, W. *Strategic Intuition*. New York City: Columbia Business School Press, Columbia University, 2007.

Duke Corporate Education. *Translating Strategy into Action*. Chicago, IL: Dearborn Trade Publishing, 2005.

Edmonson, A. and Moingeon, B. *When to Learn How and When to Learn Why: Appropriate Organization Learning as a Source of Competitive Advantage*. London: Sage Publications, 1996.

Feynman, R. *The Pleasure of Finding Things Out: The Best Short Works of Richard Feynman*. Cambridge, MA: Perseus Books, 1999. An excerpt from his lecture at the Galileo Symposium, Italy, 1954.

Fisher, A. *Critical Thinking*. Cambridge, UK: Cambridge University Press, 2001.

Flanagan, J. C. "The Critical Incident Technique." *Psychological Bulletin* 51 (1954): 327–58.

Fletcher, J. and Olwyler, K. *Paradoxical Thinking: How to Profit from Your Contradictions*. San Francisco: Berrett-Koehler, 1997.

Fry, R. and Kolb, D. "Experiential Learning Theory and Learning Experience in Liberal Arts Education." In S. E. Brooks and J. E. Althof (Eds), *Enriching the Liberal Arts through Experiential Learning*. San Francisco: Jossey-Bass, 1979, pp. 6, 70–92.

Gardner, H. *Five Minds for the Future*. Boston, MA: Harvard Business School, 2006.

Georgescu, P. *The Source of Success: Five Enduring Principles at the Heart of Real Leadership*. San Francisco: Jossey-Bass, 2005.

Gilbert, F. "Machiavelli: The Renaissance of the Art of War." In P. Paret (Ed.), *Makers of Modern Strategy from Machiavelli to the Nuclear Age*. Princeton, NJ: Princeton University Press, 1986, pp. 25–9.

Gilbert, X. and Strebel, P. "Developing Competitive Advantage." In J. B. Quinn, H. Mintzberg, and R. James (Eds), *The Strategy Process*. Englewood Cliffs, NJ: Prentice Hall, 1988, 70–79.

Glöckner, A. and Witteman, C. "Beyond Dual-Process Models: A Categorization of Processes Underlying Intuitive Judgment and Decision Making." *Thinking & Reasoning* 16 (2010): 1–25.

Gluck, F. W. and Kaufman, S. P. "Using the Strategic Planning Framework." McKinsey internal document: *Readings in Strategy*, 1979, pp. 3–4.

Goatly, A. *The Language of Metaphors*. London: Routledge, 1997.

Goleman, D. *Working With Emotional Intelligence*. New York: Random House, 2000.

Govindarajan, V. and Trimble, C. *Ten Rules for Strategic Innovators: From Idea to Execution*. Boston, MA: Harvard Business School Press, 2005.

Greeno, J. G. "A Perspective on Thinking." *American Psychologist* 44 (1989): 134–41.

Greenwald, B. and Kahn, J. *Competition DeMystified*. New York: Portfolio, 2005.

Griffin, R. W. and Pustav, M. W. *International Business: A Managerial Perspective*. Reading, MA: Addison-Wesley, 1996.

Guerlac, H. "Vauban: The Impact of Science on War." In P. Paret (Ed.), *Makers of Modern Strategy from Machiavelli to the Nuclear Age*. Princeton, NJ: Princeton University Press, 1986, 68.

Gundling, E. *Working GlobeSmart*. Palo Alto, CA: Davies-Black, 2003.

Habermas, J. *Between Facts and Norms: Contributions to a Discourse Theory of Law and Democracy*. Cambridge, MA: MIT Press, 1998.

Habermas, J. *The Liberating Power of Symbols: Philosophical Essays*. Cambridge, UK: Polity, 2001.

Haldane, J. B. S. *Possible Worlds: And Other Essays*. London: Chatto & Windus, 1927.

Hamel, G. "Strategy as Revolution." *Harvard Business Review* 74 (July–August 1996): 69–82.

Hamel, G. and Prahalad, C. K. *Competing for the Future*. Boston, MA: Harvard Business School Press, 1994.

Hamermesh, R. G. *Making Strategy Work: How Senior Managers Produce Results*. New York: John Wiley & Sons, 1986.

Hammett, P. *Unbalanced Influence: Recognizing and Resolving the Impact of Myth and Paradox in Executive Performance*. Mountain View, CA: Davies-Black, 2007.

Harris, J. *The Learning Paradox*. Toronto, Canada: Macmillan, 1998.

Harrison, R. *Strategic Thinking in 3D: A Guide for National Security, Foreign Policy, and Business Professionals*. Dulles, VA: Potomac Books, 2012.

Hellgren, B. and Melin, L. "The Role of Strategists: Ways-of-thinking in Strategic Change Processes." In J. Hendry, G. Johnson, and J. Newton (Eds), *Strategic Thinking: Leadership and the Management of Change*. Chichester, UK: John Wiley & Sons, 1993, pp. 47–68.

Henderson, B. D. *Henderson on Corporate Strategy*. Cambridge, MA: Abt Books, 1979.

Henderson, B. D. *The Logic of Business Strategy*. Cambridge, MA: Ballinger, 1984.

Heracleous, L. "Strategic Thinking or Strategic Planning?" *Long Range Planning* 31:3 (1998): 481–7.

Hilbig, B. E., Scholl, S. G., and Pohl, R. R. "Think or Blink—Is the Recognition Heuristic an 'Intuitive' Strategy?" *Judgment and Decision Making* 5:4 (July 2012): 300–9.

Hilgard, E. R. and Bower, G. H. *Theories of Learning*. New York: Appleton-Century-Crofts, 1966.

Hofstede, G. *Culture's Consequences*. Beverly Hills, CA: Sage Publications, 1980.

Hogarth, R. *Educating Intuition*. Chicago: University of Chicago Press, 2001.

Holborn, H. "The Prusso-German School: Moltke and the Rise of the General Staff." In P. Paret (Ed.), *Makers of Modern Strategy from Machiavelli to the Nuclear Age*. Princeton, NJ: Princeton University Press, 1986, pp. 290–9.

Isaacs, W. N. "Taking Flight: Dialogue, Collective Thinking, and Organizational Learning." In R. Cross and S. Israelit (Eds), *Strategic Learning in a Knowledge Economy: Individual, Collective, and Organizational Learning Process*. Woburn, MA: Butterworth-Heinemann, 2000.

Jablonsky, D. "Why Is Strategy Difficult?" Chapter 6 in J. Boone Bartholomees, Jr. (Ed.), *US Army War College Guide to National Security Policy and Strategy*. Carlisle, PA: Strategic Studies Institute of the U.S. Army War College (SSI), 2004.

James, J. *Thinking in the Future Tense*. New York: Simon & Schuster, 1997.

James, W. *Pragmatism*. New York: Longmans and Green, 1925.

Jarvis, P. *Adult Learning in the Social Context*. New York: Croom Helm, 1987.

Jelenc, L. "The Impact of Strategic Management Schools and Strategic Thinking on the Performance of Croatian Entrepreneurial Practice." Doctoral dissertation, Slovenia, University of Ljubljana, 2008.

Johnson, G. "Managing Strategic Change—Strategy, Culture, and Action." In P. Sadler (Ed.), *Long Range Planning* 25. Oxford: Pergamon Press, 1995, pp. 28–36.

Jung, C. G. *Modern Man in Search of a Soul*. New York: Harcourt Brace, 1934.

Kahneman, D. *Thinking, Fast and Slow*. New York: Farrar, Straus, and Giroux, 2011.

Kahneman, D. and Tversky, A. (Eds) *Choices, Values, and Frames*. Cambridge, UK: Cambridge University Press, 2000.

Kanter, R. M. *World Class: Thriving Locally in the Global Economy*. New York: Simon & Schuster, 1995.

Khatri, N. and Ng, H. "The Role of Intuition in Strategic Decision Making." Dissertation, Singapore, Nanyang Business School, 2011.

Kim, S. "Participative Management and Job Satisfaction: Lessons for Management Leadership." *Public Administration Review* 62 (2002): 231–42.

Kim, W. C. and Mauborgne, R. *Blue Ocean Strategy: How to Create Uncontested Market Space and Make Competition Irrelevant.* Cambridge, MA: Harvard Business Review Press, 2005.

Klein, G. *The Power of Intuition.* New York: Currency Books, Doubleday, 2003.

Knox, A. *Helping Adults Learn.* San Francisco: Jossey-Bass, 1986.

Kolb, D. *Experiential Learning: Experience as the Source of Learning and Development.* Englewood Cliffs, NJ: Prentice-Hall, 1984.

Kouzes, J. and Posner, B. *The Leadership Challenge,* 3rd ed. San Francisco: Jossey-Bass, 2002.

Lakoff, G. and Johnson, M. *Metaphors We Live By.* Chicago: University of Chicago Press, 2003.

Lehrer, J. *How We Decide.* New York: Houghton Mifflin, 2009.

Leonard-Barton, D. "Core Capabilities and Core Rigidities: A Paradox in Managing New Product Development." *Strategic Management Journal* 11 (1992): 111–25.

Liedtka, J. "Strategic Thinking: Can It Be Taught?" *Long Range Planning* 31:1 (1998): 121–4.

Liedtka, J. and Ogilvie, T. *Designing for Growth.* New York: Columbia Business School Publishing, 2011.

Lincoln, Y. D. *The Making of a Constructivist.* Newbury Park, CA: Sage Publications, 1990.

Lippitt, L. *Preferred Futuring.* San Francisco: Berrett-Koehler, 1998.

Loehle, C. *Thinking Strategically.* Cambridge, UK: Cambridge University Press, 1996.

Lorange, P. *Corporate Planning: An Executive Viewpoint.* Englewood Cliffs, NJ: Prentice Hall, 1977.

Marquardt, M. *Action Learning Solving Problems and Building Leaders in Real Time.* Palo Alto, CA: Davies-Black, 2004.

Marsick, V. J. and Sauquet, A. *Learning through Reflection.* San Francisco: Jossey-Bass, 1999.

Marsick, V. J. and Volpe, M. (Eds) *Informal Learning on the Job. Advances in Developing Human Resources, no. 3.* San Francisco: Academy of Human Resource Development/Berrett-Kohler Communications, 1999.

Marsick, V. J. and Watkins, K. E. *Informal and Incidental Learning in the Workplace.* London: Routledge, 1990.

Martin, R. *The Design of Business: Why Design Thinking Is the Next Competitive Advantage.* Cambridge, MA: Harvard Business Press, 2009.

Matejka, K. and Murphy, A. *Making Change Happen on Time on Target on Budget.* Mountain View, CA: Davies-Black, 2005.

Merriam-Webster's Collegiate Dictionary, Tenth Edition. Springfield, MA: Merriam-Webster, 2001.

Mezirow, J. *Transformative Dimensions of Adult Learning.* San Francisco: Jossey-Bass, 1991.

Mezirow, J. *Fostering Critical Reflection in Adulthood.* San Francisco: Jossey-Bass, 1994.

Mezirow, J. "A Transformative Theory of Adult Learning." In M. Welton (Ed.), *In Defense of the Lifeworld: Critical Perspectives on Adult Learning.* Albany, NY: State University of New York Press, 1995, pp. 39–70.

Mezirow, J. *Learning as Transformation: Critical Perspectives on a Theory in Progress.* San Francisco: Jossey-Bass, 2000.

Mintzberg, H. "Patterns in Strategy Formation." *Management Science* 24 (1978): 934–48.

Mintzberg, H. "An Emerging Strategy of 'Direct' Research." *Administrative Science Quarterly* 24 (December 1979): 582–9.

Mintzberg, H. "The Design School: Reconsidering the Basic Premises of Strategic Management." *Strategic Management Journal* 11 (1990): 171–95.

Mintzberg, H. *The Fall and Rise of Strategic Planning.* New York: Free Press, 1994.

Mintzberg, H. "The Fall and Rise of Strategic Planning." *Harvard Business Review* 72 (January–February, 1994): 107–14.

Mintzberg, H. and Lampel, J. "Reflecting on the Strategy Process." *Sloan Management Review* [special issue] 40 (Spring 1999): 23–4.

Mintzberg, H., Ahlstrand, B., and Lampel, J. *Strategy Safari: A Guided Tour through the Wilds of Strategic Management*. New York: Free Press, 1998.

Montgomery, J. "Probing Managerial Behavior: Image and Reality in Southern Africa." Paper prepared for the Annual Meeting of the African Studies Association, Madison, WI, October 26–November 1, 1986.

Mumford, A. *Learning at the Top*. New York: McGraw-Hill, 1995.

Nelson, R. R. and Winter, S. G. *An Evolutionary Theory of Economic Change*. Cambridge, MA: Harvard University Press, 1982.

Nonaka, I. and Takeuchi, H. *The Knowledge-Creating Company: How Japanese Companies Create the Dynamics of Innovation*. New York: Oxford University Press, 1995.

Osterwalder, A. and Pigneur, Y. *Business Model Generation: A Handbook for Visionaries, Game Changers, and Challengers*. Hoboken, NJ: John Wiley & Sons, 2012.

Palmer, R. R. "Frederick the Great, Guibert, Bülow: From Dynastic to National War." In P. Paret (Ed.), *Makers of Modern Strategy from Machiavelli to the Nuclear Age*. Princeton, NJ: Princeton University Press, 1986, pp. 91–116.

Pietersen, W. *Reinventing Strategy: Using Strategic Learning to Create and Sustain Breakthrough Performance*. New York: John Wiley & Sons, 2002.

Pink, D. *A Whole New Mind: Why Right-Brainers Will Rule the Future*. Berkeley: Penguin Publishing Group (USA) Inc., 2005.

Polanyi, M. *Personal Knowledge: Towards a Post-Critical Philosophy*. Chicago: University of Chicago Press, 1958.

Polanyi, M. *The Tacit Dimension*. New York: Doubleday, 1967.

Porter, M. E. "The Contributions of Industrial Organizations to Strategic Management." *Academy of Management Review* 6 (1981): 609–20.

Porter, M. E. "What Is Strategy?" *Harvard Business Review* (November–December 1996): 61–78.

Prahalad, C. K. and Hamel, G. "The Core Competence of the Corporation." *Harvard Business Review* 68 (May–June 1990): 79–91.

Quinn, J. B. *Strategies for Change: Logistical Incrementalism*. Homewood, IL: Irwin, 1980.

Rangan, S. and Yoshina, M. *Strategic Alliances*. Boston, MA: Harvard Business School Press, 1995.

Ray, M. and Myers, R. "The Role of Intuition in Strategic Decision Making." *Human Relations* 53 (January 2000): 57–86.

Revans, R. W. *The Origin and Growth of Action Learning*. London: Chartwell Bratt, 1982.

Roam, D. *The Back of the Napkin: Solving Problems and Selling Ideas with Pictures*. New York: Portfolio, 2008.

Rodrigues, C. A. *International Management*. St. Paul, MN: West, 1996.

Rothe, K. and Ricks, D. A. "Goal Configuration in a Global Industry Context." *Strategic Management Journal* 15 (1994): 103–20.

Rothwell, W. J. *The Action Learning Guidebook*. San Francisco: Jossey-Bass/Pfeiffer, 1990.

Rubin H. and Rubin, I. *Qualitative Interviewing: The Art of Hearing Data*. Thousand Oaks, CA: Sage Publications, 1995.

Schein, E. *Organizational Culture and Leadership*. San Francisco: Jossey-Bass, 1985.

Schneider, S. and DeMeyer, A. "Interpreting and Responding to Strategic Issues: The Impact of National Culture." *Strategic Management Journal* 12 (1991): 307–20.

Schoeffler, S., Buzzel, R. D., and Heany, D. F. "Impact of Strategic Planning on Profit Performance." *Harvard Business Review* 54 (March–April 1974): 137–45.

Schon, D. *The Reflective Practitioner*. New York: Basic Books, 1983.

Schon, D. *Educating the Reflective Practitioner*. San Francisco: Jossey-Bass, 1987.

Scribner, S. *Thinking in Action: Some Characteristics of Practical Thought. Origins of Competence*. Cambridge, UK: Cambridge University Press, 1986.

Seligman, M. and Kahana, M. "Unpacking Intuition." *Perspectives on Psychological Science* 4:4 (2009): 399–402.

Selznick, P. *Leadership in Administration: A Sociological Interpretation*. Evanston, IL: Row, Peterson, 1957.

Simon, H. *Models of Man*. New York: John Wiley & Sons, 1957.

Singley, M. K. and Anderson, J. R. *The Transfer of Cognitive Skill*. Cambridge, MA: Harvard University Press, 1989.

Sloan, A., Jr. *My Years with General Motors*. New York: Doubleday, 1963.

Sloan, J. "A Case Study of How Nine Executives Learn Informally to Develop Strategy in a Global Context." Doctoral dissertation, New York, Columbia University, 2002.

Sloane, P. *Lateral Thinking Skills*. Sterling, VA: Kogan Page, 2003.

Spitzer, Q. and Evans, R. *Heads, You Win!* New York: Fireside Books, Simon & Schuster, 1997.

Stacey, R. *Managing Chaos: Dynamic Business Strategies in an Unpredictable World*. London: Kogan Page, 1992.

Taleb, N. *Fooled by Randomness*. New York: Random House, 2004.

Taleb, N. *The Black Swan*. New York: Random House, 2007.

Taylor, F. *Principles of Scientific Management*. New York: Norton, 1967.

Teece, D. J., Pisano, P., and Shuen, A. "Dynamic Capabilities and Strategic Management." Mimeo, June 1992, pp. 12–13.

Tetlock, P. *Expert Political Judgment: How Good Is It? How Can We Know?* Princeton: Princeton University Press, 2005.

Trapp, R. and Benoit, P. J. "An Interpretive Perspective on Argumentation: A Research Editorial." *The Western Journal of Speech Communication* 51 (1987): 417–30.

Trompenaars, A. and Hampden-Turner, C. *The Seven Cultures of Capitalism*. New York: Doubleday, 1993.

Vaughan, F. "Varieties of Intuitive Experience." In W. H. Agor (Ed.), *Intuition in Organizations*. Newbury Park, CA: Sage Publications, 1990, pp. 40–61.

Von Ghyczy, T. "The Fruitful Flaws of Strategy Metaphors." *Harvard Business Review* 81 (September 2003): 1–9.

Von Krogh, G., Ichijo, K., and Nonaka, I. *Enabling Knowledge Creation*. New York: Oxford University Press, 2000.

Von Neumann, J. and Morgenstern, O. *Theory of Games and Economic Behavior*. Princeton, NJ: Elgen Books, 1944.

Vygotsky, L. S. *Thought and Language*. Cambridge, MA: MIT Press, 1987.

Waters, D. "Understanding Strategic Thinking and Developing Strategic Thinkers." *Joint Force Quarterly* 63:4. Washington, DC: National Defense University Press, 2011: 116–19.

Webster's Third New International Dictionary of the English Language Unabridged. Springfield, MA: Merriam-Webster, 1993.

Weick, K. *Sensemaking in Organizations*. Thousand Oaks, CA: Sage Publications, 1995.

Weick, K. and Sutcliffe, K. M. *Managing the Unexpected: Assuring High Performance in an Age of Complexity*. San Francisco: Jossey-Bass, 2001.

Weil, S. W. and McGill, I. *Making Sense of Experiential Learning: Diversity in Theory and Practice*. Buckingham, UK: SRHE and the Open University Press, 1989.

Wick, C. W. and Leon, S. *The Learning Edge: How Smart Managers and Smart Companies Stay Ahead*. New York: McGraw-Hill, 1993.

Woike, B. A., Bender, M., and Besne, N. "Implicit Motivational States Influence Memory: Evidence for Motive by State-Dependent Learning in Personality." *Journal of Research in Personality* 43:1 (2009): 39–48.

Yorks, L. *Strategic Human Resource Development*. Mason, OH: Thomson, South-Western, 2005.

Zuboff, S. *In the Age of the Smart Machine*. New York: Basic Books, 1988.

Index